Rainforest Radio

Rainforest Radio

Language Reclamation
and Community Media
in the Ecuadorian Amazon

GEORGIA C. ENNIS

THE UNIVERSITY OF
ARIZONA PRESS
TUCSON

The University of Arizona Press
www.uapress.arizona.edu

We respectfully acknowledge the University of Arizona is on the land and territories of Indigenous peoples. Today, Arizona is home to twenty-two federally recognized tribes, with Tucson being home to the O'odham and the Yaqui. Committed to diversity and inclusion, the University strives to build sustainable relationships with sovereign Native Nations and Indigenous communities through education offerings, partnerships, and community service.

© 2025 by The Arizona Board of Regents
All rights reserved. Published 2025

ISBN-13: 978-0-8165-5519-2 (hardcover)
ISBN-13: 978-0-8165-5269-6 (paperback)
ISBN-13: 978-0-8165-5270-2 (ebook)

Cover design by Leigh McDonald
Cover photograph by Georgia C. Ennis
Typeset by Sara Thaxton in 10.5/14 Warnock Pro with Kododa WF and Helvetica Neue Pro

Publication of this book is made possible in part by financial support from the College of Arts and Sciences of Western Carolina University.

Library of Congress Cataloging-in-Publication Data
Names: Ennis, Georgia C., 1987– author.
Title: Rainforest radio : language reclamation and community media in the Ecuadorian Amazon / Georgia C. Ennis.
Description: [Tucson] : University of Arizona Press, 2025. | Includes bibliographical references and index.
Identifiers: LCCN 2024032652 (print) | LCCN 2024032653 (ebook) | ISBN 9780816555192 (hardcover) | ISBN 9780816552696 (paperback) | ISBN 9780816552702 (ebook)
Subjects: LCSH: Quechua language—Revival. | Radio broadcasting—Ecuador—Napo (Province)
Classification: LCC PM6301 .E56 2025 (print) | LCC PM6301 (ebook) | DDC 306.442/9822309866416—dc23/eng/20250101
LC record available at https://lccn.loc.gov/2024032652
LC ebook record available at https://lccn.loc.gov/2024032653

Printed in the United States of America
♾ This paper meets the requirements of ANSI/NISO Z39.48-1992 (Permanence of Paper).

In memory of my mother and first teacher, Eilene Ennis. And for all the women—especially Serafina Grefa and the midwives of AMUPAKIN—who have mentored me in her absence.

CONTENTS

	List of Illustrations	*ix*
	Acknowledgments	*xi*
	Introduction	3
1.	Language and Ecology in the Upper Napo	33
2.	Media Ecology in the Upper Napo	75
3.	Linguistic Natures and Revitalization Ideologies	113
4.	Reanimating Kichwa in Napo's Media Ecology	141
5.	Affective Technologies and Intimate Publics	175
6.	Media and Collective Memory	201
	Epilogue	231
	Appendix: Guide to Orthographic Conventions and Morpheme Glosses	*241*
	References	*245*
	Index	*271*

ILLUSTRATIONS

Figures

1. Comparison of Napo's total population who self-identified as Indigenous and reported speaking an Indigenous language	8
2. The author with members of AMUPAKIN	20
3. The author with Serafina Grefa and Mariano Aguinda	22
4. Map of the Tena-Archidona region of Napo province	47
5. Sumaco volcano as seen from the outskirts of Archidona on the Avenida Napo	52
6. Map shows distribution of major regional dialects of Ecuadorian Kichwa	62
7. Facebook comments about ukuy, which were recirculated on the radio	76
8. Rita Tunay interviews María Narváez during *A New Path*'s first live broadcast	91
9. Mariano Aguinda takes the family radio off the shelf for evening listening while his wife, Serafina Grefa, weaves	99
10. Rita Tunay and James Yumbo interview Mario Yumbo for the radio archive	133
11. A contestant wearing "traje de muyu" dances during the cultural pageant in San Pablo de Ushpayaku	151
12. Serafina Grefa processing pita fiber by her fire	215

Tables

1. Select morphological variations in Ecuadorian Kichwa dialects — 61
2. Translated script for "Jumandi Yuyay" — 92
3. Comparison of past tense in different dialects — 105
4. Pitak Waska Ñusta, Q&A with winner Karen Pizango — 163
5. Chunta Warmi Ñusta, Q&A for Contestant 1 — 165
6. Chunta Warmi Ñusta, Q&A, response by Contestant 1 — 166
7. Chunta Warmi Ñusta, Q&A, response by Contestant 4 — 167
8. Chunta Warmi Ñusta, Q&A, winning response by Contestant 6 — 168
9. Chunta Warmi Ñusta, Q&A, response by runner-up Contestant 2 — 169
A1. Unified Kichwa Conventions and Orthography — 242
A2. Morpheme Glosses — 243

ACKNOWLEDGMENTS

My greatest debt of gratitude is to the residents of Napo who opened their lives to me. I especially thank my *comadres* Rita Tunay and Gloria Grefa for their friendship. I am grateful to the Association of Kichwa Midwives of the Upper Napo (AMUPAKIN), especially members active during my time there: Adela Alvarado, Catalina Aguinda, Olga Chongo, María Narváez, Angelina Grefa, Serafina Grefa, María Antonia Shiguango, Ofelia Salazar, Marilin Salazar, Inés Tanguila, and Gissela Yumbo. I would have a very impoverished view of life in Napo without the mornings I spent with families listening to the radio and accompanying people in their daily lives. A very special thank you to my hosts in Chaupishungo, Serafina Grefa and Mariano Aguinda, as well as to other residents who shared their knowledge with me. To my friends and colleagues in Napo, *ashka llakishkawa tukuy kangunara sumak yachachishkamanda pagarachuni.*

At the University of Michigan, Bruce Mannheim provided a constant source of motivation for understanding Quechuan linguistic and cultural practices within their lived worlds. Barbra Meek encouraged me to think deeply about the ways in which language revitalization articulates with complex sociocultural processes. Both have shaped my work profoundly. I also thank Kelly Askew, Judith Irvine, Sally Thomason, and Michael Uzendoski (of FLACSO, Ecuador) for their mentorship throughout the years, as well as their astute comments on my work. My gratitude to members of my cohort—some of my first interlocutors, especially: Adrian Deoanca, John Doering-White, Obed Garcia, Matan Kaminer, Nama Khalil, Adrienne Lagman, Prash Naidu, Sandhya Narayanan, Niku T'arhechu T'arhesi, and Warren Thompson. My thanks to Stuart Kirsch and participants in the Ethnolab workshop. I could not have asked for a more supportive group of readers as Allison Caine, Drew Haxby, Jessica Lowen, Aleksander Skylar, Jennifer Tucker, and Jessica Worl. My work also benefited from the input of members of UM's Ling Lab and Circulo Andino, including (among many): Michael Lempert, Meghanne Barker, Chip Zuckerman, Michael Prentice, James Meador, Jennifer Sierra, and Anne Marie Creighton. As an undergraduate at UM, I was immensely fortunate to work with Teresa Satterfield; her early guidance continues to inform my scholarship. Recognition is owed to the many other colleagues and friends—too many to name here—who enriched my years in Ann Arbor.

I am also grateful to the Center for Humanities and Information at Penn State University for the support of a Visiting Fellowship from 2019 to 2022, which allowed me to refine the core arguments of this book. Thank you to Eric Hayot, Pamela VanHaitsma, John Russell, Jennifer Shook, Heather Froehlich, Josh Shepperd, and Chris Willoughby. Thank you as well to Tim Ryan, Doug Bird, Chris Heaney, Tracy and Nicole Peterson, Hollie Kulago, Jamie Andreson, and other fellows and friends in State College. My thanks to Karl Swinehart and Anna T. Browne Ribeiro for their 2017 session at the American Anthropological Association meetings, when I first thought about how the past comes alive in the present. Further thanks to Erin Debenport for her encouragement. Hannah McElgunn, Nikolas Sweet, and Kamala Russell provided generous comments on chapter drafts.

Since 2022, I have been fortunate to make my academic home in the Department of Anthropology and Sociology at Western Carolina University with the gracious support of my colleagues and institution. The final writing and revisions of this book were completed upon the traditional territories of the Eastern Band of the Cherokee, though the manuscript— and I—have been guests upon many more Indigenous lands since its inception. I am especially indebted to Allyson Carter and Alana Enriquez at the University of Arizona Press, and to several anonymous reviewers for their insightful engagements with my thinking.

Over more than ten years of research and study in Ecuador, I have been lucky to join a network of scholars. My preliminary research in

ACKNOWLEDGMENTS

the Ecuadorian Amazon was supported by Foreign Language and Area Studies (FLAS) fellowships, which brought me to the Andes and Amazon Field School. Tod Swanson has provided integral mentorship for my research in Napo. I am continually thankful to Janis Nuckolls for her insights. Pieter Muysken—gone too soon—was an irreplaceable scholar of Kichwa. Thank you to my friends and fellow students of Amazonian Kichwa: Ernesto Benitez, James Beveridge, Virginia Black, Lauren Dodaro, Travis Fink, Chris Hebdon, Trisha López, Chris Jarret, Nick Padilla, Annie Preaux, Jarrad Reddekop, Alexander Rice, Bryan Rupert, Michael Severino, Lisa Warren Carney, John White, and Alí Huitzílatl. Karolina Grzech, Anne Schwarz, and Simeon Floyd have been invaluable colleagues. My sincere gratitude is owed to my comadre Eulodia Dagua, and to other teachers in Pastaza. In Quito, Susana Cabeza de Vaca and Karen Aguilar of the Comisión Fulbright del Ecuador provided indispensable support navigating grants and visas, treating me like family since 2011. Through Fulbright, I was lucky to know Kim Lewis, Heather Rule, and Sanjay Jolly, alongside many other scholars and students.

I am grateful for the financial support that made this research possible. Funding for my fieldwork was provided by a National Science Foundation Doctoral Dissertation Research Improvement Grant (DDRIG), a Fulbright-Hays Doctoral Dissertation Research Abroad (DDRA) Fellowship, and a Rackham International Research Award from the University of Michigan. Preliminary research was supported by a Tinker Field Research Grant and grants from the Department of Anthropology at Michigan. The support of a Mellon/ACLS Dissertation Completion Fellowship allowed me to complete dissertation writing. This material is based upon work supported by the National Science Foundation under Grant No. 1528496. Any opinions, findings, and conclusions or recommendations expressed in this material are those of the author(s) and do not necessarily reflect the views of the National Science Foundation.

Thank you to my father, Steve Ennis, for always encouraging me. And thank you to my mother, Eilene Ennis, for everything she taught me in our time together. I wish she could see where the path she set me on would lead.

Finally, a very special thank you to my partner, Matthew Johns, for his patient support of my journeys during the nearly ten years I have been researching and writing this text.

Rainforest Radio

Introduction

Get up.
It's time to wake up.
Are you listening?
I am going to tell you what Napo Runa mothers taught me in the
hours before dawn, when children are awakened to learn how to
become a person.
Are you really listening?

■ ■ ■

I awoke to Serafina Grefa's activity on the floor below. The glow of my phone confirmed it was shortly after three in the morning. I had grown accustomed in months prior to early morning visits to Kichwa radio programs, but this was one of my first mornings in the community of Chaupishungo. I didn't know what to expect, yet, though I would repeat this routine many times in coming months. I gathered my recording equipment and made my way downstairs into the kitchen to sit by the fire with Serafina and her family. The surrounding forest was still, the daily hum of insects quieted, though birds began to call as the hours before dawn slipped into morning. The dark was instead enlivened with the sound of Kichwa radio and light spilling from the house of Serafina's son, who lived next door.

In Serafina's kitchen and in others around Chaupishungo, women were rekindling open wood fires to heat up infusions of *wayusa* (*Ilex guayusa*). Serafina swished her first sip around her mouth and then blew the bitter liquid into the air—a protection against stinging insects during the day. Serafina and several of her adult children, their spouses, and grandchildren gathered on low benches around the fire. The floor of the kitchen was poured concrete, but the hearth was built into a sunken opening containing a pounded earth floor, with stools and benches arranged around the edge. Serafina's son-in-law Fabian asked me what I had dreamt that night. He told me about his dreams of walking in the forest, usually an unspoken reference to hunting. Serafina and her daughters wove *shigra* bags as the family exchanged stories, while her grandchildren leaned sleepily against their mothers.

Although this was one of my first visits to Chaupishungo, I was familiar with the broad outlines of these morning hours from visits to local radio programs. Simultaneously an event and a habitual time of day, the activity known as *wayusa upina* (guayusa drinking) is significant for many Napo Kichwa families. Many also see it as threatened by ongoing changes in the region, which are reshaping daily routines. Broadcasts that transposed these hours onto the air were popular features of local programming. In these events, cultural novices could experience not only the language but also the embodied actions of the wayusa upina. What I came to understand during my time in Napo was that for many Kichwa speakers, language was inseparable from place-based social practices and relationships. What many people in Napo said about language and what people there did through language suggests that for many, language was transmitted most meaningfully through embodied interactions, as just one thread of Kichwa lifeways.

Speakers of Upper Napo Kichwa (Quichua) in the Ecuadorian Amazon have increasingly turned to media, particularly radio media, to reclaim and reanimate their linguistic and cultural practices.[1] Yet, despite the enthusiasm with which new technologies of mediation have been adopted in Ecuador and around the globe for cultural sovereignty and linguistic reclamation, there are limited studies tracing how and why such media are actually produced, transmitted, received, and, possibly, recirculated (Eisenlohr 2004; Wilson and Stewart 2008; Galla 2019; Miller 2022). How—if at all—community media can contribute to language revitalization remains a pressing question.

The community media programs discussed in this book provide an ethnographic confirmation of what Indigenous activists and their al-

---

1. Orthographic choices are fraught when it comes to the Quechuan languages spoken in Ecuador (see Limerick 2017). I use *Kichwa*, following the standardized orthography of Kichwa Unificado, standardized "Unified Kichwa." The spelling *Quichua* remains widely used in English-language materials.

lies have suggested—community media are an effective and affective means of revitalizing languages and cultures. Joshua Fishman (1991) once claimed that media lack the affective and interpersonal dimensions needed to revitalize a language. Such a view assumes the passive reception of media isolated from social context, which has little to do with how grassroots media are created and used. In Napo, a complex ecology of community media supported the revalorization of not just Upper Napo Kichwa language but also social relationships and cultural practices that sustain linguistic transmission.

Media production was effective for language reclamation in Napo because radio listeners heard, and sometimes saw, their poetic practices and forms of verbal artistry, cultural activities, and face-to-face communicative relationships transposed into broadcast media. Rather than isolated moments of production, however, these radio programs were embedded in the lives of their listeners and their producers, providing a focal activity within the ecology of Upper Napo Kichwa media, the diverse strands of which are woven together to establish and sustain a mediated community of shared practices (Eckert and McConnell-Ginet 1992). In this case, the interlinked processes of radio production and reception become the mutual endeavor around which shared practices emerge.

Many of these programs focused on the stories Upper Napo Kichwa people tell about themselves—stories about who they once were, who they are now, and who they might become. Like many U.S.-based scholars who engage with Indigenous Latin America, I was captivated early in my studies by the stories my interlocutors told, as well as the various ways the narrative voices of Indigenous peoples have been transmitted—at times amplified, very often distorted (Simpson 2007)—in accounts by ethnographers, linguists, historians, missionaries, and other travelers in the Amazon.[2] Linguistic anthropologists have had an enduring interest with the ways that people tell stories and how those stories come to have meaning in different contexts (e.g., Briggs 1988; Tedlock and Mannheim 1995; Basso 1996; Ochs and Capps 2001). The case of Upper Napo Kichwa community radio demonstrates the ways that new technologies of mediation may transpose and transform both the poetic structures

---

2. In this text, I capitalize "Indigenous" to recognize the sovereignty of diverse peoples with a shared experience under settler colonialism (Alfred and Corntassel 2005, 597; Coulthard 2014, 181).

and modalities—discursive and nondiscursive, linguistic and otherwise material—of narrative practice onto the air. The production and reception of Indigenous community radio emerges as a powerful means to support linguistic and cultural reclamation and vitality.

Kichwa in Unexpected Places

The title of this book—*Rainforest Radio*—brings together two words that many still see in opposition to deepen our understanding of both. Living at the western edge of the Ecuadorian Amazon, speakers of Upper Napo Kichwa are "unexpected," to paraphrase historian Philip Deloria (2004; see also Webster and Peterson 2011), because of external expectations about Indigenous peoples there. When many people in the United States think of the Amazon rainforest, they often imagine a space that is absent of civilization, even of people. Students have told me that the first things that come to mind when they think of the Amazon are plants, wild animals, and biologists—or anthropologists—who study there. If they think of Indigenous peoples, it is in terms of uncontacted tribes. Many people I talk to are surprised that there is even radio, let alone television or cellular and Internet service, available in the Amazon. They are even more surprised when I tell them that Indigenous people not only consume media through these services but they also host radio programs, produce music videos and films, and create and share content on social media platforms like Facebook, YouTube, Instagram, and TikTok.

Napo, Ecuador, straddles the divide between the Andes and Amazon geographically, ecologically, linguistically, and culturally, challenging traditional expectations about the two regions. Like Nicholas Emlen's (2020) report of life at the frontier between the Peruvian Andes and Amazon as "just one world" and Anna Babel's view of the "in betweenness" of sociality in Lowland Bolivia, this account shows that the Amazon and Andes are linked by historical and contemporary interaction, which has shaped the land, people, and languages to be found there (Taylor 1999). Napo is a place that is neither entirely Andean nor entirely Amazonian, destabilizing the boundaries (e.g., Steward and Metraux 1948) of both.

As a Quechuan language associated with the Andean Highlands, varieties of Kichwa spoken in the Ecuadorian Amazon are unexpected because they are often ideologically erased. In a country divided into lush coast, mountainous highland sierra, and Amazonian *oriente*, Kichwa is thought of as the iconic language of the Highlands, in contrast to Amazonian language families like Chicham (Jivaroan) or the isolate Wao Tededo (Huaorani/Waorani). In 2010, approximately forty-seven thousand people spoke Upper Napo Kichwa (INEC 2010). It is likely that Amazonian Kichwa emerged through contact with Kichwa among different Amazonian populations resulting from the tumult of the colonial era (Muysken 2011). Colonial records indicate Andean Kichwa interpreters were brought into missionary "reductions" in the region, where speakers of different languages were forced together (Oberem 1980, 101). Kichwa-speaking residents around the Upper Napo are contemporary survivors of the colonial period and share cultural and linguistic practices with other Amazonian groups (Uzendoski and Whitten 2014). This linguistic history has important implications for language reclamation and revitalization projects.

Speakers of Kichwa in Napo sometimes refer to themselves as *Napu Runa*, or people of Napo, and their language as *Runa Shimi*. *Runa* means "people" or "human," while *shimi* refers to a word, language, speech, and the mouth. Fewer people identify with the term "Kichwa." Some have insisted to me that they are *not* Kichwa, but Runa. I usually refer to the language as Upper Napo Kichwa and to people as Napo Runa, or by the finer regional distinctions by which many identify. Identification of people and languages with named places or territories is an important way that Amazonian Kichwa speakers organize their social and communicative worlds.

Census data (figure 1) suggest that processes of language shift are ongoing. The 2010 Ecuadorian census recorded the total population of Napo as 103,697, with 58,845 people (nearly 57%) identifying as *indígena*. Meanwhile, in the 2010 census, 48,574 people (45.7%) reported they spoke an Indigenous language in Napo, with 47,425 speaking Kichwa (INEC 2010). This relatively large number belied an ongoing shift toward Spanish. In 2010, 60,379 people in Napo responded that their mother spoke an Indigenous language, so there were more than 10,000 people who came from an Indigenous-language background who did not report speaking an Indigenous language. Initial data from the 2022 census suggest greater language shift. By 2022, Napo's population grew to

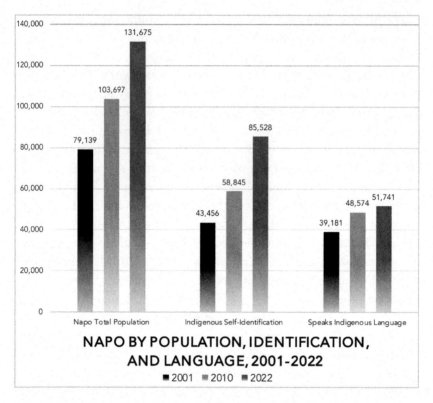

FIGURE 1 Comparison of Napo's total population who self-identified as Indigenous and reported speaking an Indigenous language 2001–2022 (data from INEC 2001; 2010; 2023).

131,675, with 85,528 people (64.9%) self-identifying as Indigenous (INEC 2023). However, a smaller percentage reported speaking an Indigenous language than in 2010. There were 51,741 people (39%) who reported speaking an Indigenous language in 2022 (INEC 2023). There is hope that the total number of speakers has not declined, even though their percentage of the population has. Census data are often a poor approximation for people's complex practices and sociolinguistic identities, but it suggests language shift is occurring. In Napo, Kichwa is transmitted intergenerationally, but in more restricted settings than the past.

Spanish, however, has become a dominant language among children and young adults, as parents encouraged them to speak it at home, while it was the primary code at school and among peers. Cultural cooperatives and media production provided spaces for what Bernard Perley has called "emergent vitalities" to refer to new domains of use and relationships created by community projects (2011, 146–47). These became sites in which Upper Napo Kichwa linguistic, cultural, and environmental knowledge were transmitted. They were also sites that spoke back to an unforeseen form of linguistic domination—the well-intentioned use of standardized Unified Kichwa in institutional media, language planning, and revitalization.

In Napo, regional speakers of Kichwa felt themselves to be oppressed not just by Spanish but by the standardized Unified Kichwa. In the Andes, institutional language planning and revitalization has depended on documentation, standardization, and classroom-based learning (Haboud and Limerick 2017; Hornberger and Coronel-Molina 2004; Hornberger and King 1996; Yánez 1991). Although an important way to reach learners and establish institutional legitimacy (Bourdieu 1991) for marginalized languages like Kichwa, standardization projects have complicated Kichwa language revitalization. Unified Kichwa is taught in Napo as a second language in bilingual education programs. It shapes the oral and written codes used in much institutional media. Grounded in the norms of Highland Kichwa, and regimented toward Spanish institutional settings, Unified Kichwa erases the sociolinguistic particularities of Upper Napo Kichwa, shaped by the region and a history of contact with other Amazonian languages. Many in Napo experienced Unified Kichwa as "another" kind of Kichwa. Much debate surrounding linguistic unification emerges from local language patterns and the connection many feel to their varieties, which regional speakers worry are being overtaken by this "other" Kichwa—a standardized variety linked to the Highlands.

These worries that children were learning "another variety" in school raise questions about how standard language is deployed and the role of classrooms in language revitalization. Many young people, who may not dominate regional forms, have adopted an oral register of Unified Kichwa, developed through their interactions with standard language education and institutional media. Anxieties over regional differentiation and belonging suggest that the adoption of Unified Kichwa is a form of language shift, as young people increasingly deploy a sociopolitically dominant code at the expense of regional forms. If revitalization is a "reshift" toward Indigenous languages as Fitzgerald (2017) suggests, it is important to consider what is being shifted to and the meanings of those forms for speakers.

Napo Kichwa people have turned to what some would also see as an "unexpected" method to confront the ongoing shift toward both Spanish language and lifeways *and* Unified Kichwa—live performances and the production of various forms of media, including radio, community cinema, television, and music. Media producers and community members sought to reclaim the practices and relationships of the past through forward-looking media forms, creating contemporary practices, as they imagined alternative futures. Napo Runa activists engaged contemporary technologies not to return to the past but to create possibilities for that past to be meaningful in the present and future. Their work shows us that a romantic return to the past is implausible if not impossible. What must be done instead is to confront disruption with all available tools to imagine emergent possibilities and vitalities for languages, cultures, and ecologies.

Remediating Endangerment

As an ethnography situated at the intersection of Indigenous media production and linguistic revitalization, my use of the term *remediation* plays on at least two meanings: its more common use in the sense of "remedying" something (Oxford English Dictionary, n.d.) and its more specialized use in media studies (Bolter and Grusin 1999) to analyze the ways that media technologies and texts are reconfigured across sites of mediation.

The first sense of remediation as remedy underlies many of the practices that I discuss. Members of a diverse Upper Napo Kichwa community of practice and their institutional and academic allies frequently seek to mitigate or "reverse" (Fishman 1991) ongoing situations of shift toward Spanish. Others seek to counter the use of the pan-Kichwa standard in institutional language revitalization projects based in standard language literacy. The efforts of many of my interlocutors in Napo to "revalorize" and reclaim sociolinguistic practices are one sense in which they are attempting to remediate language shift.

For my part, I also seek to contribute to remedying some of the taken-for-granted assumptions that have shaped the ways scholars trained within

Euro-American academic institutions conceive of language change, endangerment, and revitalization. Linguists and language advocates often approach language revitalization through particularly Western ideas of what *language* is, which also influences the methods and media they turn to for revitalization. In part stemming from Franz Boas's legacy of salvage linguistics among "disappearing" cultures, the production of grammars, dictionaries, and texts are often the first steps a concerned fieldworker takes to document a shifting language (Boas 1911; Rice 2011). Such an approach implies that language is reducible to a code—the elements of phonology, phonetics, morphology, and syntax as well as the arrangement of that code into texts. Linguistic documentation has served an important role in language revitalization projects (Spence 2018). But it also smuggles in tacit assumptions about language common among speakers of standard language cultures, such as the decontextualized and decontextualizable nature of language or the connection between a single, standard language and a unified polity (Silverstein 1996; Milroy and Milroy 1999; Milroy 2001; Flores 2013). Salvage approaches in linguistics have also resulted in linguistic extraction, leading to a "zombie linguistics," in which archived languages are disconnected from their speakers (Perley 2012; Davis 2017).

Conflicts between regional and unified forms of Kichwa invite us to differentiate between two responses to language shift that I have treated as interchangeable so far: language revitalization and language reclamation. Wesley Leonard has suggested a distinction between language revitalization and language reclamation (Leonard 2012, 2017; De Korne and Leonard 2017; see also Davis 2017). This use of "reclamation" differs from other uses in linguistics, in which a dormant or sleeping language is awakened or reclaimed through written sources. Instead, reclamation is an explicitly decolonial practice, which "begins with community histories and contemporary needs, which are determined by community agents, and uses this background as a basis to design and develop language work" (Leonard 2017, 19). Rather than beginning from a salvage paradigm with a goal of reproducing Chomsky's (1965) ideal speaker-listener in a homogenous speech community, such an approach asks what produced language shift in the first place and what constitutes meaningful ways of rekindling use.

In Napo and elsewhere, many people see serious cause for concern about ongoing processes of linguistic and cultural change. Yet the creation and consumption of Upper Napo Kichwa community radio demonstrates the contemporary vitality of many significant practices and the emergence of new modalities to sustain them. Today in Napo, some speakers worry that young people are "*mishu tukusha*" (turning into white-mestizos) or "*awalltayasha*" (becoming white). Likewise, Michael Uzendoski describes how anthropologists have foretold "the continual loss of indigenous culture in the Upper Amazon and final assimilation of indigenous peoples to mestizo society as peasants" (2005, 165). Napo Runa communities find themselves enmeshed within multiple discourses of endangerment, from both internal and external sources, in which their very personhood is in question. Yet the ways that many speakers conceive of continuities between their past and the present, as well as the forms of synthesis and renewal evidenced by Upper Napo Kichwa media, suggest that community media producers, program participants, and receptive audiences seek to define and reanimate a shared memory of their past in a present in which their conditions have dramatically changed. I also seek to "remedy" dire endangerment discourses by highlighting my interlocutors' successes in transmitting their linguistic and cultural practices across sites of production, even when they are reconfigured by the processes of transmission. The radio programs I discuss are emergent vitalities (Perley 2012, 142), because they provide new domains of use grounded in "community creativity." Along with my interlocutors, I trace the indexical connections between contemporary *runa kawsay*, "the lifeways of the Upper Napo Runa" and *ruku kawsay*, "the lifeways of the elders," evidenced in these emergent vitalities.

Processes of "remembering" (*iyarina*) and "forgetting" (*kungarina*) are central to discourse about linguistic and cultural shift in Napo.[3] In Napo, many people link the adoption of "white" lifeways with language shift. Such anxieties shape the song "Ruku Kawsay" (Lifeways of the Elders) by César Grefa, a Kichwa politician known by the stage name El Indio

---

3. Throughout this text, I utilize various versions of the terms "to remember" and "to forget" to describe processes of cultural maintenance (remembering/not forgetting) and cultural/linguistic shift (forgetting). They are placed in quotation marks to indicate the more direct citation to the terminology used by my interlocutors.

Amázonico (the Amazonian Indian). He laments the adoption of *mishu* or white-mestizo knowledge systems in the song's refrain:

Excerpt of "Ruku Kawsay" by César Grefa

Ñukanchi yachak Jumandika	Our wise Jumandi[4]
Ñukanchi yachak Jumandika	Our wise Jumandi
Shinzhi yuyayta charishkata	The powerful thought that he had
mana alita iyarisha	[by] not remembering [it] well
Mishu yuyayta apishkanchi	We have taken on white thinking
Mishu yuyay balichinchi	We exalt [give value to] white thinking

The underlined verb form *iyarisha*, "to remember," is derived from the verb *iyana*, "to think" (Nuckolls and Swanson 2020; Orr and Wrisley 1981). When combined with the reflexive -*ri* it takes on the meaning of "to remember [through reflection]." The verb *kungarina*, "to forget," describes linguistic and cultural change and continuity. Elders claim that young people have "forgotten," or, alternatively, claim that they themselves have "not forgotten." Despite these fears about contemporary processes of "forgetting," in homes around Napo today, many of the practices of ruku kawsay are remediated across generations and spaces of transmission, as contemporary families and early morning radio programs reclaim and refashion material practices and ways of speaking from the past and present. Broadcast and performance media in Napo are a meaningful way of rekindling and reclaiming language and other pedagogical projects. It is in this transmission that I locate the second meaning of the term *remediation.*

The concept of *remediation* (Bolter and Grusin 1999; Bolter 2001; Silvio 2007) describes how new media technologies appropriate and refashion the forms and techniques of prior media. Bolter and Grusin describe that "a medium is that which remediates. It is that which appropriates the techniques, forms, and social significance of other media and attempts to rival or refashion them in the name of the real" (1999, 65). However, they

---

4. Jumandi (also Jumandy) is a regional hero of anti-colonial resistance, known for his role in a major uprising against the Spanish, for which he was executed in Quito. He has been reclaimed as a central figure in Napo Kichwa politics, particularly in the Archidona-Tena region (Cognet 2021; Uzendoski 2005; see also Sawyer 2004).

largely remain focused on technologies as the vehicles of remediation. Think, for instance, of the way that photography remediated painting. I engage a more expansive view of media and mediation, grounded in Peircean realism, which proposes that all experience is mediated by semiosis (Mannheim 2018b; Ball 2014; Peirce 1955; Keane 2005). All semiotic activity—including language—is a form of mediation because there is no experience of the world prior to or apart from semiotic interpretation, interpretations that must be built up through socialization into cultural worlds. If all semiotic activity is a form of mediation, then people are also mediums of transmission, whose actions allow semiotic materials to be continually interdiscursively and intertextually refashioned. Remediation becomes a basic component of all cultural activity, as we daily draw upon and reconfigure semiotic material from various sources in our own projects of meaning making, both above and below the level of metapragmatic awareness.

Remediation is a means to explore the ways in which fashions of speaking, genres of verbal artistry, interactional routines, and material practices are enregistered (Agha 2005) across time and generations and are reconfigured within changing contexts of use. While a basic part of semiotic practice, such reconfigurations may cause considerable anxiety. For instance, in Napo, elders frequently worry that their children and grandchildren no longer wish to speak Kichwa—especially their local Kichwa—nor do they want to drink the fermented brew of manioc *aswa*. For these elders, such practices help to define a stable figure of Upper Napo Kichwa personhood, which is being reconfigured for many people through increased contact with other models of social value and practice in the settler colonial present.

Reanimating Collective Memory

The second major thread of this book concerns the ways that my interlocutors in Napo use radio and other media forms to *reanimate* linguistic and cultural practices shifting in the context of settler colonialism in the Ecuadorian Amazon. Echoing César Grefa's song, in interviews and in daily conversations many worry that young people and children are "forgetting" (or shifting) their culture and language. Upper Napo Kichwa

INTRODUCTION

media producers and performers seek to bring the past to life in a rapidly changing present—a process I call *reanimation*. They do so by animating characterological figures (Manning and Gershon 2013; Nozawa 2013; Barker 2019a) of social personhood. I analyze this as a way of *re*animating socially recognizable selves—what linguistic anthropologist Asif Agha (2005) calls enregistered figures—of their elders and their practices in the present through broadcast and other media.

A major response to linguistic and cultural shift in Napo has been mounted through institutional bilingual education programs using Unified Kichwa. Such projects, however, have contributed to producing their own sociolinguistic disjunctures, what Barbra Meek describes as "the everyday points of discontinuity and contradiction—between social or linguistic groups, within discourses, practices, or between them, even between indexical orders—that interrupt the flow of action, communication, or thought." (2010, x). In both the Ecuadorian Lowlands and Highlands, ethnographic research has shown that language standardization as a model for revitalization has led to the development of a prestige variety modeled on the standard, resistance to the standard by adherents to regional varieties, and ideological confusion for novice speakers about the "correctness" of the often-contrasting forms spoken at home and at school (Grzech, Schwarz, and Ennis 2019; Grzech 2017; Wroblewski 2012; Uzendoski 2009; K. A. King 2001).

In this context, Upper Napo Kichwa cultural activists—of varying ideological commitments—are increasingly turning toward public and broadcast media—including radio, television, and performance events such as Indigenous beauty pageants—to transmit language and culture. Thus far, anthropologists of the region have largely approached Upper Napo Kichwa media through the analytical lens of performance (Rogers 1998; Wroblewski 2014), treating events such as regional cultural pageants modeled on international beauty pageants as spaces where essentialized representations of Indigenous Amazonian culture are performed for urban, multiculturalist audiences. Past work has emphasized the "symbolic redundancy" and "invented" elements of these productions, highlighting the intertextual gaps between "performed" and "lived" realities. Yasmin Moll's exploration of contested theology and aesthetics in Islamic media production in Egypt provides an alternative approach to the contemporary mediation of "tradition," as she proposes that "practitioners reconfigure . . . tradition through engagement with the variety of normative regimes they encounter as modern subjects" (Moll 2018, 236). Like Moll, I question the analytical validity of the "invented tradition," a specter that hangs over contemporary Kichwa media production.[5] Many academic observers in Napo fixate on young women dancing in bikinis made from red, brown, and black seeds, or men who don grass skirts for musical performances—which no one wears in daily life—but which have emerged as a central component of the public register of cultural performance. Rather than treating such practices as spurious inventions, I take these forms seriously within their contexts of use, particularly as ways of imagining and animating a nostalgic past (Boym 2007; Debenport 2015, 2017) directed toward a hopeful future, within the context and constraints of the present.

The analytic of *reanimation* also reveals something new about how Upper Napo Kichwa cultural activists, media producers, and community members use media to bring particular social selves to life. Rather than focusing on these media productions as "performances," in which there may be significant gaps between performers and roles, I approach these programs as sites for the projection of chronotopic worlds that are *animated* through various forms of semiotic media (Silvio 2010; Manning and Gershon 2013; Nozawa 2013; Barker 2019a; Fisher 2019; Goffman 1974; cf. Goffman 1959). Rather than animation in the sense of drawn or computer-generated imagery, the analytic of animation emphasizes the ways that participants—both producers and audiences—breathe life into social figures and characters, which may be constructed through the lamination of different kinds of semiotic media—as in puppetry or embodied cosplay.

By combining different forms of semiotic practice, of which speech is just one modality, radio producers and participants reanimated social figures who inhabit a time-space of the past, the present, and a hopeful fu-

---

5. Moll suggests that the "invented tradition is analytically suspect," as such reconfigurations are key to the production of discursive traditions (2018, 236). Moreover, the idea of the "invented tradition" assumes the necessity of continuity between a past origin or original state, creating the stakes for the "last" ideologically pure representative of a particular culture or language to vanish, while also circumscribing the possibility of creativity and transformation.

ture, in which linguistic practices, contexts of use, and social relationships have been reconstituted. Linguistic anthropologists have largely drawn upon the Bakhtinian concept of chronotope—inseparable expressions of time, space, and personhood (Bakhtin 1981b [1938]; Agha 2007; Inoue 2004)—in relation to language, exploring how linguistic practices allow speakers to draw listeners across time and space. The preference of radio producers to remediate embodied productions into aural radio media points to the significance of nonverbal modalities for constructing and calibrating chronotopes (Hartikainen 2017; Eisenlohr 2015; Moore 2016).

The analytics of remediation and reanimation speak to a concern shared between Native American and Indigenous studies and linguistic anthropological approaches to language shift and reclamation to consider not only the negative aspects of language and cultural shift—perceptions of absence in the context of settler colonialism—but also emergent sites of synthesis, renewal, and vitality (Vizenor 1994, 2009; Perley 2012; Davis 2017, 2018). As Barbra Meek observes, "language revitalization involves not only the reconstitution of some grammar, but of the indexical orders that link a grammar to a complex of meaning emergent through a world of experience" (2010, 50). Remediation and reanimation reconstituted indexical connections where they had been ruptured by—often forced—cultural and linguistic shift. This is one way that my interlocutors used mass media to sustain and reawaken significant forms of interaction and genres of practice (Garrett 2007, 2005).

Multimodal and Multi-sited Ethnography

This research explores the social effects of Upper Napo Kichwa media, which requires understanding not only the production of these media, but how such media are embedded in daily communicative practices. I almost missed what was most important about language activism in Napo when I arrived in 2015. At the start, I was focused on the importance of media for *language* revitalization. Although I had visited Napo several times to study Kichwa and conduct preliminary research, I still could not see how the Upper Napo Kichwa mediascape was concerned with more than language. Instead, I was interested in how broadcast media like radio contributed to language revitalization in the context of tensions over standardized varieties like Unified Kichwa and regional varieties like Upper Napo Kichwa. Both beliefs about language—ideologies of how one should speak—and the actual use of different varieties on the air are important aspects of media production in Napo, which I discuss at various points in this book. Community-produced broadcast and performance media allowed people that did not usually have access to media production—often rural and elder Kichwa women—to be heard more widely. On community media, they spoke publicly in what many referred to as "their variety"—the Kichwa micro-lects that ideologically distinguish regions, settlements, and even families.

But to understand reclamation in Napo more deeply, I had to learn to see language—and media produced to transmit it—as more embedded in other social practices and relationships. Initially inspired by prior ethnographic studies of the social embeddedness of media, I wanted to understand how the social circulation of forms of speech beyond mobile discursive "texts" was facilitated by radio media (Hirschkind 2006; Fisher 2016; Ginsburg, Abu-Lughod, and Larkin 2002; Abu-Lughod 2004; Wortham 2013; Wilson and Stewart 2008; Spitulnik 1997). Besides snippets of discourse, how do narrative practices, styles, registers, and other bundles of linguistic features circulate—if at all—between face-to-face interactions and radio-mediated communication? Several practices, I found, were recontextualized in media. Group storytelling, sound-symbolic ideophones, and different genres of song might appear on the air, alongside more innovative styles of speech such as the *saludo*—the popular "shout out" to named listeners—or *yachachina*, local news segments and announcements. Other material practices and embodied interactions could also be recontextualized in radio media, a seemingly aural platform.

Ethnographic methods, moreover, have proven to be particularly valuable for studying language shift and reclamation. Mufwene (2017) notes that despite a great deal of attention in disciplinary linguistics to the topics of language endangerment and revitalization, the causes motivating people to shift from Indigenous and other minority languages to dominant, frequently colonial, languages remain undertheorized. He observes that many linguists make vague gestures to "colonization" or "globalization" in disrupting Indigenous and other marginalized languages, rather than "the adaptions their speakers make in response to their changing socioeconomic ecologies" (2017, e203; cf. Meek 2010, 42).

Linguistic anthropologists, grounded in ethnographic fieldwork methods, have long been concerned with understanding the social, economic, and political forces and regimes of value within which speakers of minority languages are enmeshed. This study draws inspiration from linguistic anthropologists who connect the study of language shift and change to the ways that languages are ideologized within broader political economies (Irvine and Gal 2000; Gal and Woolard 2001; Kroskrity 2000; Kroskrity and Field 2009). Susan Gal (1979), Don Kulick (1992), and Barbra Meek (2010) all provide nuanced ethnographic examples of the ways that larger sociolinguistic and economic frameworks influence the transmission of minoritized languages between generations. Ethnographic research can provide insight into questions of ongoing interest: Why do speakers of minoritized languages, despite many well-established programs aimed at reinvigorating or reawakening heritage languages, continue to shift to dominant, colonial languages, such as Spanish, and English? And what practices support the ongoing transmission of linguistic and cultural forms, even within settler-colonial institutions that devalue Indigenous ways of being in and speaking with the world?

In Napo, I initially drew upon the call in multi-sited ethnography to "follow the thing" (Marcus 1995). Radio was the first "thing" I followed around the cities of Tena and Archidona, visiting radio stations tucked into the offices of the Catholic church in Tena, hidden away in homes with rooms converted to studios, or in spare closets that had been repurposed in the municipal building in Archidona. On several of these programs, I was invited to speak—in Kichwa—about my research in Napo and the importance of language maintenance and revitalization. I became a regular guest cohost of the program *Mushuk Ñampi* (A New Path), one of the most widely listened to programs in Napo during its time on the air from 2014 to 2019. Like the daily cohosts Rita Tunay and James Yumbo, I kept a notebook to write names and messages from listeners I met around Napo. I was recognized less frequently than my colleagues, but by the end of my fieldwork in the summer of 2017, I was regularly asked if I wasn't "Jordy from the radio," or the *runa shimi rimak rancia warmi* (the Kichwa-speaking white-European woman), whom they had heard on the

FIGURE 2 The author with members of AMUPAKIN. Bottom row, L–R: Gissela Yumbo, Ofelia Salazar, Serafina Grefa, María Antonia Shiguango, Marilin Salazar, Adela Alvarado, María Narváez, Inés Tanguila, Catalina Aguinda, María Tapuy, Olga Chongo. Top: Mayra Shiguango and the author. Photo by Trisha Lopez with the author's camera.

air. When I affirmed, they would ask for a saludo, often directed to their family or to their community.

Beyond daily observation and participation at radio programs, I carried out research at a women's health and cultural center, the Association of Kichwa Midwives of the Upper Napo (Asociación de Mujeres Parteras Kichwas del Alto Napo, AMUPAKIN). The multigenerational members and volunteers of AMUPAKIN (figure 2) were frequent participants in the Upper Napo Kichwa media industry. I followed media in public spaces around Tena and Archidona, and into the daily life of rural households. In each space, I audio and/or video recorded interactions. I also used methods like survey and free interviews, conducted both in private and in communal settings, and elicitation tasks focused on storytelling with speakers of different ages. I followed my hosts into their forest gardens, learning about plants, animals, and local history. As part of my work with AMUPAKIN, I also participated in the Napo media industry. At AMUPAKIN's request, I applied for and received funding for a narrative arts project from the Ecuadorian Ministry of Culture and Patrimony. Our work on this project included filming, transcribing, and translating the stories of elder members of AMUPAKIN and their husbands about their environmental knowledge. This experience allowed my interlocutors to reflect on language standardization, writing, knowledge transmission, media, and ecological socialization, informing how I understand the place of language and media in Upper Napo Kichwa social life. In each site where I conducted research, I sought communal and individual consent for participation. Unless requested by my interlocutor, I do not use pseudonyms for the people in this book, in recognition of their roles as knowledge producers and teachers. Kichwa knowledge is usually contextualized within the relationships in which it was transmitted, a citational practice I attempt to maintain here.

My work with women emerged from my position within a gendered and racialized social world. Until relatively recently, Napo Runa society was deeply organized by gender (Guzmán Gallegos 1997; Galli 2012; Mezzenzana 2017). Men and women ate communally but separated by gender. AMUPAKIN's founder María Antonia described how in her childhood, male visitors to her family's home would sit on low wooden benches to converse, while women sat quietly together on the floor. Although my racial ascription (*rancia* or *tsala*, white, European) as well as my nationality (U.S. *gringa*) allowed me to move in spaces often closed to women, especially Napo Runa women, this was not a comfortable experience. I felt uncomfortable in recognition of how my race in a racialized society (Weismantel 2001; Canessa 2012; Roitman and Oviedo 2017) affected perceptions of my authority in comparison to my Napo Runa teachers. I also felt uncomfortable as a person with a body that could be—and was—gendered and sexualized by some male interlocutors. My status as a powerful outsider, however, meant that I was insulated from gendered violence in Napo in ways that some Kichwa women were not (see Galli 2012). In the households where I explored radio reception, I was drawn into the social world of women. Although I have developed important friendships with Runa men in Napo, Runa women have remained my closest interlocutors.

Radio was the "thing" I followed to the household of Mariano Aguinda and his wife Serafina Grefa (figure 3) in the Kichwa community of Chaupishungo. It was in their household I realized the "thing" that

FIGURE 3 The author with Serafina Grefa and Mariano Aguinda. July 17, 2019. Photo with author's camera by unknown.

I—and others in Napo—were following was not really radio, or even language, but the reweaving of their communicative world. The questions that had puzzled me when I began my research on radio—Why focus on "culture" and not language? And why spend so much energy on events that most people will only listen to?—began to make sense when I understood that my Kichwa interlocutors were teaching me—but more importantly, each other—to live what they called *ali kawsay*, "a good life," through speech and behavior.

I met Serafina and her family through AMUPAKIN, which sometimes arranged home stays with members. Serafina had not hosted a student before. She later told me she was wary to accept me into her home, though she ultimately did. The group's coordinator charged her to treat me like a daughter who still needed to be taught how to care for herself in the forest and the rivers. After I had lived in Chaupishungo for several months, Serafina accompanied me to visit and interview her neighbors. She sometimes recounted to them her hesitancy to take on a *rancia ushi*, a white daughter. Would I speak Kichwa? Would I eat their food? Would I drink the fermented manioc brew aswa? Even though I was a rancia, she assured them, I had learned to be a good daughter—I spoke Kichwa, I gladly drank aswa, and even ate *uchu*, a spicy sauce that enlivens boiled manioc, plantain soup, and steamed fish. These were significant practices elders believed young people were abandoning. Most importantly, I was not *killa* (lazy). I woke up every morning around three o'clock to sit beside the fire with Serafina, and a group of her adult daughters, teenage foster children, and young grandchildren, drinking guayusa, and listening to the radio and conversation. I had even tried to learn to weave shigra. I remained clumsy, though, while Serafina and her daughters deftly wove knots they described as "daughters" upon "mother" threads to produce shigra, strong mesh bags carried by men when hunting and by women while foraging in the forest or as their purse in town.

Although I never became a weaver, as I watched Serafina and her daughters weave during the wayusa upina, I also came to understand why this time was so important for the radio and other cultural reclamation projects in Napo—it was a site of everyday pedagogy, where children were explicitly and implicitly taught their elders' social and place-based knowledge. It was a time when children learned to be Napo Runa and when Napo Runa adults and elders reaffirmed their connections to each other and to their communicative world.

Community Media and Collective Memory

Language activists and allies (e.g., Camp and Portalewska 2013; Ginsburg 1997; Wilson and Stewart 2008) have called for the use of media as a method to amplify the voices of speakers of marginalized languages. Yet, the specific effects of the production, reception, and circulation of such media on speakers' daily practices largely remains an open, context-dependent question. Indeed, ethnographic research exploring the ways that linguistic and cultural practices are transposed into new contexts of mediation (Peterson 2017, 1997; Choksi 2018; Debenport 2015; Webster 2017; Fisher 2019) has shown we cannot assume that community media have the same effects and meanings in all settings of linguistic and cultural shift. Through the first in-depth ethnographic and linguistic study of Upper Napo Kichwa media ecology (Postman 2000; Fuller 2005; Lum 2005b), I show that these radio programs can expand how anthropologists understand the production and reception of media, the cross-cultural formation of publics, Amazonian narrative and collective memory, and the methodologies and effects of language reclamation.

Careful attention to the interlinkages between the creation and consumption of Upper Napo Kichwa radio dissolves any analytical or methodological divide in media studies associated with the production and reception of media, as these processes are inseparable among a mutually constitutive community of producers and consumers of Upper Napo Kichwa media. Radio programs are not decontextualized production events. They are embedded in producers' and consumers' lives and relationships. Media can only be understood as a method for community-oriented language reclamation with attention to spaces of production, reception, and their overlap. Many of the routines and practices remediated on Upper Napo Kichwa community radio are unintelligible without attention to the historical and contemporary contexts of use that they seek to reanimate on the air. Such reclamation media are often grounded in the verbal artistry and poetics of the familial sphere, challenging the focus on stranger sociality, rational debate, and political action typically associated with discussions of "publics" and the "public sphere" (Warner 2002; Habermas 1989; Anderson 1983).

The reception and subsequent interpretation of media are also not transparent processes. The formation of publics around media is an issue of cross-cultural relevance (Gal and Woolard 2001). Upper Napo Kichwa radio media shows that participation in a public is not always organized, as Warner describes, "as a relationship among strangers" (2002, 74). Rather, such media can involve an interactional "private," or in Debenport's words, "practices with texts among select groups of known individuals" (2015, 142). The recirculation of aural and oral media among an entangled population of producers and consumers reveals how public and private spheres of interaction are laminated in radio programs, hailing both known and unknown interlocutors. Listeners' different linguistic codes—standardized and regional—may identify them with or exclude them from the various publics and privates that coexist in Napo, depending on their subject position(s). Print and film practices have been more

INTRODUCTION   25

widely explored in relation to the formation of Indigenous publics.[6] Upper Napo Kichwa radio media, however, respond to both the oral poetics and the embodied textual practices (Uzendoski and Calapucha-Tapuy 2012) of Kichwa narrative and other verbal artistry.

The cross-cultural formation of publics is also relevant to understand how members of the different audiences addressed by Upper Napo Kichwa broadcast media engage with these media. Prior analysts in Napo (Rogers 1998; Wroblewski 2014) have considered the ways in which Indigenous media is directed to and received by multicultural audiences, with an emphasis on "essentialized" formulas. However, many signs deployed in cultural performance are not seen as essentialized icons of a pristine indigeneity by my Upper Napo Kichwa interlocutors. Instead, they are described as a way of honoring and remembering the practices of the elders, as well as imagining a world free from white social and material domination. The midwives of AMUPAKIN complained sometimes when they saw young women who wore shoes in cultural presentations like parades or beauty pageants. In contrast, AMUPAKIN's elder members rarely wore shoes during presentations. Is this another case of strategic essentialism, and the presentation of a materially—and ideologically—pure form of indigeneity for public audiences (Conklin and Graham 1995)? I suggest that it is not, or at least not entirely, nor for everyone. Rather, it is grounded in what I have called the remediation and reanimation of the embodied habits of their mothers and grandmothers. Elder women remember a time before rubber boots were worn in the forest and have shown me—reanimating the memory through the channel of their own bodies—the way that their mothers used a machete to clear the ground of thorns when they would harvest peach palm. Within the different semiotic systems held by members of various publics, a barefoot woman in traditional dress might signify an essentialized In-

---

6. Some notable works include Debenport's (2015) ethnography on "Keiwa" dictionaries and soap operas; Peterson's (2017) work on Navajo film and Twitter feeds, as well as an earlier article (1997) on radio; Webster on Navajo poets and poetics (2009), and the use of YouTube to overcome textual constraints (2017); Choksi (2018) on Santali writing in and on real and virtual sites; and LaPoe and LaPoe (2017) on storytelling and (digital) news media in Indigenous North America.

digenous femininity, but for many of the women who participate in such productions, it is a sign of one's respect for the practices of the past in a materially distinct present. Remediation and reanimation speak to the production of historical consciousness in Napo, as well as what is happening in these media productions, at least among a significant portion of their audience.

Radio media draw attention to how chronotopes (Bakhtin 1981b [1938]) of the past are brought to life in the present among speakers of Upper Napo Kichwa. The ways that historical narratives, through the "words our elders left behind," are transposed onto the radio addresses debates regarding the interrelationship of myth and history in Amazonian historical consciousness (Gow 2001; Hill 1988; Fausto and Heckenberger 2007). External distinctions like "myth" and "history" had very little to do with the knowledge that had been handed down by their elders for many people I knew. Practices like live-broadcast wayusa upina radio programs evidence a preference for constituting the past as a knowable world within the present. In Napo, the past is not continually forgotten in pursuit of progress—or at least it is not ideologized that way. Upper Napo Kichwa narrative practices—including ideophony, intertextuality, and formal dialogism—contribute to make the space-time of the past knowable, and even inhabitable, in the present. This is not to say that my interlocutors did not recognize differences between the past and the present. Many would comment on how clever and knowledgeable the elders of the past had been—for instance, regarding their knowledge of natural materials and crafts—in contrast with their own contemporary practices. Their claims occurred in the context of clearly identified changes between their own lives and the collective memories of the past projected through the transmission and retransmission of "the words our elders left behind." Despite these barriers to accessing the social and material lifeways of their elders, many insisted that they continued to "remember" (maintain) their elders' practices and stories by living (K. *kawsana*) or existing (K. *tiana*) with them—that is, animating them or giving them life—in the present.

My interlocutor's focus on the remediation of embodied practices in aural media directed at linguistic and cultural revitalization draws attention to the ways that an understanding of language revitalization as the reconstitution of a decontextualized, formal code may be inadequate to reconstitute the spaces where a code once had meaning. For good or bad, linguists and (linguistic) anthropologists have been some of the primary academic advocates for language revitalization (Hill 2002; Perley 2012; Palmer 2017). Linguistic anthropologists have also been particularly reflexive regarding the role of dominant or hegemonic ideologies in shaping social practices (Bauman and Briggs 2003). Sympathetic scholars have sometimes turned to methodologies for revitalization grounded in standardizing, text-based approaches to language, which have influenced the approaches many groups take to language revitalization. This is not to create a simple dichotomy between text-based revitalization practices and other modalities, nor between academic fields. Text remains an important modality in a larger methodological toolkit.

In Napo, however, speakers frequently express beliefs such as "Kichwa is pronounced just as it is written," one of the main reasons written standardization has been extended into oral standardization. Text-based approaches to the revitalization of predominantly oral languages also carry significant contradictions. It is worth examining their effects within the ideological assemblages and ecologies of language (Kroskrity 2018; Dauenhauer and Dauenhauer 1998; Hill and Hill 1986) where language shift, revitalization, and reclamation occur.

Some disjunctures in the revitalization of Upper Napo Kichwa emerge from the standardization of an oral language for use in formal education. The "unification" of regionally diverse Ecuadorian Kichwa varieties has created debates around social value and authenticity similar to other contexts (Jaffe 1999; French 2010). Such contradictions are intimately related to how many Napo Runa ideologize linguistic differentiation, socialization, and respect for elders. These were ideologies frequently remediated on radio programs in Napo. They were especially visible in the focus of the producers of *A New Path* on the reanimation of linguistic practices as embedded in contexts of use and the dialogic authority of elders on their monthly live broadcast of the wayusa upina. Upper Napo Kichwa radio programs attune us to the ways that alternative modalities and methods for linguistic and cultural revitalization respond to the complex linguistic ecologies that surround speakers of shifting languages. In the case of Napo, community broadcast media contribute to the articulation of a multivocal, dialogic public sphere grounded in the intimate social routines of Napo Runa family life.

To make claims about the efficacy of community revitalization media, it is imperative to trace how community radio media are produced, consumed, and recirculated in the complex social and linguistic ecologies of the Upper Ecuadorian Amazon. Rather than assuming that media are an effective method for linguistic and cultural revitalization, I show that they are one because the production and reception of Upper Napo Kichwa radio media are embedded in speakers' daily lives and communicative practices. They are linked into broader social and economic processes in the Ecuadorian Amazon, as the nascent Upper Napo Kichwa media industry provides a new economic outlet for residents of Napo and has opened new domains of use—which are often tied to self-consciously "traditional" domains—for Kichwa. Closely linked to community tourism cooperatives, cultural activism and performance groups, and a variety of social and political organizations, Upper Napo Kichwa radio media help weave together some of the diverse strands of the Napo Runa social world. Such interlinked spaces are increasingly drawing young people and their elders together to reclaim and reanimate significant linguistic and cultural practices. These radio programs are contemporary sites of regional Kichwa vitality.

Plan of the Book

Upper Napo Kichwa radio highlights the need to understand media and reclamation within their contexts of production and reception. The following chapters move across different spaces of production and reception to describe how a nostalgic past is constituted, circulated, and, sometimes, contested in media events directed toward the reclamation of language within contexts of use, rather than just language as a code.

The first chapter provides an overview of processes of extractive and settler colonialism that have shaped language in Napo since the first arrival of Europeans in 1538 through my fieldwork in 2015–2017. The Ecuadorian Amazon is home to several other Indigenous languages, creating a multilingual linguistic ecology within which Upper Napo Kichwa likely developed in the colonial period and is now spoken. I also introduce an unexpected source of disruption for Napo Kichwa linguistic practices—the standardized variety known as Unified Kichwa. For many in Napo, Unified Kichwa fits into an already complex linguistic landscape, where variations in phonology, morphology, and lexicon mark regional linguistic histories. I further trace different forms of contemporary colonial expansion—missionary education, wage labor, roads, settlers, agricultural development, resource extraction, among others—to their effects on linguistic and social practices. Until the 1920s, Napo remained relatively peripheral to the colonial and post-independence state. The next century would see Napo undergo a series of social and environmental changes, spurring language shift toward Spanish and eventually Unified Kichwa. Any possibility of reversing or mitigating language shift also requires understanding the conditions driving that shift in the first place.

Building on this historical and ethnographic context, chapter 2 introduces the ecology of local media in Napo and explores the different languages and varieties used within Napo's media ecology. The chapter introduces how Kichwa radio media articulates with other media technologies in Napo, including social media. I follow the transmission of a Facebook comment about flying reproductive leaf-cutter ants leaving their nests onto the radio, and among audiences who recirculated the notice that this local delicacy was coming into season. I also pay particular attention to the ways Kichwa-speaking residents of Napo evaluate their own and others' speech in different settings and explore how language relates to social categorization in the Amazon. I conclude by introducing examples of "our Kichwa" and Unified Kichwa at different community radio programs in Napo. In doing so, I identify the ways radio programming links different genres of media, participants, and linguistic varieties across an emergent ecology of Amazonian media. This chapter contributes to understanding variation within what is often taken as a single language (Ecuadorian Kichwa), as well as the interweaving of communicative modalities involved in seemingly singular media technologies like radio.

Told through various realizations and stories of the wayusa upina—the drinking of guayusa (wayusa) tea—chapter 3 explores the ideological, ontological, and pedagogical conflicts at stake in Kichwa language reclamation. The wayusa upina refers to the intimate, predawn hours when multigenerational families drink guayusa, converse, prepare for their day, and instruct children in the proper comportment of Kichwa lifeways.

Widely recognized by Kichwa people for its pedagogical importance, the wayusa upina has emerged as a central trope in Napo Kichwa media, repeated in glitzy beauty pageants, invoked on early morning radio programs, and regularly performed on the air in elaborate radio plays. I use different historical narratives and contemporary instantiations of the wayusa upina to show that Napo Kichwa people conceive of language as planted by elders in the hearts and minds of younger listeners, which will grow only if tended and remembered. It is these "words the elders left" that many in Napo sought to reclaim and remember in the face of language shift toward Spanish and toward Unified Kichwa. Language was as much about listening as about speaking. Such understandings of language socialization, as well as the beliefs about linguistic identity introduced in the previous chapter, conflict markedly with the underlying assumptions of text-based approaches to revitalization promulgated through standard language projects.

Chapter 4 examines the role of embodied performance in cultural reclamation, with a particular emphasis on women's performance. Since the late 1980s, bilingual educators in Napo have used cultural-beauty pageants featuring young Kichwa women to glamorize Kichwa cultural practices and promote a formal register heavily influenced by Unified Kichwa. I provide a new view of Kichwa cultural pageantry, which emphasizes the ways producers and participants sought to animate and reanimate—or semiotically bring to life—language alongside different forms of cultural practice. The chapter compares two cultural events in the township of Archidona, which were sponsored by the administration of the Kichwa mayor Jaime Shiguango—the cultural-beauty pageant for the Intercultural Peach Palm Festival and the administration's monthly wayusa upina performance, live-broadcast at four o'clock in the morning from communities around Archidona. In both, producers and hosts sought to recalibrate cultural performance to include voices that they thought had been ignored—those of more rural audiences and elder speakers. I analyze the different forms used by participants in each. Cultural performance and broadcast media are a multimodal method of reclamation, which afford the emergence of multiple fashions of speaking. Such performances may be taken up in unpredictable ways by the publics who interact with them.

Around Archidona, listeners in Kichwa households frequently heard their friends, family members, and neighbors speaking on the air as they drank their morning tea. Chapter 5 analyzes the circulation of several significant genres of Kichwa verbal artistry across face-to-face and otherwise mediated sites of production, with a focus on women's affect and songs of lament. Upper Napo Kichwa radio and music are an effective and affective means of stimulating conversation in Napo Runa households, which extends the communicative reach of regional speakers. Based in an intimate ethnography of radio reception in the household of Serafina Grefa and her multigenerational family, I trace the ways different genres of radio media remediated face-to-face practices, served as sites of commentary, and initiated further discussion, particularly around elder women's social and environmental knowledge. Understanding the interactional effects of Kichwa radio media also requires an understanding of the broader linguistic and media ecology in which it is produced.

Napo Kichwa community media provide a site for participants to reanimate collective memories fractured by the expansion of extractive and settler colonialism in the region. As a focused case study, in chapter 6, I follow the production of *pita* fiber across four sites of production: in Serafina Grefa's household in Chaupishungo, at regional beauty pageants, on a morning radio program, and on- and off-stage at AMUPAKIN. Pita fiber occupies a central place in Napo Kichwa history: it was one of the first products extracted as colonial tribute; in the early 1900s, Napo Kichwa people traveled by foot to sell it in the markets in Quito; today, products woven from pita feature prominently in cultural pageantry and are frequently sold to tourists. Yet, its production is declining among younger generations, who more frequently recycle plastics for use in weaving. I track the ways pita is produced and discussed in these different settings to suggest that community media are sites where participants seek to revalue and reinvigorate the practice within contemporary socioeconomic conditions. They do so be reanimating well-known figures of personhood, crafted through memory and contemporary practice, who often speak with the voices of their elders. By following radio and language across Napo, I came to see that what I—and others in Napo—were following was not really radio, or even language, but the reanimation of their social worlds and collective memories for use in the future.

The book concludes with the sudden death of one of the central figures of this text in November of 2020. I reflect on the ways social media and songs of lament contributed to circulating news of the death of Serafina Grefa, who was one of the core members of AMUPAKIN during my research in Napo and my host mother in Chaupishungo. Serafina's death highlights both the urgency of transmitting "the words of our elders" that motivates many people in Napo as well as the unexpected ways that different genres of media continue to circulate and animate the Upper Napo Kichwa social and linguistic world. Radio became a part of a broader ecology of media in the region, which contributed to reclaiming language alongside other modalities of cultural practice. The production and reception of radio media shows us the importance of community-based activism for reclamation, as well as the diversity of practices and positions within Indigenous communities. Ultimately, the story of Amazonian Kichwa radio and the people who produced it in the Upper Napo has important implications for how we understand the social dimensions of language shift and reclamation, as well as the day-to-day mediation of cultural and material-environmental change.

Set at the frontier of the urbanizing Amazon, this book tunes in to the story of a dedicated group of radio hosts and community members who gave shape to the early morning hours of their listening audience. Explicitly oriented toward members of a rural, regional public and the revalorization of "our own language," the radio program *A New Path* remediated and reanimated these "words our elders left behind" on a live, radio-broadcast production of the early morning guayusa-drinking hours. Due to the multivocal affordances of radio media, however, participants in these programs animated dynamic, and at times contested, chronotopes and figures, which established a polyphonic public sphere, in which multiple fashions of speaking could emerge. These programs, in turn, were anchored in "the words our elders left behind," a collection of wide-ranging historical, familial, and personal narratives, songs, and embodied practices. Although many of the practices remediated on the radio are undergoing shift, these radio programs reinvigorated the linguistic and otherwise embodied practices of their listening audience, dialogically strengthening the words of counsel and other practices of still-present elders. These nostalgic media events were also hopeful projects, in which participants sought to reclaim and reanimate their elders' knowledge and history in both the present and the future, among an electronically mediated community of practice, which converged in the ecology of Upper Napo Kichwa media.

CHAPTER 1

Language and Ecology in the Upper Napo

Serafina Grefa was born in 1947, living most of her life near the Inzhil-laqui River, in foothills nestled between Andean mountains and Amazonian floodplains. During her lifetime, as well as those of her friends and family living around the towns of Tena and Archidona, social life and language underwent dramatic transformations tied to settlement and extraction. Walking together over the several miles between her home in Chaupishungo and the town of Archidona, Serafina reflected on changes in the landscape. As a child, she and her family had visited Archidona using pathways on the banks of the rivers to traverse the forest. As an elder, Serafina walked a gravel road to reach the paved highway that leads to Archidona or Tena. Closer to the main road are the homes of settlers and fields deforested for cattle grazing or other agricultural projects.

Serafina and her family confronted everyday forms of settler disruption to their material environment, which also had consequences for their linguistic worlds. Although many young adults in Serafina's household spoke Kichwa with their elders, several of the youngest children were Spanish-dominant and did not always respond to their grandmother's Kichwa. Even more surprisingly, teenage foster children in Serafina's home were introduced to "another kind" of Kichwa at the high school they attended in nearby Tena, a trend that caused considerable concern in many families around the province. The situation in Napo highlights how expected and unexpected forms of coloniality (Quijano 2000; Roche 2019)—the hegemonic afterlives of colonial power relationships—may shape the linguistic, social, and material worlds of minoritized peoples, with serious consequences for their communicative practices.

During a lunchtime interview squeezed in between other meetings, the mayor of Archidona remarked to me, "The goal of the radio is to strengthen and transmit culture." Jaime Shiguango, one of the few Kichwa men to hold the municipal office in Archidona, had used Ecuadorian state funds for cultural and other development projects to create a radio program, which he called *Mushuk Ñampi*—A New Path. This was also the slogan for his administration, in power between 2014 and 2019. He continued, explaining that culture included "food, dance, Kichwa sport, what's called hunting, the *pajuyuks*, or the transmission of powers, shamanism, natural or ancestral medicine, and how to survive in the rainforest." The municipal radio program encouraged listeners to "reconnect to these skills" by collecting stories about them and staging live broadcasts each month based in residents' remembrances. I was puzzled. Why would a radio program, with a primarily listening audience, take the transmission of embodied practices as their central goal? Shouldn't a radio show, which most people would only experience by listening, care more about language, than how to survive in the rainforest? These were not the scripted grammatical lessons or dialogues I had imagined, belying my own expectations of educational media. What I came to understand was that for many Kichwa speakers, language was inseparable from place-based social practices and relationships. What many people in Napo said about language and what people did with and through language suggests that language was transmitted most meaningfully through embodied interactions, as one thread of Kichwa lifeways.

When Mayor Shiguango first introduced me to the idea that his radio program sought to transmit culture and not just language, I was confused. But this idea of how to subsist in the rainforest was in fact central to the show's daily programming, as well as to monthly live-broadcast radio performances they carried out with communities around the province of Napo. The people I worked with in Napo were certainly concerned about language, especially shift toward Spanish as well as toward the standardized Unified Kichwa, but they also had very pressing concerns like access to land, food security, and employment (see also Shulist 2018). Adults worried that children did not speak Kichwa and that they were becoming "white" in other senses—including the foods they consumed and the daily activities that engaged them. This chapter explores how settler colonialism has reshaped the ecologies—social, material, linguistic—of Upper Napo Kichwa speakers and the effects this has had on their linguistic practices. Surprisingly, well-intentioned but top-down revitalization projects meant to valorize Kichwa and counteract shift toward Spanish also involve their own forms of coloniality as they interact within the changing material and linguistic ecologies of the Upper Napo. The environmental and linguistic ecologies of Napo shape the methods and media utilized in the various language revitalization and reclamation projects discussed in this book.

Contemporary speakers of Upper Napo Kichwa engage in a diversity of lifestyle and subsistence practices, as many people work as civil servants, educators, and in other urban professions. Until recently, however, Upper Napo Kichwa people were best known for engaging in forest-based subsistence, focused on the growth of key crops in their *chagra* (garden). Many households are organized around individual husband-wife pairs with their children, and sometimes an elder or other family member. In the past, however, Upper Napo Kichwa people lived in multigenerational patrilocal residences. These were generally large, palm-thatched buildings, where members of an extended family (*ayllu*)—generally an elder couple, their single adult children, their sons and wives and their children—all lived together (Oberem 1980, 219). Hunting, gathering, and swidden agriculture occurred on a family's lands, with boundaries marked by streams, rivers, and custom (Oberem 1980, 219, 257). Many families now supplement their diets with trade goods like rice, but staple crops still include *lumu* (manioc), *chunda* (peach palm), and *palanda* (plantain). Semidomesticated plants and fruits are enjoyed seasonally. Men once hunted larger animals with blowguns and rifles, while a variety of traps and nets were used to capture smaller mammals, birds, and fish. However, limited game is to be found in the regions around Archidona and Tena. Hunters are lucky to encounter large rodents like the *siku* (agouti) or *lumucha* (paca). As midwife María Antonia Shiguango told me, "We are not within our old forest, and that is our sadness."

Families once awoke before dawn, often by three o'clock, to prepare to hunt or work in the forest. While they drank infusions of guayusa, they would converse, discuss their dreams—which were a source of knowledge about the future—recount narratives, make music, and prepare for their days. However, the introduction of wage labor and formal schooling, alongside material changes in the rainforest, have reshaped the early morning routines of the wayusa upina, "the drinking of wayusa." Many of these practices live on in elders' narratives and in some contemporary households, particularly in rural areas, where residents proudly claim they "remember" the lifeways of their elders. Increasingly they also live on in broadcast media.

Linguistic ecologies are linked to the material and social ecologies that surround them, which shape language choices in important ways. This chapter explores some of the ways language and ecology have been discussed popularly and in the field of language endangerment. I suggest that we instead understand language endangerment as a form of language oppression (Taff et al. 2018; Albó 1979; Roche 2019; Davis 2017). By exploring the link between language and ecology in Napo, I do not suggest an abstract framing of biological endangerment, nor a deterministic understanding of the influence of environment on language. Rather, I am interested in exploring how people, their languages, and their lifeways overlap, interweave, and are influenced by the processes and ideologies of settler colonial states.

This chapter introduces several ecologies in Napo. I highlight three overlapping forms of social and environmental disruption stemming from settler colonialism that have driven language shift toward Spanish in the Ecuadorian Amazon—extraction, settlement, and missionization. Yet, the ecology of languages in the Upper Amazon includes less expected forms of domination. In a multilingual and multidialectal landscape, Kichwa speakers in Napo confront language shift toward Spanish and the use of the standardized variety Unified Kichwa in institutional revitalization projects and bilingual education. Many activists, parents, and grandparents worry that if their children are learning Kichwa, it is a foreign variety, imported from the Highlands and taught in school. Standardized Unified Kichwa has entered an already complex ecology of language with unforeseen consequences, which also contribute to contemporary linguistic and cultural activism in Napo.

Ecology and Language Endangerment

Settler colonialism has reshaped life in Napo. This is evident in the following narrative excerpt from a story by a Kichwa man named Patricio

Cerda, told when he was in his forties. The excerpt is drawn with permission from a collection of narratives I produced with the Association of Kichwa Midwives of the Upper Napo and their families (AMUPAKIN 2017) about their environmental relationships. Patricio described the transformations to both ecosystems and knowledge stemming from the settlement of a place known as Llaucana Cocha (The Saltlick Lake) into the community of San Pedro:

Excerpt from "Llaucana Cocha" (The Saltlick Lake) by Patricio Cerda (AMPUAKIN 2017)

Rukuunaga payna rikukpi	According to the elders,
kuna timpu nikpiga	in these times,
ashka runauna kambiarishka.[1]	many people have changed.[1]
Mana ñawpa kwinta sacha.[2]	The forest is not like before.[2]
Mana ñawpa kwinta kucha.[3]	The lagoon is not like before.[3]
Payna aychawara apisha	When they catch fish,
takura shitakpi	they use dynamite,
manzharin.[4]	and [they] get frightened.[4]
Chingarin kucha,	The lagoon disappears,
urayma talirin	it spills over downriver,
aychawa, shikitu, tukuy.[5]	the large and small fish, everything.[5]
Chi amus rishka, rikpi,	Its amu (spirit being) has left too.
kuna llakta, llakta tukukpi,	When they left, it became a community,[1]
llambu chingarin	and everything is lost,
aychawas, ruku sachas. . . . [6]	the fish and the deep forest too. . . . [6]

---

1. I have translated this using a singular, gender-neutral "they." In Napo Kichwa, the third-person pronoun "pay" does not encode gender and could be translated as he/she, depending on context. Kichwa speakers generally discuss *amu* as appearing in cross-gendered form. However, because the speaker does not make a designation for the spirit, I have attempted to maintain the gender-neutral structure of Kichwa.

Shinakpi ñukanchi kuna rikukpiga	So now we see,
llambu kungarisha riushkanchi,	we have been forgetting everything:
ña, ruku sachama rina,	going to the deep forest,
illapa apina,	carrying a rifle,
chigunara. . . . [9]	those things. . . . [9]

San Pedro Llawkana Kucha nishka	The community is now called San
urilla llakta, kuna llakta rashka	Pedro,[2]
llambu.[17]	but it is still known as Llaucana Cocha.[17]

There are several significant threads to this story. The use of dynamite for blast fishing referenced in line 4 is likely adopted from settler neighbors and further enabled by the arrival of extractive industries in the region, as many Kichwa men worked in crews clearing the forest for roads and pipelines. It contrasts with fishing techniques using nets or the *barbasco* plant (*Lonchocarpus utilis*), which stuns the fish and allows

---

2. This transcript is modified from a transcription and translation produced in conjunction with the Association of Kichwa Midwives of the Upper Napo (2017) from the book and video project *Relating to Our Forest*. In general, the present translation breaks up the sentences into smaller constituents to emphasize the internal structure in Kichwa. This line, however, maintains the original translation to Spanish provided by the storyteller's son, which reads: "Aunque la comunidad ahora se llama San Pedro, todavia [*sic*] se conoce como Llaukana cocha." I have utilized the older, Spanish-derived orthography largely utilized by the transcriber for the English translation. Here I follow a mixed orthography, which utilizes many of the norms of Unified Kichwa while also representing many of the local particularities in speech, which define what many people call "their language." This is a departure from how some of my Kichwa colleagues in Napo prefer written Kichwa (or Quichua), which would instead be written in a Spanish-influenced orthography sensitive to local dialect features. Such debates animate this text. I have chosen this mixed orthography with recognition that transcription is also a political act (Bucholtz 2000). I am inspired by Zora Neale Hurston's approach to representing the vocal diversity of oral storytelling in *Barracoon* (2018). I also draw upon the linguistic anthropological tradition of ethnopoetics (Uzendoski and Calapucha-Tapuy 2012; Tedlock 1983) to highlight the poetic structures of Kichwa in translation, rather than the poetic structures of the hegemonic language of translation (in this text, English).

them to be gathered easily from the water (see also Kohn 2002, 113). In line 17, Patricio describes the establishment of a community called San Pedro—note the Catholic name of the town—on the site of a hunting and fishing area, pointing to the region's history of missionization and settlement. Patricio further indicates that the loss of the ecosystem leads to a loss of cultural knowledge gained through practice. In the analysis of Kichwa speakers, ecological changes linked to settlement, missionization, and extractive practices are also linked to the loss of cultural and environmental knowledge.

Since I began research in Napo in 2014, I have found that environmental concerns were at the forefront of many people's daily lives. In turn, I observed that environmental changes were linked to cultural and linguistic changes. Serafina's grandchildren, for example, sometimes did not know the names for animals or plants that she recognized readily, as they were no longer part of their daily experiences (Ennis 2023). As Sapir (1912) noted, vocabulary is an interface between language users and their environment. Viewed through the lens of settler colonialism, the destruction of the Amazon rainforest and the disruptions of Indigenous languages and lifeways there can be analyzed within the same frame. Shaylih Muehlmann argues that "what language obsolescence and environmental degradation chiefly share is their deep involvement in the creation and structure of social inequality" (2016, 57). In Napo, the structure of sociolinguistic and environmental inequality is shaped by settler colonialism.

Although colonialism manifests differently in different places and times, it centrally involves access to Indigenous land, achieved through dispossession and genocide. Scholars identify several kinds of colonialism—extractive, settler, internal, external, planter, and others—but as Max Liboiron suggests, all of these assume in some way the right to access and use Indigenous lands (2021, 7–9). For environmental philosopher Kyle Whyte, one of the most significant ways settler colonialism manifests is by "undermin[ing] Indigenous peoples' social resilience as self-determining collectives" (2018, 125). Patrick Wolfe (2006) has defined settler colonialism in terms of the logic of elimination of the native in order to access territory. In the Ecuadorian Amazon, elimination has less to do with physical displacement or genocide of Indigenous peoples by colonizers, although these have been involved. Rather, control of native populations has been managed through material transformations in the daily environmental conditions under which people make their lives (Muratorio 1991; Macdonald 1999).

Environmental discourses are prevalent both in the Amazon and in considerations of Indigenous language endangerment. Indigenous Amazonians are very often treated in popular discourse as unique defenders of the environment, while their linguistic and cultural knowledge is described as the precious heritage of all of humanity. A headline on *National Geographic's* website proclaims, for instance, that "Indigenous peoples defend earth's biodiversity—but they're in danger" (Raygorodetsky 2018). The NGO Terralingua, co-founded by anthropologist Luisa Maffi in 1996 to investigate "biocultural diversity" (Maffi 2005), explicitly links environmental and cultural endangerment. UNESCO's Indigenous Languages Decade (2022–2032) is framed "to draw attention to the *critical situation* of many indigenous languages and to mobilize stakeholders and resources for their preservation, revitalization, and promotion" (UNESCO n.d., emphasis added). Although frequently well-intentioned, such discourses highlight an ongoing link made between Indigenous peoples, Indigenous languages, and the environment that reinforces the sense that they are on the verge of disappearance—an ideological position key to the settler colonial project of Indigenous erasure (O'Brien 2010; A. Simpson 2011). Such discourses are especially prevalent surrounding the area where I work on the urbanizing edge of the Ecuadorian Amazon, a region known for its abundant beauty as well as oil development, mineral conflicts, and deforestation (Sierra 2000; Sawyer 2004; Riofrancos 2020). In considering this link, I wish to explore the relationship between Indigenous Amazonians and their environments, as well as between languages—alongside their speakers—and their surrounding ecologies during language shift and reclamation.

What does it mean to speak of ecologies in relationship to language and culture? Often referring to the study of relationships between organisms and their surroundings, the concept of ecology has been widely influential and debated throughout the history of environmental anthropology (Milton 1997; Orlove 1980). Anthropologists have moved from environmental determinism (Steward 1955), to viewing humans as organisms within self-regulating ecosystems (e.g. Rappaport 1967a, 1967b), to an emphasis on the ways issues of power and inequality shape ecological relationships and practices at both global and local levels (Wolf 1972; Biersack 1999; Kottak 1999; Kirsch 2006). Rather than a singular ecology, anthropologists now explore ecolog*ies* extending beyond the human to include more-than-human beings (Kohn 2013) and global flows of power (Chao 2022; Kirksey 2015; Tsing 2012). In Napo, understanding the ways that material and organic ecologies have been reshaped in the context of Ecuadorian settler colonialism illustrates the sociopolitical and ideological conditions under which people mobilize different languages and linguistic varieties.

Ecological approaches in linguistics first described the relationship among languages and linguistic varieties (Voegelin and Voegelin 1964; Haugen 1972). As in environmental anthropology, the ecological metaphor has taken on increasingly broad meanings, giving rise to a diverse field of study at the interface of language and environment (Fill and Mühlhäusler 2006; Fill and Penz 2017). I draw upon Einar Haugen's concept of an ecology of language, or "the study of interactions between any given language and it's environment," where "the true environment of a language is the society that uses it as one of its codes" (Haugen 1972, 325). Although Haugen described language as a way for users to relate "to nature, i.e. their social and natural environment," he was clear that the environment of language was distinct from the referential environment it described (Haugen 1972, 325). The true ecology of language, according to Haugen, was instead psychological, relating to the interactions of language varieties within the mind of a user, as well as sociological, relating to its interaction with other language varieties. Mufwene (2001) largely takes up this psychological and sociological perspective in considering language evolution and language ecology.

As many scholars—Haugen included (1972, 326)—have noted, the comparison between biotic and linguistic ecologies is not seamless (Mackey 2006). Although languages are sometimes compared to organisms (Mufwene 2001, 148), they are more often described as expressive tools of their speakers, or as structures (Haugen 1972, 326). Mufwene, however, has argued for understanding languages not as individual *organisms* within an ecology (likened to individual idiolects), but as a Lamarckian *parasitic species*, which depend on its hosts (language users) and their sociocultural systems for life (2001, 16). Language change in this view becomes analogous to evolution, an adaptive response to changing environmental conditions, which can be modified by a wide range of factors, both internal and external (Mufwene 2001, 17). While Mufwene does point to the "physical environment" (2001, 156) and socioeconomic conditions in shaping linguistic ecology, external language contact and internal linguistic variation are the most significant ecological factors for his analysis of language change.

The social environment of a language can include, as Mufwene states, "whether socioeconomic conditions in a particular polity favor or disfavor usage of a particular language" (2001, 153). Yet, part of a language's sociological environment also includes the material environment in which language users engage their linguistic varieties, which shape and are shaped by socioeconomic conditions. Mühlhäusler (1995) makes this link explicit in his examination of language diversity and linguistic ecology in the Pacific Islands, arguing that "habitat destruction" is the main contributor to linguistic change and the loss of linguistic diversity. In the colonial settings Mühlhäusler describes, habitat destruction upended local communicative networks as people were forced to migrate to new territories (1995, 187). Where Mühlhäusler identifies "imperialism" as the driver of both linguistic and biological destruction, I see the related forces of settler colonialism at work.

In Napo, both linguistic and biotic ecologies are disrupted by the spread and growth of new settler ecologies, ones that are—among other dimensions—environmental, material, and social. I use ecology in the expansive sense deployed by environmental philosopher Kyle Whyte, who describes them "in terms of their makeup of qualities of relationships," which he defines as occurring between humans, other-than-human beings like plants and animals, other entities that may be spiritual, and landscapes (2018, 134). Relationships are integral to ecologies, whether they be biological, social, or linguistic. An ecology is much more than just the biotic and abiotic environment or the trophic levels linked in an ecosystem. The bundles of linguistic practices and features we describe as languages exist in relationship to each other, just as much as human and other-than-human beings exist in various relationships to each other in what English speakers abstractly call "the environment." Ecologies are here related to the interwoven relationships between linguistics forms, practices, ideologies, speakers, communities, other-than-human plant and animal beings, spiritual entities, and organic and inorganic environments. These ecologies also include various forms of communicative media and technologies, addressed in chapter 2.

Ecological metaphors have been mobilized through framings of language endangerment as analogous to—and related to—biological endangerment (Dorian 1989; Hale et al. 1992; Fishman 1991). In the 1980s and 1990s, scholars sought to foment greater concern for the precarious position of many Indigenous and minoritized languages by drawing on the discourses and interests of the environmental and conservation movements. Languages were explicitly likened to species (e.g., Krauss 1992), as endangered as the flora and fauna falling victim to the Anthropocene. Maffi (2005, 2002) describes a process of biocultural endangerment and links the loss of language and culture to the decline of biodiversity. Where ecologists might consider conservation or restoration, concerned linguists have promoted processes of revitalization, which has been described as a process of "reversing" language shift (Fishman 1991; Grenoble and Whaley 2006) among "vanishing voices" (Nettle and Romaine 2000).

Linguistic anthropologists have explored the underlying assumptions of many of these discourses of language endangerment (Hill 2002; Kroskrity 2011; Duchene and Heller 2008). Jane Hill (2002) highlighted ways that languages are treated as the intangible cultural heritage of all of humanity, instead of systems of communication that provide daily meaning to individuals. Hill's exploration of the hyper-valorization of Indigenous languages as intangible human heritage echoes the ways the Amazon is described as the environmental commons for all of humanity, most notable for its biodiversity and ability to store carbon (Gatti et al. 2021). Meanwhile, the needs of Indigenous residents to make a life there are not often discussed, much as the needs of Indigenous-language speakers to materially reproduce themselves are often ignored. Jenny Davis (2017) highlights a similar tendency to erase the colonial conditions that produce language endangerment, as if such processes just occurred naturally. Bernard Perley (2012) identifies a methodological overreliance in the field on preservation (or conservation) through documentation in inaccessible archives, creating what he calls "zombie languages." Removing language from its contexts of use can have serious ideological and practical effects. While recognizing the limitations of the discourses of endangerment, I use these ecological metaphors as an invitation to consider the relationship between language and various ecologies, those that are environmental, social, and linguistic.

Understanding language shift in relation to settler colonialism requires a political framing. Yet, naming a so-called driver of language shift often leaves open a lingering question about what to do about that driver. To paraphrase Gerald Roche, if urbanization is identified as causing language shift, should speakers of endangered languages return to the countryside? If it is economic development, should they renounce money? (2020, 166). Neither seems a tenable solution. By naming settler colonialism as a significant driver of language shift, however, I do suggest that one of the most important responses is decolonization. Tuck and Yang (2012) argue that decolonization is not just a metaphor. For many, the return of land and sovereignty is the urgent goal of decolonization. But I also understand decolonization as an ongoing and unfinished process, with social, political, economic, ideological, epistemological, and ontological dimensions (Smith 2012; Thiong'o 1998; Fanon 1968).

One way to ideologically decolonize language endangerment—or to "re-language" it as Barbra Meek (2025) has suggested—is to name the major causes of language shift more explicitly. I follow a framework of language oppression, or what Alice Taff and her colleagues have referred to as the "*enforcement* of language loss by physical, mental, social, and spiritual coercion" (2018, 863, original emphasis). Economic or material coercion are also on this list, as they shape the possibilities of the social, environmental, linguistic worlds within which people live. Benjamin Frey (2013) describes language shift in terms of a framework of "verticalization" (Brown 2022), in which it is the vertical connections between external (settler) institutions and local communities that lead to the slow dissolution of language vitality. "As social networks reorient themselves toward the external society in which they are embedded," Frey writes, "people begin using the language of that society more frequently" (2022, 139). In Napo, resistance to missionary boarding schools in the late 1800s (Muratorio 1991, 84–85) eventually gave way to settler education and wage labor (Erazo 2013, 35–39). Napo's increasing ties to settler institutions promoted the verticalization of its linguistic ecology, in which Spanish became an increasingly dominant language.

A framework of language oppression points to manifestations of coloniality in language revitalization projects, as top-down methods can function as another form of oppression. Wolfram and Schilling-Estes (1995) describe the endangerment of regional varieties of English, threatened by more powerful and more standard forms. Language revitalization projects in Napo raise similar questions about the ways that regional (or nonstandard) varieties are addressed by language revitalization. For many people in Napo, the standardized Unified Kichwa is also a "foreign" imposition, knowledge of which is required for employment in the bilingual school system as well as for use in institutional politics and much media. Language revitalization projects can, perhaps surprisingly, be a form of language oppression.

If language oppression of various kinds is at the root of language shift, then it is also worth reconsidering how we understand the usual response to endangerment—language revitalization. In this account, I distinguish between language revitalization and language reclamation (De Korne and Leonard 2017; Leonard 2017). This way of understanding language reclamation differs from language revitalization, which often relies more on the perspectives and methods of academic linguistics rather than the ways languages are most meaningful to speakers. This use of the term emphasizes an orientation toward speakers' and signers' linguistic rights and goals in the face of oppression. In this account, Indigenous and otherwise minoritized languages are not unintentionally or passively endangered. Rather, they are actively oppressed by the settler colonial disruption of their ecologies or forms of interrelationship. It is such disruptions that many activists in the Upper Napo sought to address through community media. But just how has settler colonialism reshaped life in Napo, and what effects has this had on the ecology of languages there?

Kichwa and Settler Ecologies

To understand Upper Napo Kichwa media as sites of revalorization and reclamation, it is necessary to understand the ruptures created by colonialism in the Ecuadorian Amazon. Jenny Davis (2017) has noted a central tendency in linguistics research to downplay or erase the colonial histories and policies that create situations of language shift. Yet, as Barbra Meek reminds us, "while language endangerment is first and foremost about the often violent replacement of one linguistic code by another, it is also about the rupturing and replacement of sociocultural practices and everyday interactions, resulting in the disintegration of the speech community or social networks that sustained the code" (2010, 3). In Napo, norms of development often serve to foster colonial assimilation. Where boarding schools once aimed to inculcate Spanish, government policies aimed at reducing poverty and increasing childhood education may now rupture the practices that sustain Kichwa as a code of daily interaction. In Napo, the environmental disruption caused by extractive industries and the arrival of new settlers both limits and expands the material conditions under which Indigenous Amazonians may live as self-determining collectives (Whyte 2018; Uzendoski 2018). Settler colonialism has reshaped the relationship of many Amazonian communities to the land, forest, and waters around them, which has also had consequences for spaces of intergenerational transmission of language, verbal art, and other forms of knowledge.

Settler Colonialism—Then and Now

Napo's capital of Tena, as well as neighboring Archidona (figure 4), have grown dramatically over the last hundred years. Tena has expanded particularly rapidly. The population of its urban center grew from 2,106 in 1974 to 23,307 in 2010, while the total population of the canton doubled in the same period, growing from 29,712 to 60,880, according to census data (INEC, n.d.-a). Meanwhile some eleven kilometers (6.5 miles) away, Archidona's population grew dramatically. Officially becoming a canton in 1981, the new administrative unit of Archidona had a population of 15,010 in the 1982 census, which grew to 24,969 by the 2010 census. Archidona's urban center grew from 1,714 in 1982 to 5,478 in 2010. Migrants to the region have settled beside—and sometimes displaced—Indigenous Amazonians. According to the 2010 census of the 103,697 people living in Napo, self-identified Indigenous residents made up about 57 percent of the population, mestizo and white residents accounted for a combined 41 percent, while 1.6 percent of the population identified as

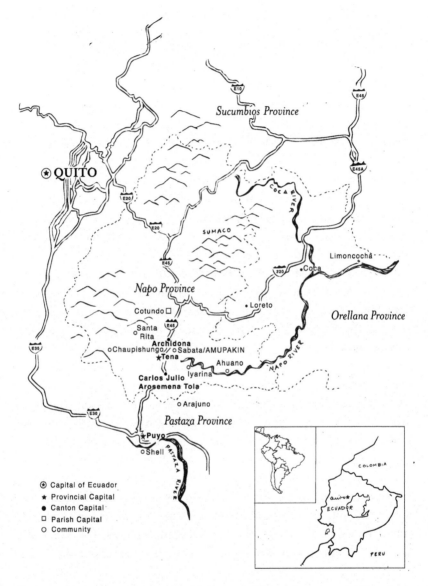

FIGURE 4 Map of the Tena-Archidona region of Napo province. Map shows significant regional locations discussed throughout this text. Map design by Mia Loia (WFH).

Afro-Ecuadorian.[3] Archidona had an even larger proportion of Indigenous residents, with 80 percent of the population self-identifying as Indigenous in 2010 (INEC 2010). Even in a majority Indigenous province, settler Spanish language and social practices dominate public life.

Speakers of Upper Napo Kichwa living in the Ecuadorian Amazon are the survivors of colonial violence and more recent national policies aimed at the erasure of their lifeways (Oberem 1980; Renard-Casevitz, Saignes, and Taylor 1988; Muratorio 1991; Macdonald 1999). An uprising led by Amazonian shamans, including the "anticolonial hero" Jumandi in 1578 (Oberem 1980, 85–89), centers many contemporary projects to resist settler colonial domination (Cognet 2021). Before the province was called Napo, Spanish chroniclers called the area Quijos, referencing a regional cultural complex (Oberem 1980, 330). Upheaval caused by epidemics, violence, and forced labor reshaped local populations. The colonial Spanish administration regularly resettled groups to provide labor in regions whose populations had fled or succumbed to epidemics (Oberem 1980, 99; Renard-Casevitz, Saignes, and Taylor 1988).

At the time of colonial contact, the area comprising present-day Napo province was densely populated. Based on colonial documents, Oberem estimated that when the Spanish conquered the region in 1559, there were some twenty-six thousand inhabitants of the Quijos region (1980, 40–41). By 1768 the Indigenous population had fallen to slightly below two thousand, before slowly beginning to recover (Oberem 1980, 46). While some of this population loss can be credited to the epidemics gripping the region throughout the colonial period, Quijos groups are reported to have fled colonial and missionary encroachment, seeking refuge first in the Andean Highlands in the early years of the Spanish conquest, while from the 1600s onward they appear to have looked for safety in the dense forests to the east (Oberem 1980, 98, 43). Amazonian Kichwa-speaking populations emerged from this period of upheaval and

---

3. The 2010 Ecuadorian national censuses contained the demographic categories *Blanco* (white), *Mestizo* (mestizo); *Indígena* (Indigenous); *Afroecuatoriano* (Afro-Ecuadorian); *Montubio* (a primarily coastal population); and *Otro* (other). In 2010, the white population of Napo was 2.7 percent, the Mestizo 38.1 percent, the Indigenous 56.8 percent, the Afro-Ecuadorian 1.6 percent, Montubio 0.6 percent, and other 0.2 percent (INEC, n.d.-b).

LANGUAGE AND ECOLOGY IN THE UPPER NAPO

the settlement of culturally and linguistically diverse populations in missionary "reductions." During the colonial period, activity within the Jesuit Mission of Maynas—a vast region including the Upper Napo—has been described as sporadic, partly due to the small number of missionaries and their relative lack of funds (Taylor 1999, 225). Contemporary missionary activity since the 1920s has been more intense, helping to reshape daily life in Napo (Oberem 1980; Muratorio 1991). For much of postconquest history, Napo remained more geographically inaccessible and therefore relatively peripheral to the colonial state, at least in comparison with ongoing contemporary settler activity in the region.[4]

More recently, Napo has become anything but peripheral to the Ecuadorian state. In the late 1800s and early 1900s, populations in the Upper Amazon were again disrupted by the forced relocation of an unknown number of people eastward during the rubber boom (Oberem 1980, 116–17; Erazo 2013, 34–35). One of my interlocutors reported that her grandfather had been a rubber tapper but had returned to Napo. Many suffered under the rubber industry (Reeve 1988), but at least some people in Napo highlighted stories of their strength during the period. While colonial systems of economic and social control such as the *encomienda* and *reducción* came to an end at the turn of the twentieth century, white-mestizo landowners, officials, and missionaries still found ways to extract labor and resources from Indigenous populations.

Between the 1920s and 1950s, Upper Napo Kichwa families were subject to a system of debt-peonage under a *patrón* (Sp. "owner, master,

---

4. Alongside clerics and Dominican priests, Jesuits have been an important, albeit discontinuous, presence in the region. By the mid 1700s, the majority of Quijos were converted to Christianity, but "the Indians could not have had great knowledge of Christian doctrine, because at times years passed without priests visiting the smallest populations in their large parish districts" (Oberem 1980, 105). While Jesuits were expelled from Spanish territories in 1767, they returned to Napo in 1869, but their missionary efforts were sporadic. Jesuit priests in Archidona exploited their position, using it to extract goods from their Indigenous congregants, in part resulting in a violent uprising against the Jesuits in 1892 (Oberem 1980, 114–15). After the Ecuadorian state finally and definitively expelled the Jesuits from the region in 1896, the Ecuadorian government invited the Italian Catholic Josephine Order to establish missions in Napo in 1922 (Oberem 1980; Spiller 1974; Muratorio 1991, 1995).

guardian") of a landed hacienda estate (Oberem 1980, 117). Children were often given to the patrón to be raised in exchange for their performance of household tasks, while owners regularly relocated populations to work their lands (Oberem 1980, 118). The hacienda system of debt-peonage ended as new missionary schools, government policies, agrarian reform, and petroleum development in the region increased Upper Napo Kichwa people's access to wage labor (Perreault 2000; Muratorio 1991; Macdonald 1999). The effects of this period linger in Napo. I met middle-aged people who had spent time being *criado* (Sp. "raised") among the white-mestizo families who owned the haciendas where their parents worked. Since the early twentieth century, and with increasing rapidity since the 1950s, the material, linguistic, and social ecologies of the Upper Napo have been affected by three interlinked aspects of the settler colonial system: mineral extraction, missionization, and land reform.

Mineral Extraction

Extraction drives several forms of environmental disruption in the Ecuadorian Amazon (López et al. 2013). These include extraction of oil (Sawyer 2004; Riofrancos 2020), of resources like gold (Galarza et al. 2021) and gravel from local rivers (Aguirre et al. 2021), of timber—most recently balsa for use in the production of wind turbines (Sierra 2000; Dalmases 2021), and of agricultural products (Jarrett, Cummins, and Logan-Hines 2017; Lu 2007). These contribute to two major sources of environmental and linguistic change: environmental degradation and the growth of a settler cash economy in Napo and neighboring regions.

Petroleum and other forms of mineral extraction have also shaped national policies and daily life in the Ecuadorian Amazon. Early oil exploration in the region first provided opportunities for men to work as guides in the forests, while it also cleared the paths that the Josephine missionaries would travel in 1922 (Muratorio 1991, 166). Between 1938 and 1948, Shell Oil carried out intensive exploration in the region that would eventually be separated from Napo to form the province of Pastaza. After Shell Oil exited the region in the late 1940s, the Texaco-Gulf consortium secured a contract to explore 1.5 million hectares in 1964, helping to establish petroleum as a central feature of social and economic life in much of the Ecuadorian Amazon (Perreault 2000, 111).

Development in Napo intensified between 2007 and 2017 during the presidency of Rafael Correa, whose "Citizens' Revolution" was partly funded by Amazonian oil (Riofrancos 2020). The discovery of large reserves of heavy crude petroleum in Napo accelerated development in the region and created conflicts in communities divided over the financial resources promised by mineral extraction (Uzendoski 2018; Erazo 2013). However, processing of the heavy crude reserves proved more difficult than expected and the developer Ivanhoe Energy officially ceased production in the region in 2015 (Uzendoski 2018, 368).

Napo has seemingly been less affected by extraction than other Amazonian provinces, where major conflicts over oil and mineral resources have attracted international attention. Yet, the infrastructure for such projects—and the larger petroleum industry of which they are part—mark the landscape in Napo in the network of paved roads that fans out toward the oil fields in the east as well as the pipelines that carry the oil from the Amazon to the coast. A highway now winds from the national capital Quito, over the often-frigid Andean *páramo*, before descending into Napo's mountainous, tropical rainforest. It was this rugged landscape that some elder residents of Napo describe their parents and grandparents traversing for days on foot to carry trade goods to and from Quito, while more distant familial histories recount that the Napo Runa were pressed to work as porters of both cargo and people, whom they carried in chairs strapped to their backs until the 1800s (Oberem 1980; Muratorio 1991; Erazo 2013). In the early 1970s, Archidona and Tena became connected to Quito with a major highway, reducing the time needed to travel to the capital from days to a matter of hours (Perreault 2000, 168; Erazo 2013, 31). These roads facilitate access between rural *comunidades* and the centers of Tena and Archidona (figure 5), drawing many young people toward the cities and the opportunities they offer.

Elder midwife Catalina Aguinda remembered this period of road building as we wound through the mountains on a journey to Quito. Looking out the van window at a passing mountain, Catalina told me the mountain was known as *Gringo Changa*, "Gringo's Leg." The mountain's name embedded stories of the highway's construction, as well as Napo Runa understandings of the "masters" or spiritual owners of places (Kohn 2007). This is a process that linguist anthropologists have described as intertextuality (Bauman and Briggs 1990; Briggs and Bauman

FIGURE 5 Sumaco volcano as seen from the outskirts of Archidona on the Avenida Napo, the main road leading through Archidona. April 11, 2017. Photo by the author.

1992; Hill 2005; Bakhtin 1981a) to understand the ways that snippets of discourse—or texts—can be decontextualized, recontextualized, and embedded within new forms and contexts. Catalina's story is similar to how Keith Basso (1996) describes Apache knowledge and social pedagogy, such that a name can evoke a story and a lesson learned from that place. Describing the mountain as a *gringo*, Catalina evoked the history of Runa workers consumed by the spirit of the mountain, who is known to have appeared from inside the mountain as a gringo speaking incomprehensible English. This is an excerpt of how she explained this history, which had been shared by her elders:

Catalina Aguinda describes road construction in Napo, October 16, 2016

CA: Ñawpa cartera raushka uraspi,₁
    kay cartera pay tractor
      allaushkaibi,₂
    shina ranushka nin.₃
    Payna takua tukyachisha tukya-
      chisha rinushka nin.₄

CA: Before, in the time when they
    were opening the roads,₁
    when the tractor was digging
      there for this road,₂
    this is what they say happened.₃
    With dynamite they went on
      blasting and blasting, it is said.₄

'Narakpi chi bolqueta apasha riushka runaunara tukuy wañchishka nin.$_5$

Chi, shuk bolqueta, ali bolqueta, atun bolqueta, shuk tractor, shuk moto nivelador, chi shuk pala mecanica ninun.$_6$

Chi aukunara tukuy chingachishka nin kay urkui.$_7$

Shinarakpiga kay payguna takura tukyachinga nisha shitakpis mana wañushka nin.$_8$

Chi urku mana tukyan, mana pakirin.$_9$

'Nashkaimi shuk tuta shamushka nin.$_{10}$

Wardian anushka nin.$_{11}$

Payuna wakachishkara shuwanungami nisha kuiraungama.$_{12}$

Llukshisha rikukpi tiashka nin allpa allashkai gringo.$_{13}$

Atun gringo tiashka ninun.$_{14}$

GE: Imasnara rikurin chi atun gringo?$_{15}$

CA: Chi gringo.$_{16}$
Chi urkumandak llukshimusha tian nin.$_{17}$

GE: Chi paywa supay?$_{18}$

CA: Ari, paywa supay.$_{19}$
Pay shina runa tukusha tianmi nin.$_{20}$
Ña runa tukusha tiakpimi tapunushka.$_{21}$

So then, it is said, that [mountain] killed all the people who were in the truck.$_5$

There, a dump truck, a nice, big dump truck, a tractor, a bulldozer, and they say, a backhoe.$_6$

Those things, all of it was made to disappear, it is said, inside this mountain.$_7$

When that happened, they threw dynamite wanting to blow it up, but it didn't die, it is said.$_8$

That mountain didn't burst, it didn't break.$_9$

When it was like that, he came one night, it is said.$_{10}$

They were the guards, it is said.$_{11}$

They were to guard what others would want to steal.$_{12}$

When they went out to look, there was sitting, it is said, in the excavated earth a gringo.$_{13}$

He was a big gringo, they say.$_{14}$

GE: What did this big gringo look like?$_{15}$

CA: That gringo.$_{16}$
He came out of the mountain to be there, it is said.$_{17}$

GE: [Was he] its spirit [devil]?$_{18}$

CA: Yes, its spirit [devil].$_{19}$
He had turned like that into a person, it is said.$_{20}$
As he had become a person, they questioned him.$_{21}$

Shina tapukpi imarashara tiaun- gui nisha,[22]	Like this they asked saying, "what are you doing?"[22]
tapunukpi pay inglesllai riman.[23]	But when they ask, he responds only in English.[23]
Ingles mana intindinchi nin nisha rimakuna aka ñawpa rukuguna.[24]	"We don't understand English," it is said, saying [this] our elders spoke.[24]
Kwintashkara uyakani.[25]	And I heard their conversations.[25]
Shinami nisha, shina shuk kawsak gringomi tiaun nisha Gringo Changa ninun chi urkura.[26]	They say there is a gringo living [there], so they call that moun- tain "Gringo Changa" (Grin- go's Leg).[26]

Road construction—and its connection to foreigners—are central to how Upper Napo Kichwa people historicize settler colonialism and environmental changes in their region. This history marks the landscape in the names given to places. Catalina further explained that both the Napo Runa workers and the equipment that disappeared inside the mountain are known to still be there, working for the gringo spirit who controls the mountain, building more roads inside.

Extraction and other development contribute to the growth of a cash economy in Napo, as the extractive and agricultural industries became an important source of wage labor for residents of the Upper Napo. Ofelia Salazar, a midwife in her forties, reflected on how a trade economy in Napo had been transformed into a cash economy. "In the old times with smoked fish, or bringing a basket of firewood, or with some other kind of exchange, that's how they would give the healing gifts," she said. Ofelia continued, "but in this time, there is none of that. But in this time, there is money" (AMUPAKIN 2017, 170). Napo Runa are sometimes seen as more "peaceful" or "assimilated" than other Amazonian groups due to missionization (Taylor 1999, 194–95, 236). This dynamic meant Napo Runa men were recruited early on to work as guides for oil companies in less settled regions. Macdonald (1999) reports that by the 1970s, virtually all the Kichwa men of the township of Arajuno were employed by the oil company. During my research, young men in Napo sought to acquire jobs with oil or mineral companies in Napo or nearby provinces, while young women might seek employment in local offices or the tourist industry. Speaking Spanish is seen as a prerequisite for most employment in the settler economy. Many people hope that their children will also learn English or other international languages, like Chinese. Despite recognition of pollution and other effects, the employment and economic opportunities offered by extractive and agricultural industries are also attractive to many people. The growth of a wage economy in Napo was an important way for families to escape debt peonage on the holdings of settlers. And families today require money for all sorts of things—school uniforms and other clothes, home goods, body care products, groceries, utilities, and even traditional medicinal services, as Ofelia suggested.

The extraction of oil and other resources like gold and gravel is incredibly ecologically damaging. Opening roads and cutting the forest disrupts animal populations, while byproducts of extractive industries contaminate water sources used for drinking, bathing, and fishing. Contrary to popular discourse, these are ecologically damaging activities that some Indigenous people might support or even engage in (Lu 2007; Erazo 2013). In the 1960s and 1970s, some families used new wages and agricultural development loans to purchase cattle and clear pastures across Amazonian provinces. Agricultural development loans offered by the Ecuadorian government required Indigenous people to put their newly demarcated landholdings into active production. Like more recent development projects in Ecuador, these programs were also funded by oil exploitation in the Amazon (Macdonald 1999, 74–75). More recently, gold extraction is dividing local communities. Kichwa and other Indigenous Amazonians also engage in reciprocal relationships with their ecologies, developed from long periods of interaction and intimate knowledge of the rainforest (Jarrett, Cummins, and Logan-Hines 2017; Descola 1994). Profound social inequality can lead people into choices that challenge the straightforward narratives of environmentalists regarding the Amazon.

The ecological disruption entailed by extraction and settlement in the Amazon is one way, as Kyle Whyte puts it, that "settler populations are working to create their own ecologies out of the ecologies of Indigenous peoples" (2018, 135). These activities disrupt the ecosystems in which Indigenous Amazonians were once able to subsist in the rainforest. Extraction, as an instrument of settlement, was partly enabled by missionization—another way that settler colonialism has reshaped the Upper Napo.

Missionization

Extractivism in the Amazon coincided with increased missionization. Italian Catholic Josephine missionaries arriving in Napo in the 1920s are reported to have followed the trails cut by oil companies exploring the region, while missionary maps aided exploration in the 1940s (Muratorio 1991, 166). Evangelical Protestant missionaries were active in Napo through the Summer Institute of Linguistics and other projects (Orr 1978). Many missionaries sought to "civilize" and settle Indigenous groups around missionary schools and centers. The attitude of at least some missionaries toward Kichwa residents of Napo is revealed in Bishop Maximiliano Spiller's description that white agricultural settlers in the region "earn a living honorably and provide an example of civilization and morality to the *indio*" (1974, 19). It is left unsaid that these are qualities that must be modeled for and imparted to Indigenous peoples rather than values that might be equitably exchanged or even learned from Indigenous peoples.

One of the most obvious ways missionaries affected Amazonian Kichwa practices was by encouraging settlement. Josephine Catholic missionaries were important in the foundation of Kichwa villages and towns around Napo, as seen in Patricio's story. Until roughly the 1960s, Napo Runa households maintained more mobile residences, preferring to travel between small, familial settlements and dispersed hunting and agricultural lands, where they sought refuge from the demands of missionaries and other colonial agents (Oberem 1980; Macdonald 1999; Muratorio 1991). Variations of this practice continue today, as people travel between homes in urban centers and homes near agricultural lands. More permanent settlements around the resources of schools and missionary centers became increasingly attractive as agrarian reforms led to significant changes in land tenure and social organization. In Archidona, a missionary boarding school was complemented by several day schools built between the 1960s and 1970s in the surrounding countryside. Many families settled around these schools (Erazo 2013, 52–53). Oral histories broadcast on Upper Napo Kichwa radio reference the role of missionary priests in establishing Kichwa settlements in the area during a period and process called *llaktachina*, "settlement" (literally, "to make a community"). Changes in residence and settlement have transformed daily life for many, contributing to the rupture of the material conditions that sustained the practices of ruku kawsay—the lifeways of the elders.

Catholic missionaries in the region have been integral in establishing patterns of language shift toward Spanish. Josephine missionaries focused on establishing Spanish-language boarding and day schools, as well as technical programs in mechanics, carpentry, and handicrafts. A retired teacher and activist reflected that when they spoke Kichwa, Catholic missionary priests told them, "[You] have to abandon that, [you] have [to] study in Spanish." Many contemporary elders tell stories of their own or their parents' time at the missionary boarding school in Archidona, where they were actively discouraged from speaking Kichwa. The effects of these policies have reverberated across generations. One woman in her early fifties described that she makes "some mistakes" when she speaks in Kichwa, because her parents encouraged her to speak only in Spanish once she entered school. Her father had studied with the Josephine priests, while her mother was raised with the Dorothean nuns. The priests later sent her father to establish a school near Coca. There, students were tasked with clearing a square meter of grass with a machete when they spoke in Kichwa. She joked, "My father always had a well-maintained schoolyard."

Despite their role in encouraging shift toward Spanish, as well as the "civilization" of local populations, Catholic and other missionaries occupy a complex position in Napo Runa society.[5] Unlike most other non-Indigenous residents, some priests have learned Kichwa, while the regional Josephine Catholic radio station broadcasts a morning and evening Kichwa-language program, which features music, local news, and cultural commentary, alongside daily prayers and religious content in

---

5. Muratorio indicates that missionization aimed at assimilation of Napo's Indigenous residents, as "the Josephines promoted an evangelizing ideology of Indian *integration* into regional and national development through productive labor" (1991, 163 emphasis in original). Many of my interlocutors were critical of missionaries, particularly their role in rupturing linguistic and cultural practices. Yet, many people in Napo are deeply faithful; some even describe missionaries as providing a "civilizing" influence, leading to improvements in women's lives. It is important to recognize missionaries' role in cultural shift and the real significance of Catholicism (and other faiths) for many.

Kichwa. Such broadcasts are also an important way that regional speakers engage with their language and contribute to establishing an Upper Napo Kichwa-speaking public sphere.

Land Reform and Settlement

Land reform and the arrival of new settlers supported the growth of a material infrastructure of extraction and the social infrastructure of missionization. With a population of more than one hundred thousand people in 2010, Napo has grown dramatically since 1962, when the province was home to roughly twenty-four thousand people (INEC, n.d.-b).

The redistribution of "unused" lands has transformed land tenure in Napo. Since the 1960s, Ecuadorian government policies have focused on the large-scale settlement of the "vacant lands" (*tierras baldías*) of the Amazon by both white-mestizo and Indigenous settlers from the Highlands and coast.[6] So-called vacant land was defined as any territory without a formal owner in the land registry. However, Upper Napo Kichwa families had traditionally managed land through a series of customary, informal agreements in which members of an extended family claimed large areas, with boundaries marked by rivers and streams (Oberem 1980, 257). But even prior to the intensive land reform beginning in the 1950s, Oberem suggests that Kichwa residents of Napo had "to defend themselves from the whites who want[ed] to denounce part of the Indian lands under the pretext that they comprised vacant land" (Oberem 1980,

---

6. Such policies have their antecedents in the 1936 *Ley de Tierras Baldías y Colonización* (Law of Empty Lands and Colonization), which established colonization of "uncultivated" and unclaimed lands as a principal strategy to alleviate the poverty created by the Highland hacienda land tenure system (Becker and Tutillo 2009). In contrast to the debt peonage practiced by Lowland hacienda owners, Highland Indigenous communities were subject to a system known as *huasipungo*, where they "were tied to the hacienda, and in return for their labor were provided with a marginal landholding for their own use" (Perreault 2000, 98). Despite early reforms, the inequality engendered by the hacienda system was evident in the first national land census in 1956, which revealed that only 0.4 percent of Ecuadorian landholders held 45.1 percent of agricultural land, while 73.1 percent of small landowners held only 7.2 percent of cultivated land (Macdonald 1999, 66).

119). Further reforms in the 1960s and 1970s have transformed traditional familial territories into a sometimes-contentious system of private and cooperative landownership. These changes have also altered systems for inheritance and subsistence. Parcels are divided into ever-smaller units among subsequent generations, while cattle ranching and small-scale cash agriculture have taken on new importance in the region.[7] It is partly the lack of land for traditional agriculture and the limited game nearby leading many people toward wage labor. For many families, it is not possible to practice forms of subsistence that were common a hundred or fifty years ago.

Except for missionary schools, none of these would seem at first to be sources of linguistic oppression. Yet, these material changes are ways that language oppression is enforced. Elimination of native languages and lifeways can take many forms. One of them is the disruption of the social and material ecologies within which people live and interact. These are forms of settler oppression with which you may be more familiar. There are subtler ways that colonialism has reshaped ecologies in Napo—ones that more directly intervene in language.

Linguistic Ecologies of the Upper Napo

Settler colonialism has reshaped linguistic relationships in the Upper Napo. One of the most obvious ways is through the spread of a social and interactional world in which Spanish is required. A less expected way has been through the transformation of several regional Ecuadorian Kichwa dialects into a standardized institutional language, an effort that has been led by Kichwa activists and their academic allies, and increasingly taken up by the Ecuadorian state, with unforeseen consequences. For many speakers of Upper Napo Kichwa, the standard Unified Kichwa entered an already complex ecology of language, with variable results.

Being Napo Runa for many people means engaging in a range of cultural practices associated with Kichwa groups from the headwaters and banks of the Napo River. These regional designations are linked to local

---

7. For further details, see Macdonald 1999, 1979; Perreault 2000; Muratorio 1991; Becker and Tutillo 2009; Jarrett 2019.

varieties of runa shimi, "human language." Speakers make fine distinctions between their varieties, with some phonological, morphological, and lexical features varying between neighboring communities, as well as between Archidona and Tena (Grzech, Schwarz, and Ennis 2019; Muratorio 1991). Many of these variations are still poorly described, so that features taken for granted as diagnostic of different dialects can vary rather widely, in ways that are not well analyzed.[8] Further comparative analysis of variations in lexicon, phonology, and syntax will help to clarify regional linguistic histories. Such information can help to refine reclamation practices within a complex linguistic ecology, where sustaining regional variation has emerged as an important goal for many speakers.

The importance of territorial identification for speakers is reflected to some degree in classifications offered by linguists and ethnographers. Carolyn Orr (1978) of the Summer Institute of Linguistics introduced one of the most influential classification systems for the Quechuan languages spoken in the Ecuadorian Amazon. This system divides the languages into three main areas: Loreto/Napo, Tena (spoken in the areas around Tena, Arajuno, and Ahuano), and Bobonaza/Pastaza, based on morphological, phonological, and lexical variations. Table 1 highlights some of the significant differences in morphology and phonology that distinguish the three main dialect regions within the Lowlands, with a more general sketch of Highland Kichwa, alongside standardized Unified Kichwa (Orr 1978; Orr and Wrisley 1981; Carpenter 1982; Ministerio de Educación del Ecuador 2010a):

Among the Amazonian regions, Lower Napo Kichwa patterns more closely with the forms of the Highlands and Unified Kichwa, while Napo and Pastaza Kichwa share some innovations. Quechuan languages are what linguists call agglutinative, meaning that words and sentences are formed by joining suffixes such as those contained in table 1 with lexical roots. Although the differences between these morphemes may seem

---

8. For instance, according to Orr's widely referenced description, in the Highlands the locative morpheme is -pi; in Pastaza/Bobonaza and Tena Kichwa it is contracted to -i; and in Loreto/Napo it is -pi. However, I have encountered a great deal of variability in the locative among speakers; speakers from the Pastaza region frequently use -i, -bi, and the form -ibi, while speakers from Archidona vary between the expected -i and -bi/-pi, with a few also incorporating -ibi.

LANGUAGE AND ECOLOGY IN THE UPPER NAPO

TABLE 1 Select morphological variations in Ecuadorian Kichwa dialects

	Upper Napo Kichwa (Tena-Archidona)	Pastaza Kichwa	Lower Napo Kichwa	Highlands (Imbabura)	Unified Kichwa
Past TAM	-ka-	-ra-	-rka-	-rka-	-rka-
Locative	-i / -bi	-ibi	-pi	-pi	-pi
Continuative	-u-	-u-	-hu-	-ku-	-ku-
Same-subject reference	-sha	-sha	-sa	-shpa	-shpa
Purposive	-ngax/-ngawa	-ngawa	-ngapa	-nkapax	-nkapak
Plural	-una / -guna	-guna	-kuna	-kuna	-kuna

See Appendix 1 for a list of morphemes used in transcription in this text.

small, their combination in use can produce significant differences and difficulties in communication across dialects. The past tense of the verbal copula—that is, the word that would translate to *was* in English—in Upper Napo Kichwa is *aka*. This contrasts with the past tense of *karka* used by both Highland Kichwa speakers as well as speakers of Lower Napo Kichwa. During a survey interview I conducted on linguistic diversity in Napo, Mariano Aguinda, a Kichwa speaker from the Archidona area in his early seventies, detailed the ways that such differences could complicate communication between dialects. He laughed to remember that speakers in Loreto—a township to the north of the Tena/Archidona area—used forms such as karka. He further reproduced an exchange, which he contrasted with what "we" speak:

Mariano Aguinda describes differences between Archidona and Loreto Kichwa, April 18, 2017

MA: Chi ñukanchi "chibi chura-kanchi" tapunchi.₁ Payna "chipichu karka," ninun.₂ \<ha ha\> "Mana chipichu karka," nin.₃ "Kaypimi karka," nisha shina rimanun chiguna.₄

MA: We ask, "chiBi churakanchi" [(should) we have] put it there?"₁ They say, "chiPichu karka" [was it there?]₂ \<ha ha\> [They] say, mana chiPichu karka [it wasn't there].₃ They say kayPimi karka [it was here], that's how those ones talk.₄

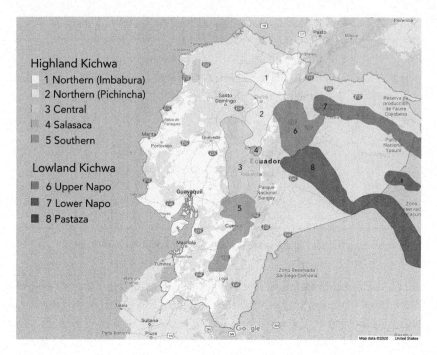

FIGURE 6 Map shows distribution of major regional dialects of Ecuadorian Kichwa. Gratefully adapted with permission from Richard Aschmann (2020). Map data from Google Maps.

According to Mariano, speakers from Loreto are part of the same *muntun*, or kinship group as the Highlands. His evaluation reflects the different morphological and phonological forms embedded in this exchange. In Upper Napo Kichwa, the words for "there" and "here" are *chibi* and *kaybi*, respectively. However, in contrast, Mariano identified the forms *chipi* and *kaypi* in use around Loreto, particularly in line 2.[9] Further, the third-person singular past-tense karka also contrasts with the past tense aka used in Upper Napo Kichwa. Mariano joked that not understanding, he and his companions had put the item in question on what they identified as karka.

---

9. I have not analyzed the speech around Loreto. Orr and Wrisley (1981, 3) list *chaipi* (chaypi) as the form in use in the Limoncocha area. Mariano may be misremembering the form, or his quote may represent another, possibly still undescribed, regional variation.

Unified Kichwa and Highland Kichwa have multiple correspondences, which helps to impart the sense to many in Napo that they are interchangeable, and they are distinct from local varieties. Figure 6, meanwhile, shows the geographic division between Highland and Lowland Kichwa populations, as well as eight significant dialect areas, five in the Highlands and three in the Lowlands, which spread along some of the major river systems.

Ecuadorian Kichwa is less a single language than a collection of closely related dialects spoken across the Andean Highlands and into the Amazonian Lowlands. Both scholars and speakers identify several differences between the Highland and Lowland varieties (Grzech, Schwarz, and Ennis 2019; Nuckolls and Swanson 2020; Orr 1978; Carpenter 1982). As one of my interlocutors in Napo explained, "there are really many varieties, even though they are runa shimi." Such differences are partly linked to the history of colonialism in the Amazon, which saw Kichwa arrive as a missionary language in the context of the profound upheaval of Indigenous, but non-Kichwa speaking, populations there (Muysken 2011). They also have important implications for language revitalization projects in Ecuador.

Historical Ecology of Language

The most probable social and linguistic history of Napo challenges easy binaries between Andean Highlands and Amazonian Lowlands. The presence of Kichwa in the Ecuadorian Amazon can in part be explained by contact with, and possible conquest by, the Inka empire prior to the arrival of the Spanish (Oberem 1980, 50–54). Moreover, the Spanish conquest ruptured—at least partially—a robust regional trade network that is thought to have spread throughout the Andes and Amazon toward the coast (Renard-Casevitz, Saignes, and Taylor 1988; Hornborg 2005; Uzendoski 2004). Prior interaction in this multilingual, interregional network may have facilitated the later emergence of Kichwa as a lingua franca in the region (Oberem 1980, 314; Muysken 2011). Consequently, the varieties of Kichwa spoken in Ecuador belong to the larger Quechuan language family, which is spoken by several million people, with a geographic range that encompasses much of western South America, stretching from southern Colombia to northern Argentina. Although generally referred to simply as Quechua, the language family is diverse, with varying degrees of mutual intelligibility among different varieties (Muysken 2000; Emlen and Adelaar 2017; Heggarty and Beresford-Jones 2010). The language family as a whole is not immediately endangered, but smaller, regional varieties such as those spoken in Napo are threatened both by a shift toward Spanish and by the well-meaning, top-down imposition of standardized Unified Kichwa in institutional settings (Grzech 2017; Uzendoski 2009; K. A. King 2001; Haboud and Limerick 2017). Regional Quechuan varieties like those spoken in Napo are likely shaped by their long histories of interaction with speakers of other Indigenous languages, contributing to a rich dialectal mosaic.

Evidence suggests that pre-Colombian inhabitants of Napo were not speakers of Quechuan languages. Oberem (1980) describes the area corresponding to present-day Napo province along with parts of the contemporary provinces of Sucumbíos and Orellana as inhabited by a cultural group identified as the Quijos. Some scholars have suggested that the Quijos may have been associated with the Barbacoan Highland Chibcha cultural group (Steward and Metraux 1948; Renard-Casevitz, Saignes, and Taylor 1988). Oberem (1980, 314), however, remained hesitant regarding this affiliation, which has been based on archeological, rather than linguistic, grounds. Based on current evidence, the original language(s) spoken in this area remain unclear. There is a very significant history of contact among speakers of different Indigenous languages in the contemporary Ecuadorian Amazon. Colonial-era documents show that the Quijos' regional neighbors were speakers of Tukanoan, Tupian, Zaparoan, and Chicham (or Shuar-Candoan) languages (Renard-Casevitz, Saignes, and Taylor 1988; Oberem 1980; see also Adelaar and Muysken 2004). What can be ascertained from the colonial records is that the Quijos comprised four major cultural areas, shaped by particular material and cultural practices, with some groups being more closely associated with the Highlands and others with the Lowlands (Oberem 1980, 330). Such histories of contact are likely conserved in regional lexicons for flora and fauna, which differ between Highland and Lowland varieties of Kichwa, given the varied environmental zones in which speakers of regional Kichwas live.

Colonial-era activity has a significant role to play in the story of Kichwa in the Ecuadorian Amazon. Intended to aid in the goal of missionization, *reducciones* brought together various small populations and isolated groups to form a larger settlement (Oberem 1980, 84). Moreover, missionaries were often responsible for training Indigenous interpreters, likely aiding in the spread of Kichwa beginning in the 1660s (Oberem 1980, 101). Missions likely provided a central point of contact among disparate groups who were "reduced" into them, such as a population of Zaparoan-speaking Oas who were resettled by Jesuit missionaries at Santa Rosa along the banks of the Napo (Oberem 1980, 43).[10] Far from displaced migrants from the Highlands as they were once viewed (Uzendoski and Whitten 2014, 2; Whitten 1976), Upper Napo Kichwa speakers are part of a regional interactional sphere implicating multiple linguistic and cultural groups that stretches westward toward the Andean Highlands and eastward toward the Amazonian Lowlands. This history affects contemporary language activism, as Lowland varieties of Kichwa were likely shaped by speakers of Amazonian languages, whose descendants survived the upheaval and turmoil of the colonial period as Kichwa speakers. Although Highland and Lowland Kichwa are related, their innovations reflect distinct regional and social histories, which many people recognize as part of their familial inheritance.

Contemporary Ecology of Language

Kichwa is one of thirteen Indigenous languages spoken in Ecuador. The predominant Indigenous language spoken in Napo is Amazonian Kichwa. Other languages widely spoken in the Ecuadorian Amazon include: the Chicham language family (Shuar, Achuar, and Shiwiar in Ecuador and Aguaruna and Huambisa in Peru) (Kohlberger 2016); the isolates Wao Tededo (Huaorani) (Peeke, Levinsohn, and Orr 1991; Peeke 1973) and Cofán (A'ingae) (Dąbkowski 2021); and the Tukanoan language grouping of the Siona-Secoya (Adelaar and Muysken 2004, 453). In some regions, Amazonian Kichwa has replaced Indigenous languages with smaller populations, including Zaparoan languages like Andoa (Adelaar

---

10. In neighboring Pastaza province, moreover, the Canelos Kichwa likely emerged from the confluence of Highland Kichwa refugees and a small Zaparoan group around the Dominican mission at Canelos, which further attracted Quijos *émigrés* and other Zaparoan people (Renard-Casevitz, Saignes, and Taylor 1988, 276).

and Muysken 2004, 451–52). Lowland Ecuadorian Kichwa has slowly spread eastward, particularly as Amazonian Kichwa peoples have journeyed in search of less settled regions.

Napo's Indigenous population is composed of active and passive speakers of Upper Napo Kichwa, as well as Kichwa speakers from neighboring Amazonian provinces, and more recent Kichwa migrants from the Highlands. Speakers of other Amazonian languages, primarily Wao Tededo and Chicham, also live in the Archidona-Tena area, some of whom have married into Kichwa families (see also Uzendoski and Whitten 2014). A large population of Waorani live in the southeast of the canton of Tena, on the border with Orellana and Pastaza provinces, which are also home to large Amazonian Kichwa populations. The Pastaza region includes speakers whose families might once have spoken Zaparoan or Chicham languages, but who have more recently shifted to Kichwa, as well as contemporary speakers of Chicham.

It is difficult to estimate the number of speakers of Kichwa in Napo, especially as the notion of "speaker" can encompass so many different degrees of competency and affiliation with a language (Meek 2017; Davis 2018; Dorian 1977). As discussed in the introduction, in the 2010 national census, more than forty-seven thousand people self-identified as Kichwa speakers. Uzendoski and Whitten have estimated that there are some 150,000 Amazonian Kichwa spread across the provinces of Napo, Pastaza, Sucumbíos, and Orellana (2014, 1). Although a large population of speakers remains, ongoing patterns of shift to Spanish and the use of the standardized Unified Kichwa in bilingual education create a complex situation in which Upper Napo Kichwa is seen as increasingly threatened.

Processes of identification and differentiation through language are complex. Speakers of Amazonian Kichwa generally refer to their language as runa shimi or in reference to their regional territories, for example, *Tena shimi* or *Archidona shimi*. Ethnographers have offered various names for Kichwa-speaking groups in the Amazon, including the Canelos Kichwa—speakers of Bobonaza Kichwa according to Orr and Wrisley, centered around the mission of Canelos—and the Quijos Kichwa—speakers of Orr and Wrisley's Tena Kichwa (Oberem 1980; Whitten 1976). Others have used the ethnonym *runa*, writing, for instance, of the Napo Runa (Uzendoski 2005; Macdonald 1999), a classification closer to how many people talk about themselves on a daily basis. While the "Quijos Kichwa" are sometimes discussed in reference to contemporary populations of Kichwa speakers in Napo, fewer people there identify with this designation. In recent years, a group of families in the mountains near Archidona have recuperated Quijos identity as the Nación Originaria Quijos (NAOQUI).

In Napo, few people describe themselves or their language as "Kichwa," instead preferring the ethnonym *runa*, "human being/person." One of the primary valences of this is "human being," understood to include Upper Napo Kichwa and culturally and linguistically related groups. Kichwa people also describe a contrastive category of *auka*, "outsiders," which comprise neighboring Indigenous groups, such as Wao Tededo and Chicham speakers. Differentiation between runa and auka is often said to relate to key social practices tied to colonialism, including runa acceptance of Christianity, wearing clothes, and eating salt.[11] Bilingualism and multilingualism among Indigenous languages is common in some regions of the Ecuadorian Amazon, but remains under-described. However, my primary interlocutors in Napo generally did not claim familiarity or knowledge of any variety of *auka shimi*.[12]

The distinction between runa and mishu (white-mestizo) populations in Napo is also significant for the contemporary ecology of language in Napo. Several terms describe white-mestizo settlers, which include *awallta* (from *awallakta*, "highlander") *irakcha* (lord);[13] *blancu* (Sp. "white"); tsala (K. "pale"); and mishu (U.K. "mestizo"). Although Ecuador takes part in the larger Latin American discourse of *mestizaje*—cultural and racial admixture between European and Indigenous populations—as Mary Weismantel suggests, "in actual practice within specific social con-

---

11. Muratorio (1991, 43) recounts an origin story, in which the runa and auka became different groups after the runa accepted baptism and began to eat salt, while the auka refused salt and fled into the forest. Auka has also been translated as "savage" and is considered by some to be a derogatory term.

12. While my work was primarily in the Kichwa-dominant regions of Archidona and Tena, greater bilingualism between Wao Tededo and Runa Shimi is to be found in other parts of Napo and further east. Similarly, Kichwa and Chicham bilingualism is quite common in various regions of Pastaza.

13. My interlocutors explained that this is a contraction of *ira akcha*, "greasy hair," for the shininess of European hair. However, due to common phonological processes in Napo, I suspect it may be a local remnant of the term *huiracocha*, "lord," used to refer in the colonial period to Spaniards (Oberem 1980, 33).

texts, there is no intermediate or 'mixed' racial category: race operates as a vicious binary that discriminates superiors from inferiors" (2001, xxxi).[14] While many of these terms might translate in English to "mestizo," I translate them as *white* or *white-mestizo* when they refer to people who "maintain a 'white' lifestyle" (Oberem 1980, 28), in contrast to a runa lifestyle. Significant differences in lifestyle run upon fault lines of language, subsistence, alimentation, and bodily habitus.

The "vicious binary" between white and Napo Runa has partly been maintained by a division—at times sharp, at times permeable—between Spanish and Kichwa language and lifestyle. In Napo today, despite Kichwa's constitutional co-official status with Spanish, the number of white-mestizo Spanish speakers who have learned more than a few phrases in Kichwa is still negligible. It is Kichwa speakers who are expected to learn Spanish. Food, likewise, has separated mishu from runa, such that drinking aswa—a manioc mash fermented by chewing a small portion and returning it to the mass, which is mixed with water and drunk throughout the day—also serves as a significant line of social differentiation.

Despite stereotypes about the isolation of Amazonians, Upper Napo Runa have an ongoing history of interaction with people of different backgrounds. Besides Kichwa-speaking runa from other regions, the members of other "auka" Indigenous groups, and white-mestizos, Upper Napo Kichwa speakers regularly interact with people they call rancia and *gringu*, phenotypically white foreigners, who might arrive as tourists, students, volunteers, investors, researchers, missionaries, or otherwise as travelers.[15] While categories like mishu are less often about phenotypic markers of race, categories like rancia, as well as *negro/a* (Sp. "Black"), *yana* (K. "Black"), or *chino/a* (Sp. "Chinese"), are used to make racialized categorizations based on physical features and perceived nationality. A small population of Afro-descended people, who are becoming increasingly active in public life, also lives in Napo.

Upper Napo Kichwa is still widely utilized in daily life, but children and young people in the area face increasing pressure from Spanish,

---

14. Huarcaya (2018, 416) further defines mestizaje as "assimilation into mainstream culture."

15. According to Oberem, *francias* was a common term for European and North American foreigners (1980, 33). This word has been increasingly Kichwaized in Napo, so that today it is pronounced "rancia."

which is the dominant language of most public and institutional interactions. Moreover, daily patterns of use suggest that intergenerational transmission of Kichwa has been increasingly ruptured. Elder residents of rural communities, particularly women with less access to formal education, may still be monolingual in Kichwa. Most people in Napo have some degree of bilingualism with Spanish. Spanish is most often used by children and young adults in their daily interactions. Although some children understand speech in Kichwa, they often respond to their parents and grandparents in Spanish. Patterns vary between communities and families. Upper Napo Kichwa is generally used among adults and some young people but much less frequently by children and adolescents. Many young adults in the area continue to recuperate their use of spoken Kichwa, suggesting possibilities for a more hopeful future for the use of Kichwa.

When I interviewed Kichwa speakers about how they understood regional variations, I found that for many people, regional varieties were closely linked to regional identities. My interviewees recognized regional variation between the Highlands and Lowlands, as well as within the Lowlands. And although they suggested regional differences could produce difficulties in communication, they were generally understanding and accepting that people in different areas had their own "ways" or "types" of speech. Regional linguistic variations, moreover, were understood to be inherited through the speech of their elders. Speaking according to one's regional way was often a sign of respect for family history. These regional linguistic varieties comprise an ecology of language—ways that linguistic practices and qualities are related to each other and to broader understandings of social life. They also include relationships to other Indigenous languages spoken in the province, like Wao Tededo and Chicham. This ecology of language has been interrupted by Spanish in missionary boarding schools and by the introduction of the "formal," standardized variety of Unified Kichwa.

Unified Kichwa in Napo's Linguistic Ecology

Regional speakers in Napo associate Unified Kichwa with the speech of the Highlands, often describing it as a foreign imposition, linked to the national government and its institutions. This is evident in the claim by

Rita Tunay that the government had mandated study of Unified Kichwa. During my research, Rita was a widely popular cohost of the radio program *A New Path*. One afternoon, when we were discussing language and the radio, she explained that people in Napo perceived that "today the government has decreed in writing to study runa shimi." "However," she continued, "it seems like they have commanded to study this language from the Highlands, what we call Kichwa Unificado (Unified Kichwa)."

A young man similarly explained to me that while studying at a bilingual education school in the nearby province of Coca, he had learned what he described in Spanish as "another Kichwa." However, when he returned to Napo, he explained, "[my grandmother] told me it isn't like that, it's another way." After learning Kichwa from his grandmother, he concluded that the Kichwa he had learned in school was "mixed" with "Kichwa from the Highlands" and that it "sounded different." His grandmother, meanwhile, described in Kichwa that the form he learned was *llutachishka* (K. "Unified;" literally "stacked/glued together"), while his friend offered the Spanish descriptor "*Unificado.*" For many people, Unified Kichwa is simply not the same as what they refer to as "our own Kichwa" (*ñukanchi kikin shimi*).

Despite the diversity of Kichwa across regions, Ecuador has only one official standard for writing Kichwa, Unified Kichwa. Ecuador is notable for having recognized the Indigenous languages Kichwa and Shuar as "official languages of intercultural communication" in the 2008 constitution (*Constitución de la República del Ecuador* 2008 art. 2). Yet, the official Kichwa used in the constitution as well as other written and oral contexts can vary considerably from that spoken daily in households in Napo and the Andean Highlands. One of the most significant features of Unified Kichwa is that it is based on a linguistic reconstruction of a historical form of Kichwa, thought to be spoken before regional fragmentation (Montaluisa 2018, 292; Salomon 1983). This form shares much in common with the contemporary Highlands and diverges significantly from many of the practices of the Lowlands. Yet, even among Highland speakers, Unified Kichwa can flatten regional variations and remains controversial throughout Ecuador (K. A. King 2001; Andronis 2004).

Unified Kichwa has increasingly been deployed as a language of the Ecuadorian state. It is the code in which the Ecuadorian constitution was translated into Kichwa and was the form used by former president Rafael Correa and his translators to address Kichwa-speaking constituents. Knowledge of Unified Kichwa is generally mandatory for bilingual educators, and it is the oral and written form often taught in bilingual education programs at public schools. It is also the form preferred by many politicians and educators for public speech (Limerick 2020) and, until recently, has been the dominant code of performance media like the cultural beauty pageants overseen by the bilingual school system. The ways Unified Kichwa has been positioned in Napo lead some people to see it as a "formal" or more correct form of Kichwa, while others worry that "their own" language is being lost. These debates shaped the context of language education and media production in Napo and demonstrate seemingly unexpected ways that settler colonial ideologies and practices can shape language revitalization.

Conclusion

Disagreements over the linguistic codes used for language revitalization are taking place in the context of ongoing shift of Kichwa toward Spanish, which has been wrought by the contemporary arrival of major roads, oil and mineral extraction, missionization, formal schooling, and new Highland settlers following land reform. These changes have reshaped life for residents in Napo over the last fifty years, leading away from forest-based agriculture and hunting on traditional lands toward urban settlements, wage labor, and institutional education.

Beginning from the assumption that language is a decontextualizable system may lead us to focus on how marginalized language communities are utilizing that language, rather than the social and material conditions to which they are responding through their language practices. When I have discussed that Napo Kichwa people feel themselves to be oppressed by national language standardization, some have commented that if people in Napo really cared about their dialects, they would have taught to their children. The argument continues that at least the language standardizers are doing something, in contrast to the "failure" of regional speakers, who are supposedly letting their languages slip away. This stance ultimately shifts the blame to Kichwa families who fail to teach their language and their children who fail to acquire it correctly (Meek 2011). Yet, it ignores the reasons that language practices began to change in the first place—the reworking of Indigenous ecologies into settler ecologies (Whyte 2018).

In Napo, I saw Kichwa speakers make dynamic choices about language and language socialization practices that respond to an assemblage of language ideologies and ontologies (Kroskrity 2018; Ennis 2020), as well as material constraints. With land reforms, a subsistence Amazonian lifestyle has become increasingly difficult to maintain and less attractive to young people (Macdonald 1999; Shenton 2019). The expanding settler economy and society in the region has helped clear forests for intensive agriculture and contaminated rivers with the extraction of oil, gold, and other resources, at the same time as missionary and state-run education has expanded (Muratorio 1991; Kohn and Picq 2020; Sawyer 2004; Uzendoski 2018). Bernard Perley notes a tendency toward victim blaming in the rhetoric of language endangerment and revitalization but warns against thinking of Indigenous language communities solely as passive victims (Perley 2012, 136). Shifting toward Spanish may be many people's response to a settler social world where Kichwa and other Indigenous languages have been actively suppressed in education, labor, and many other settings.

Language shift in Napo, like in many other regions of the world, is directly and indirectly tied to both extractive and settler colonialism and other forms of domination. In Napo, missionary boarding schools helped disrupt intergenerational transmission of language and other forms of knowledge. These schools were also intended to "pacify" local populations and ease the transition to massive resource extraction in the Amazon (Muratorio 1991, 166–67). Contemporary state-run Spanish-language schools and ongoing social, economic, territorial, and environmental marginalization have encouraged shift toward Spanish and entrance into the wage labor economy. Many people describe the loss of traditional ecological practices and lifeways as a collective "forgetting" of their elders' knowledge. In Napo, cultural activists are turning to performance and broadcast media as grassroots, multimodal methods to reclaim and reweave intergenerational transmission of language and more than language, despite the various forms of disruption and oppression they still confront.

The turn to Spanish in many Napo Kichwa households has been driven by necessity. This resulted from the interruption of the forms of ecological—and thus material and economic—interrelationship that give rise to social continuance in the Upper Napo. Unified Kichwa interacts with Napo's local ecology of languages as an institutionally and economically dominant form, which has also interrupted the transmission of regional varieties of Kichwa. The importance of the work of language activists around bilingual education and standardization in the context of profound social and educational inequality should not be minimized. Yet, their work also reveals how hegemonic assumptions about linguistic diversity and political unification can shape language revitalization projects, which may ignore or even magnify the oppression of regional varieties. Language revitalization can involve coloniality in its assumptions. The need to choose a single variety for widespread revitalization is one example. We can thus look to ways that communities are reclaiming their languages outside of some of these more institutional structures. One of these is through an ecology of regional media, in which Kichwa speakers mobilize a diversity of ways of speaking and interacting with each other.

Various state, religious, and economic actors have contributed to the rapid development and urbanization of the areas surrounding the town of Archidona and the provincial capital of Tena over the last century, particularly since the 1960s. Today, however, an elderly generation remembers with deep nostalgia the way life was "before," while young cultural activists utilize such memories as the basis for defining and enregistering "our own" language and culture in media. It is such use of community media, particularly radio media, for grassroots linguistic and cultural reclamation in the Upper Ecuadorian Amazon that is the primary focus of this book.

CHAPTER 2

Media Ecology in the Upper Napo

It was a cool October morning, the air lightly chilled from overnight rain. Serafina and I had slept at the Association of Kichwa Midwives of the Upper Napo for her shift, on call in case of a birth. As at her own home, Serafina and the other midwife awoke before dawn to light a fire and brew a pot of guayusa in AMUPAKIN's kitchen. Her colleague's husband tuned the radio to *A New Path*, which was an important source for local news.

During their daily live program, the hosts and producers of *A New Path* regularly communicated with their listeners through their Facebook page, where the two-hour program was livestreamed. Their Facebook page served as the channel where audience members left messages on livestreams or sent direct messages with announcements or requests for a saludo (shout-out) on the air. That morning, as Serafina was simultaneously preparing to return home around five o'clock in the morning, Mayor Jaime Shiguango left a comment written in Spanish on the program's Facebook livestream. The message announced that the *ukuy*, a seasonal delicacy of flying reproductive leaf-cutter ants, were leaving their nests near his house (figure 7).

This news was reported—in Kichwa—by hosts James and Rita to their listeners. This was how Serafina overheard it, as she ended her shift at AMUPAKIN. Hearing the news about ukuy, Serafina mused that people would go out to look, and commented on the behavior of ukuy. As we left AMUPAKIN and walked to the main road into Archidona, we saw a group of children circling a puddle, searching for the plump ukuy to put

FIGURE 7 Facebook comments about ukuy, which were recirculated on the radio. Adaptation by the author of a screenshot from October 6, 2016.

into plastic bags. Serafina commented that they were looking for ukuy, which are attracted to lights. She then said good morning to a young man waiting at the bus stop and told him that she had heard on the radio that the ukuy were out. And she repeated the news to her family when she arrived at home, leading several young children to rush outside to search for the seasonal treat.

This morning shows how radio articulated with other technologies and forms of face-to-face communication in Napo, contributing to a broader ecology of media there. Radio media in part facilitated the circulation of mediated texts (Spitulnik 1997), which evoked listeners' experiential knowledge. The local ecology of media in Napo also responded to many people's understandings of language and communicative practices. Oral, aural, and embodied forms of mediation extended and amplified a community of practice in Napo. It was in this articulation that I came to understand how the broader ecology of media in Napo helped to revalorize and reclaim language by recontextualizing the embodied pedagogies and interactional routines linked to sociocultural transmission. This ability to remediate significant sites of socialization helps to explain how local radio and other forms of media were mobilized to revalorize local environmental knowledge, alongside local language varieties. This chapter introduces radio's central place in Napo's ecology of local media.

Ecologies of Media

Media in Napo can be understood as an ecology, much like the interaction among language users and their varieties, as well as the relationships between biotic organisms and abiotic systems. Napo's ecology of media is comprised of a plurality of practices with communicative technologies and forms that exist in relationship to each other and to their users. This view emphasizes how media interact with each other, as well as how humans interact with media and with each other through mediation, including both face-to-face interactions and technologically mediated communication. Although I arrived in Napo focused on radio, I soon realized it was inseparable from other media production, circulation, and reception in Napo.

There were several Napo-based radio programs, broadcast on both FM and Internet stations. There was also a wide range of media forms and technologies in circulation, which intersected with radio at various points. Especially popular were genres of regional Kichwa music, performed live and shared through recordings on personal media devices. These could circulate on CDs, DVDs, USB drives, or cell phones with Internet access through file sharing and social media platforms. Live performance genres included music, dance, cultural demonstrations and other pageantry, and parades. Many pageants and other live events were simultaneously live-broadcast over the radio. For those with access to televisions, the one-hour program *Rayu Shinalla* (see Wroblewski 2022) was broadcast in Kichwa weekday mornings, and there were shorter segments of local news and variety programs sometimes dedicated to content in Kichwa or other Indigenous languages. Community films and videos were also in circulation, especially music videos. These media forms were shared via social media and other websites. Preferred platforms included Facebook, WhatsApp, and Internet radio on websites. At the time, there was some use of Instagram and YouTube, which has increased alongside the use of apps like TikTok since the conclusion of my primary fieldwork in 2017. Finally, people interacted with different forms of written media, including books, grammars, dictionaries in Kichwa, as well as short messages and announcements, some of which could circulate online or on the radio. Media ecologies, however, are not reducible to an inventory of equipment and technical capabilities. They include the social relationships enabled through radio and related events, as well as the ways of living and feeling stemming from interactions with media and other people through media (Fuller 2005).

These media forms often recontextualized, or remediated, each other. Radio media in Napo remediated not only different genres of face-to-face interaction, but also live performances and pageantry. Several radio hosts in Napo sought to produce content meant to be listened to at well-known times of day—especially the early morning, which remediated face-to-face interactions that might otherwise be disappearing from peoples' lives. It is such complex interactions between media and people that draw me to the metaphor of ecology for media, rather than the metaphor of landscape implied by Appadurai's (1996) concept of "mediascapes." For Appadurai, mediascape referred to the distribution of infrastructure to produce and disseminate images of the world, as well as the actual "images of the world created by these media" (1996, 35). Mediascapes, although encompassing interconnected media, imply a terrain created at a distance through which audiences move. An ecological view of media instead emphasizes the entanglements between forms, events, and people that are treated as separate in some disciplines. Think of the institutional fragmentation of media into radio studies, television studies, and film studies. The lifespans of such media forms are further divided into production, distribution, and consumption, while communities are atomized into "producers" and "consumers" of media. In Napo, these forms, events, and people are interconnected within the local ecology of media.

Media may create environments (Postman 2000; McLuhan 1964), but they do not tyrannically determine people's behaviors within them. Rather, they may afford certain actions, affective states, or habits of thought over others. The media ecology in Napo was also shaped by multiple ideologies about language, mediation, and interaction in Napo, which influenced the relationship among media forms. In utilizing a framework of media ecology, I am interested in exploring the *effects* of media on human sociality (McLuhan 1964), but not in retreading academic debates that position literacy as the inevitable evolutionary outcome of orality, nor that posit a "Great Divide" between so-called primarily oral and literate societies (Goody and Watt 1963; Ong 1982; Lum 2005a). Literacies and their social effects are multiple (Heath 1982; Besnier 1995; Ahearn 2001). Print literacy, however, continues to be seen by many as the ultimate form of communication that all people, including Indigenous Amazonians, should eventually embrace.

For Upper Napo Kichwa speakers, oral language is already imbued with its own forms of textuality (Uzendoski and Calapucha-Tapuy 2012). In Napo, linguistic ideologies link inscription and textuality to embodiment rather than the decontextualization of knowledge in writing and print. One elder counseled a young apprentice to guard what she had spoken in her heart, where it would grow throughout her life, and help guide her actions. Significantly, the elder claimed that writing—and even video recording—was insufficient to maintain such knowledge. Anthropologist Michael Uzendoski and community scholar Edith Felicia Calapucha-Tapuy (2012) emphasize that Upper Napo Kichwa verbal art is a form of "somatic poetry" that is embodied through a multimodal aesthetics capable of transcribing intertextual meanings in landscapes, bodies, and the mind. Many Upper Napo Runa embrace understandings of inscription and textuality that go beyond print literacy, and which are not always compatible with inscription in audio and video files.

Media ecologies are shaped by the interaction among those who mobilize them, their ideologies of how different media work and relate to other forms of communication (Gershon 2010), and the affordances of various media. The orthographic script used in writing often influences the ways Kichwa speakers pronounce or read a written message. The script does not determine this. One could learn to match written scripts to regional variations, even within a "deep orthography" like that of Unified Kichwa (Limerick 2017), in which several regional variations may be linked to a single standardized grapheme. Ideologies of literacy and beliefs about how letters correspond to sounds provide a marked influence on how Kichwa people interact with text. Print literacy is not incompatible with Amazonian indigeneity. Although some may disagree with language standardization, many adult and elder Kichwa people in Napo are proud to have learned to read and write, as they remember how literacy and education were used to exclude Kichwa people from full sociopolitical participation in Ecuador until the late 1970s (Picq 2018, 89). There are, however, significant issues in the reception of print literacy in Napo, due to the role of standard language ideologies in the development of Unified Kichwa and top-down language revitalization projects.

Producers of the program *A New Path* were engaged in a sometimes-contentious reclamation movement. They sought to publicly remediate and therein "revalorize" and reclaim practices, symbols, and discursive forms seen as threatened by shift toward Spanish and urban lifeways, as well as by the introduction of Unified Kichwa in well-intentioned language-revitalization practices centered on state-run bilingual education and institutional media production. This chapter contextualizes the radio programs and linguistic and cultural practices analyzed in this book by exploring the ecology of media in which Kichwa-language media was produced, circulated, and evaluated. In exploring three Napo Kichwa radio programs, I focus on the relationship between radio and print media, and how these modalities intersected with the Upper Napo's sociolinguistic ecology. However, I remain attentive to the ways radio and print interact with other technologies, modalities, and genres of media in Napo, as well as the sociopolitical and economic contexts that shape their use.

Radio in Napo's Media and Linguistic Ecology

Radio has been a popular, widespread, and inexpensive media technology in Napo, and Ecuador more generally. Upper Napo Kichwa–language radio shows are a well-established feature in a media ecology that is dominated by Spanish-language programming. Article 36 of Ecuador's Communications Law enacted in 2013 requires that 5 percent of daily programming "express and reflect the cosmovision, culture, tradition, knowledge, and wisdom of Indigenous, Afro-Ecuadorian, and Montubio communities and nationalities" (*Ley Orgánica de Comunicación*, 2013). This requirement is often met with Kichwa music and programming.

Four stations based in Tena—*La Voz de Napo* (The Voice of Napo), *Radio Ideal* (Ideal Radio), *Radio Arcoíris* (Rainbow Radio), and *Radio Olímpica* (Olympic Radio)—broadcast talk-radio and music programs with Upper Napo Kichwa hosts during my research. Some stations played automated mixes of Kichwa music in the predawn hours when station owners imagine Kichwa audiences to be attentive to the radio. Napo's airwaves were shaped by regional satellites of national, Spanish-language stations such as Radio Canela (Cinnamon Radio), which did not have regular programming in Kichwa. While traveling in taxis or passing by a radio, I sometimes heard short segments in regional or national varieties of Kichwa or other Indigenous languages, such as Chicham or Wao Tededo. Such clips were unpredictable, minimizing their role in establishing a receptive public. It was daily programs such as *A New Path* and stations like La Voz de Napo to which my interlocutors tuned their radios.

The Voice of Napo

Since the 1960s, alongside other forms of infrastructure, Western media technologies have played an increasing role in Napo. Padre Mario Perín had arrived in Napo from Italy in 1966, eventually learning Kichwa and becoming a popular host at the Catholic station. According to Father Perín, two-way radios were first used by missionaries to communicate between Tena and distant settlements (see also Macdonald 1979, 6). This point-to-point communicative infrastructure grew into the Catholic Josephine radio station, La Voz de Napo, founded as a short-wave station in 1970 as reliable hydroelectric energy arrived in Tena (Spiller 1974, 297). The station acquired an AM (amplitude modulation) frequency in 1998 and began transmitting as an FM (frequency modulation) station in 2010. The station's current range throughout Napo, Pastaza, and Orellana provinces is extended to national and international audiences by simultaneous digital transmission. Listeners may call in from communities around Amazonian Ecuador and more distant regions in the Highlands and coast, though Napo is the best represented province among listeners. The station's more distant listeners were generally residents of Napo who had moved for work or school, and who called in or wrote over Facebook to request songs and send messages to their families in Napo. Although the Josephines played a role in cultural and environmental transformations in the region, there are many ways in which they have supported the causes of Napo Kichwa communities. La Voz de Napo's programming is a popular site of local Kichwa-language media production.

The Voice of Napo broadcasts two programs in Kichwa: a morning show informally called *Wayusa Upina*, "wayusa drinking," broadcast between five and six o'clock in the morning, and from six to eight in the evening, a "runa shimira rimana," or "Kichwa-language" program. Their remaining programming is in Spanish. During my research, both programs were hosted by Gloria Grefa, a Kichwa speaker from the Talag region to the east of Tena.

Gloria was in her early twenties when we met in 2015. Born in Napo, Gloria had been raised for part of her childhood and adolescence by a Spanish-speaking foster family in the capital city of Quito. She once described to me how she continued to read the Catholic *Devocionario Quichua* while she was living in Quito, helping her to maintain her understanding and use of Kichwa. After returning to Napo to reconnect with her natal family, Gloria worked as a volunteer and apprentice at La Voz de Napo. Between 2013 and 2015, she worked in the communications department of the provincial government of Napo as a translator and media professional. In 2015, after her two-year government contract ended, she returned to take a paid position at La Voz de Napo as their Kichwa-language radio host.

Before dawn and past dark, in a second-floor studio in a building next to Tena's central San Jose Cathedral, Gloria would sit in front of the computer used to manage the radio program, answering phone calls and text messages from her audience, while she queued up songs and spoke lovingly into the microphone. Gloria had a high, clear voice that some listeners would describe as *mishki*, "sweet," though others commented she had a *llaki*, "sad," tone to her voice, a descriptor that evokes the pain of love and empathy. She saw her job at the radio in terms of the affective labor of bringing joy (*kushiyachina*) to her listeners with her voice and with Kichwa music. She also counseled them (*kamachina*) about religion and significant cultural practices like drinking aswa (manioc chicha) and wayusa, speaking in runa shimi, and respecting one's elders.

Although a fluent speaker of Upper Napo Kichwa (alongside Spanish), Gloria's speech was influenced by the extended period she had spent in the Highlands, her work in government settings, and the orthography of the Kichwa texts with which she interacted on the air. Like other radio hosts, Gloria had to mediate between the expectations of audience members who aligned with standardized forms of speech, and those of her regional audience. Her on-air broadcasts often included standardized words, such as the term *mashi*, "comrade/co-worker," used in institutional contexts. But she also addressed her listeners as family members. She once told me that she imagines she is speaking with her family on the air, using forms recognizable to them.

Gloria was the Voice of Napo's most frequent Kichwa host, but the Italian priest Father Mario hosted a half-hour religious segment on Monday nights, speaking in both Spanish and Kichwa. Throughout La Voz de Napo's history, priests with some command of Kichwa have hosted the programs, sometimes assisted by regional Kichwa speakers. Listeners in Napo spoke fondly of Father Mario, as well as his predecessor Father Humberto Dorigatti, one of the earliest hosts of the program, who had arrived in Napo in 1947.[1] Only a few contemporary priests seem to have learned Kichwa, and it was uncommon in Archidona for other priests to carry out services in Kichwa.

La Voz de Napo's programming focused on religious education; local, national, and international news; messages; and religious and popular music, and thus drew together several media genres and modalities. Italian Josephine priests and nuns had recorded several Kichwa-language devotional songs, like "María Ñukapa Mama" (K. "My Mother Maria"), which Gloria played alongside hits from Upper Napo Kichwa groups like Los Playeros Kichwas (Sp. The Kichwa Beachboys), Patricio Alvarado and his band Llaki Shungu (K. Loving/Sad Heart), or Kambak (K. Yours). Gloria used her platform to discuss linguistic and cultural change, but the focus of her shows, particularly those in the evening, was reading prayers from the *Devocionario Quichua* and the daily gospel and passages from the Bible in Spanish that she simultaneously translated into Kichwa on the air. La Voz de Napo was an important site for local organizations and regional listeners to transmit messages. Gloria always had a large

---

1. I attempted to interview Padre Humberto in September 2016 at the retirement home where he resided in Archidona but found that he was no longer capable of participating in interviews at his advanced age. He died in February 2017, an event which I and others in Napo learned about on the radio.

stack of papers for her segments of yachachina (news)—personal or organizational messages and announcements that had been dropped off by listeners or by local government representatives. Regardless of the language they were originally written in, Gloria generally translated these items into Kichwa. Death announcements of local congregants and catechists were also a regular part of the program, accompanied by prayers for the departed's soul. Like other local radio hosts, Gloria kept a small notebook where she wrote the names of people she interacted with in her daily life in Napo, who regularly requested a *saludushka shimi* (K. "shout-out," literally "greeting" from Sp. *saludar*, "to greet"). Like other Kichwa radio programs in Napo, Gloria's shows were imbricated in listeners' everyday interactions, as her voice lovingly accompanied them in their daily prayers, alerted them to the death of a distant family member, or provided them with energy in the early morning hours.

Amazonian Power

Listeners tuning in between five and six o'clock in the morning might find both Upper Napo Kichwa and Spanish in use on the bilingual program *Antisuyu Ushay/Poder Amazónico*, "Amazonian Power," hosted by Fernandisco and his colleague Mancino—known here by their radio names. Fernandisco is a founding member of the popular group The Kichwa Beachboys, whose songs are played on many stations and at public events. Their program was broadcast from the ground floor of a home converted into the studio and offices of the radio station. The station owner occupied the back rooms of the house and rented out the apartments above. At the start of my fieldwork, Radio Olímpica also had an evening Kichwa program, *Wasima Tigrashun* (K. "Let's Return Home"), focused on messages and music. Napo's media ecology is constantly shifting, and shortly after I began research, this program was cut from the schedule for lack of advertising revenue. Later, *Antisuyu Ushay* was also cut for lack of funding, though the duo eventually returned to the air with a new evening program. Neither received a wage for their work at the radio, "gifting" their time to the owner of the private station that broadcast their program. They supported themselves and their families through jobs in Tena's municipal offices.

While the hosts of other Kichwa-language programs largely seemed to imagine their audience as Kichwa-dominant elders and families listening in the rural countryside, the hosts of *Antisuyu Ushay* spoke more explicitly to a bilingual, urban public. As Mancino described, the program above all was intended to "valorize" the language for those living in the city or nearby who "did not want to know Kichwa nor the majority of our practices." The hosts switched regularly between the use of Upper Napo Kichwa language and music to frame the program, and informational content in Spanish, which they often summarized in Kichwa. Their programs shared a focus with others in Napo on Kichwa music, though they also played Spanish-language music, uncommon on other programs. They also transmitted messages received as text messages or via Facebook (usually written in Spanish), local and national news, *consejos del buen vivir* (Sp. "advice for good living"), and *cuentos y leyendas* (Sp. "stories and legends") of the region, which they worried were being forgotten.

Fernandisco and Mancino saw the radio as an important means to raise what they described as the "self-esteem" of Kichwa speakers in the area. Although the program was bilingual, Fernandisco hoped that the greater use of Kichwa on the program would "influence" listeners and contribute to the revalorization of the language, in the face of the social and economic pressure to learn languages like Spanish or English. They frequently used translation from Kichwa to Spanish, or Spanish to Kichwa, to tell the time or to translate messages. This modeled the fluent use of both languages and emphasized that Kichwa belonged on the airwaves alongside Spanish. They were also committed to speaking in regional varieties of Kichwa and sometimes corrected my own use of standardized forms that I had learned at other radio programs.

Mancino and Fernandisco were, respectively, in their early and late fifties during my fieldwork and their personal backgrounds are illustrative of the social setting of contemporary settler colonialism in the region. Mancino was from a rural community located several hours' travel by foot and boat from Tena. His parents had married when his mother was twelve and his father was fourteen, and together had gone to work on a hacienda for a *pata* (K. from Sp. patrón, "landowner"). As a child, Mancino's mother had sent him to Tena to live with the *patrona* of the hacienda, "in order to learn proper morals" like "politeness" and "respect." It was during this three-month period with the patrona that Mancino was first introduced to electric light, amplified music, and cars. Fernandisco was from a Tena Kichwa family and had watched Tena expand from a missionary town surrounded by Kichwa settlements to a bustling frontier city, a history he would remark upon when we walked together through town. He had learned Kichwa as his first language. However, at three and a half years of age, his family had placed him in an *internado*, a boarding school run by nuns. Yet, he had "never forgotten Kichwa," even after six years in a Spanish-language boarding school, which he attributed to his early exposure at home.

Fernandisco and Mancino disagreed somewhat on the role of parents in teaching Kichwa to their children, although both had experiences with being forced by their surroundings to learn Spanish. Fernandisco emphasized the importance of early childhood education in Kichwa, while Mancino was more supportive of the idea that parents teach their children Spanish from a young age. As he argued, in his own case, when he had learned Spanish, he spoke it "badly," which caused his interlocutors to laugh at him. Parents are frequently concerned that children will speak Spanish with an accent or with other markers that it is their second language if they are not explicitly taught it from a young age. Like many parents I encountered, Mancino supported efforts to help young children learn Spanish as a necessity for contemporary life in Napo. The bilingual format of their radio program responded to some of these tensions surrounding the dual role of Kichwa and Spanish in Napo, particularly among their imagined listening public.

Fernandisco and Mancino's history of involvement with radio media is also illustrative of the ways that radio has been used for development projects in the region, which have coincided with a broader emphasis on the use of media to "give voice" (Fisher 2016) to marginalized peoples around the globe. They briefly had a program together on Radio Arcoíris in 2004. Fernandisco emphasized, however, that 2005 was the year their program was born, when the Spanish NGO Ayuda en Acción (Help in Action) arrived in Napo. According to Fernandisco, one of the NGO's primary strategies to propel regional development was through radio programming. Fernandisco and Mancino hosted a program called *La Llave del Futuro* (Sp. "The Key for the Future"), focused on health, education (particularly language), political organization, regional economic development, and agriculture. As their programs have come and gone at different stations according to the availability of ever-shifting sources of funding, they have added cultural change and environmental conservation to their programming. Fernandisco described their program in terms of a widespread, international ideology of the positive potentialities of community media to develop and shape the awareness of their listening audience around major social issues (Powdermaker 1962), with a particular emphasis on linguistic and cultural shift.

A New Path

The Kichwa-language radio program *Mushuk Ñampi,* "A New Path," arrived on Napo's airwaves in July of 2015. Unlike many other Kichwa-language radio shows, the program *A New Path* was not produced by an established radio station. Rather, it was funded, produced, and streamed by the Municipality of Archidona. The majority-Kichwa town of Archidona did not have any established radio stations, as all of Napo's stations were located in the capital of Tena, some ten kilometers to the east.[2] The Municipality of Archidona's Department of Communications partnered with two stations in Tena, the commercially licensed station Radio Arcoíris and the community-licensed station Radio Ideal, to broadcast their program, with a reach that included Napo and the neighboring provinces of Orellana and Pastaza. The program was simultaneously live-broadcast on Facebook, which afforded its temporary archival online.[3] Social media provided another channel between radio hosts and listeners. Those with computers or mobile phones might comment on the show on Facebook during the live-broadcast or send messages to the hosts via direct message.

---

2. Archidona did not have a radio station during my fieldwork, but Fernandisco and Mancino described working at a station, Radio Líder, in Archidona during the period Ayuda en Acción was active in Napo. The mediascape in Napo, however, shifts frequently. During my fieldwork, the Municipio de Archidona had begun the process of acquiring the license for a public radio frequency, but this project did not come to fruition.

3. This informal archive disappeared when Jaime Shiguango's term as mayor ended. The incoming administration eventually removed most of the records of the public broadcasts, projects, and programming conducted during Shiguango's tenure.

Other hosts included linguistic and cultural reclamation as a theme of their programs, but it was one of the most explicit goals of the hosts and producers of *A New Path*. When the show was launched, its two twenty-something cohosts, Rita Tunay and James Yumbo, prerecorded the program for broadcast between four and six o'clock in the morning, when many families listen to the radio. They soon switched to a live-broadcast format due to audience response. Listeners attempted to contact the hosts during the show to request shout-outs and other messages. This genre was an extremely popular feature of all Kichwa-language radio programming in Napo. The content of the program was largely directed by its two Kichwa-speaking hosts, with oversight by Dario Lopez, the show's non-Kichwa director, as well as by Jaime Shiguango, the Kichwa-speaking mayor of Archidona between 2014 and 2019. Dario sometimes commented that *A New Path* sought to expand Kichwa-language programming to focus on content beyond personal messages and music. Indeed, their programs focused most explicitly on cultural reclamation.

For the young Kichwa hosts of *A New Path* and Voz de Napo, media represented a pathway to greater financial stability. Both Rita and James were employees of the Municipal Department of Communications, with Rita serving as a secretary and communications professional, while James edited photos, audio recordings, and videos for promotional materials. Like Gloria, both received a salary for their labor at the radio and the municipal offices, helping to establish Kichwa-language broadcasting and media production as a viable career path for young people in the area. The demands of their job were often grueling. Each weekday, Rita and James would arrive a few minutes before four o'clock in the morning at the Municipal building in Archidona. The overnight security guard opened the doors as we arrived, often still heavy with sleep. James arrived on a motorcycle from the small house nearby where he rented a room. Rita arrived via bicycle from the one-room apartment a few blocks away that she sometimes shared with her parents when they visited from their rural agricultural community. They were sometimes tasked with hosting performance events like beauty pageants lasting late into the night, then hosting the radio program the following morning. Since the conclusion of my fieldwork in 2017, James and Rita have continued with their public careers. James has remained active as a regional media producer and host, including for the administration of Rita Tunay. Rita was elected vice-prefect of Napo in 2019, likely bolstered by her popularity on the radio. She became prefect of Napo (2019–2023) soon after due to the health-related death of her running mate, Edison Chavez. I explore her rise in local politics via the media industry in chapter 4.

A New Path was so popular partly because it remediated regional linguistic practices. During an interview, program manager Dario emphasized that while he provided technical direction and production help, *A New Path* was "their own program" with a "community basis." Despite not speaking Kichwa, Dario was a supportive and respectful member of the municipal team, and he took significant direction from the young Kichwa-speaking hosts of the program. James, for instance, suggested that they include a segment of *asichina* (K. "humor/jokes"). Joking is an important genre of face-to-face communication in Napo, as Kichwa speakers, both men and women, delight in telling narratives of how a man received his *burla shuti* ("nickname," but literally "joking name"), and—with less frequency on the radio—*uchu shimi* (literally "spicy words") focusing on ribald humor. Although Dario was initially skeptical, they had very positive audience response to the jokes. According to Dario, the program had come to belong to the people of Archidona, who shaped its content and participated actively in its production.

Unlike other stations with dedicated, professional studios, *A New Path* was first produced in a narrow storage closet at the back of a small office housing the communications department. As the program's popularity grew, the recording studio was moved from the small closet to a larger office, albeit also a former storage room. The room was decorated with printouts of the days of the week, months of the year, and numbers in Amazonian Kichwa, which are usually discussed with Spanish loan words.[4] Promotional photos from cultural events, as well as pamphlets and flyers were also taped to the wall.

While Rita sat at one desk, responsible for much of the talk on the program, her cohost, James, would sit at a desk across the room from her, managing the computer program that queued songs and other audio

---

4. These terms often reinforced Amazonian Kichwa dialects and knowledge and did not coincide with the Unified Kichwa dictionary (Ministerio de Educación del Ecuador 2009). For example, October was named as *Ukuy* (Flying leaf-cutter ant) in reference to the season when the ants emerge.

recordings. They would often confer with each other, predominantly in Spanish but sometimes in Kichwa off the air, while they conversed on the air in Kichwa. Although most of the program was in Kichwa, both James and Rita are fluent speakers of Spanish, having completed high school and some post-secondary schooling in Spanish-language institutions. Many other Kichwa-speaking staff at the municipality had similar educational experiences. The municipality offices were often a Spanish-language space of interaction, though the young staff members would switch into Kichwa to laugh and joke with each other, or to speak with middle-aged and elderly visitors.

A New Path was a complex, multi-voiced radio show, which incorporated various kinds of programming, as well as different speakers. The shows can be divided into two kinds of programming—their regular, daily programs, and their monthly live performances of the early morning wayusa-drinking hours. Both their daily and monthly programs followed a script, written in Spanish, which guided the action of the program. The script often served more as a guide than its strict minute-by-minute organization might suggest, as community leaders and residents of Archidona might stop by the show unplanned to make an announcement and stay for a short interview on the air.

The program mixed Kichwa-language music and community recordings with institutional promotion and information, drawing together different media genres and types. Such segments highlighted the work done by the Municipio on behalf of the residents of Archidona, while also transmitting information on new regulations and public health. Other segments focused on local announcements, described as yachachina, as well as songs and recordings of jokes and stories from local communities. They were occasionally joined by live performers, including César Grefa, a politician and singer from the nearby canton of Arosemena Tola. Grefa is also the singer of "Ruku Kawsay" (Old Lifeways), the haunting song about cultural change discussed in the introduction, which he sang live on the radio during his visit.

In March 2016, about six months after the start of their show, *A New Path* introduced an innovative monthly program (figure 8), which remediated an existing regional emphasis to demonstrate significant cultural practices as part of public events. Although the wayusa upina is a part of daily practices, it has also become a central aspect of commu-

FIGURE 8 Rita Tunay interviews María Narváez during *A New Path*'s first live broadcast wayusa upina program at the Association of Kichwa Midwives of the Upper Napo, March 3, 2016. Photo by the author.

nity celebrations, as community leaders and members travel from house to house, beating drums, blowing on large snail shells, and awakening neighbors with steaming pots of guayusa (see also Jarrett 2019).[5] *A New Path*'s programs remediated the practices of these communal celebrations and more intimate realizations of the wayusa upina among the gathered members of intergenerational, kinship-based residence units. The program described in table 2 celebrating the anti-colonial resistance of Jumandi began with the members of the Wayra Churis (K. "Sons of the Wind") arriving on foot, wearing traditional dress, while they beat drums, blew large snail shells, and sang, echoing public gatherings. Other programs, meanwhile, might see one of the hosts seated with a microphone next to an open fire, as a gathered "family" reanimated the processes of waking and calling out for wayusa. These programs were some-

---

5. Muniz (2022, 150–51) discusses the incorporation of live wayusa upina programming on Radio Jatari in Arajuno as part of significant events. The wayusa upina is part of a widely circulating repertoire in Amazonian Kichwa political and performance spaces.

TABLE 2 Translated script for "Jumandi Yuyay," November 16, 2016

Technical Script of the Live Radio Program *Mushuk Ñampi* (A New Path)

Themes: Institutional
Hosts: 2 JAMES AND RITA
Duration: 120 minutes
Air date: 11/06/2016 (Wednesday)
Genre: Kichwa Programming
Transmission schedule: MONDAY TO FRIDAY 4:00 to 6:00 A.M

Hour	Minute by #	Operator	Detail	Time	Guests
	Minutes	SECTION 1			
04H00	0	Opening bumper	Program intro	50 SEC.	
		Musical break	**One song will be played** live by the group Challua Anga Churikuna (K. "Sons of the Fish Eagle")	2 minutes	
		Greetings by the background speakers Host 1 (Rita) Host 2 (James)	**Introduction Welcome** greeting to the listening communities, and we emphasize the theme of JUMANDI YUYAY (K. "Jumandi's Philosophy"), we thank the cultural actors (waira churi, amupakin, yumbo takis, challua anga churikuna, Chunta kuru wasi) for their participation; they intervene with a welcome greeting: **1. MAYOR**	3 minutes	

	8 minutes	**Musical break**	A song will be played	2 minutes	
		Host 1 (Rita)	We return to the program with moving speech and give	5 minutes	**ACT #1**
		Host 2 (James)	way to the **RITUAL of blowing the snail shell** under the care of the **waira churis** and their respective explanation.		
			Responsible for narration:		
04H14		**live JOKE**	Mr. Nelson Chimbo	**2 minutes**	
04H22		Host 1 (Rita)	Sending greetings and moving speech we return to	**8 minutes**	**ACT #2**
		Host 2 (James)	the program to begin with the demonstration and explanation of the **wayusa upina** under the care of the indigenous group waira churis.		
4H24am		**Live musical break**	**Challua Anga Churikuna**	**2 minutes**	
4H30		Host 1 (Rita)	We return to the program and right away speak with Mr.	6 minutes	**ACT #3**
		Host 2 (James)	Fernando Espinoza on the topic of:		
			- Jumandi's leadership		
04H30am		**live JOKE**	Mr. Nelson Chimbo	**2 minutes**	

times hosted in the courtyard of the municipal offices, but more often they were held in rural communities around Archidona and transmitted through a mobile Internet connection to partner stations. These shows drew in a range of participants, including ad hoc groups of community leaders and residents, as well as members of cultural revitalization and community tourism organizations, skilled in the presentation of traditional cultural practices.

Like their daily counterparts, *A New Path*'s monthly program followed a script, which Rita developed in consultation with members of the hosting community. In the early days of these programs, participants were given greater freedom in planning. After a particularly disorganized program in one community, Rita spent more time preparing with participants, visiting before the broadcast to review the script and to discuss expectations that the practices be treated as sacred. Although the individual programs could vary a great deal, depending on their setting and participants, the first page of the script for the program broadcast on November 16, 2016 (table 2), provides a sense of how they are organized to include multiple participants, genres of performance, and modalities of interaction, including musical performances, live interviews, jokes, and other demonstrations. The original formatting is maintained in this translation.

Like other radio personalities in Napo, the hosts of *A New Path* reached their audiences over the radio each morning and cultivated face-to-face interactions with individual listeners as they moved through their work and personal lives. These monthly live programs brought Rita and James into close contact with the residents of local communities. Their jobs at the Municipio were another source for interaction, as Rita was often the first point of contact for Kichwa-speaking residents who visited the Department of Communications to leave messages and announcements. Beyond interactions in the Municipio, twice-weekly visits to communities around Archidona provided another source of interaction with listeners. On Tuesday and Thursday mornings following the program, Rita and James would travel from Archidona's urban center to one of the many rural communities spread throughout the canton to record the speech and stories of their listening audience. Although these visits were important ways for Rita and James to connect with their listeners, connections they enjoyed and cultivated, they could also be frustrating experiences. Despite their best efforts to arrange the meetings ahead of time, they sometimes found upon their arrival that the community president had not convoked a meeting with community members, or that people had grown tired of waiting, and had already left for the forest or town to begin their day's work.

The ongoing production of language reclamation media for the radio is reconfiguring ideologies of public and private speech and information in Napo. At times, elder speakers demurred from recording with the program, claiming that they did not know any stories. Such avoidance may reflect different understandings of what makes a "story" and how it is told (Mannheim and Van Vleet 1998), as well as different orientations to knowledge. While some kinds of talk, such as messages, jokes, and nickname narratives were easier to elicit, some of the team's difficulties in recording may have been linked to ideologies of secrecy and value surrounding storytelling, which forms the basis for many people's social and personal power. Stories are intimately linked to the knowledge, and power, of *rukuguna*, "elders." Stories also inform the specialized knowledge of *yachakguna*, a social category often glossed in English as "shamans," but meaning literally "ones who know"—the scientists, doctors, and scholars of Upper Napo Kichwa communities.

Rita described in an interview that local beliefs about storytelling initially conflicted with the program's plan to establish an archive of community recordings for use on the air. As she explained, when they began carrying out recording sessions in rural communities, some people told them, "My knowledge is my own, I don't want to share it." Rita went on to describe that many people requested payment for their stories. However, she reported that after "counseling" such people, she had slowly been able to change their minds by telling them, "We must teach our knowledge. We must transmit it to children. When we die, where will all the knowledge be left? Who will know it?" Rita's acceptance of the necessity of recording once-secret knowledge for wider transmission was echoed by others, who advocated for recording elders' stories to be remembered and known in the future.

As the program's popularity grew, the community recording sessions drew more participants. Rita and James were greeted as local celebrities, and many communities prepared wayusa, fermented manioc aswa, or small meals for them. Recording sessions generally took place in a community meeting house, soccer field, or other communal space. As public events, co-present listeners might comment on a narrative or clamor to make their voices heard in the next recording. While the decontextualized versions of these stories on the radio appear monologic, they often layered the traditional dialogic setting of Upper Napo Kichwa storytelling into the recording. Rita recorded these stories on a small audio recorder or her cell phone. James later edited them to include background music, or to cut out some pauses, asides, and questions. Rita took careful notes about the organizational history and leaders of the community during visits, alongside the names (and nicknames) of participants. These names later circulated intertextually across radio programs, as hosts sent them greetings and reminded them to get up to drink wayusa. These radio-mediated shout-outs recirculated in face-to-face interactions, as friends and family commented that they had heard one directed to a particular person or relayed a message directed to them on the radio.

I came to know the importance of such messages while in Napo. While my work with Gloria at La Voz de Napo was mostly as a silent observer, I was a regular guest host on *A New Path*. The cohosts requested that I assist them on the show, primarily with messages directed to individual listeners in the area. They sometimes interviewed me on the importance of linguistic transmission and revitalization. Rita and James told me that at the beginning of my time with the program, some listeners disapprovingly thought that I was an incompetent young Kichwa speaker. When it was revealed that I was a rancia (foreigner of European descent), listeners were impressed that I had learned so much Kichwa, beyond common tourist phrases like *ali punzha*, "good morning," and *ñuka shutimi an*, "my name is." As my linguistic abilities grew, I appeared on the program more regularly, as well as on stage at Kichwa beauty pageants where Rita and James were frequent hosts. As a foreign researcher who had learned the language, my presence was used to underscore the value of Kichwa. After more than eighteen months in Napo, listeners would sometimes recognize me from the radio, when they encountered the rancia who spoke Kichwa in town or their communities. I devoted a section of the notebook I carried to requests for shout-outs from listeners around Napo. *A New Path*'s program developed and amplified face-to-face and radio-mediated interactions between listeners and hosts.

Another important outcome of *A New Path*'s community recording sessions was the production of an informal digital archive of regional recordings of elder and adult community members. These recordings were housed on computers at the Municipio. I was given a copy of some, though not all, of the edited files produced for the daily program. The files I received are divided into a number of folders, which are also indicative of some of the significant genres transmitted on the radio: Nicknames (16 files); Stories and Legends (37 files); Recovered Audio (20 files); Community Humor, containing a number of files marked "*pikante*" (Sp. "hot; spicy"), likely in reference to the descriptor uchu shimi, literally "spicy word," for bawdy jokes (6 files); Jokes in Kichwa (19 files); Ancestral Narratives (3 files); and two folders containing the original unedited recordings from specific communities. Despite the best intentions of radio producers, this archive was somewhat haphazardly managed, and portions were inadvertently lost. These community recordings were very popular with listeners. In the community of Chaupishungo, radio listeners often stopped their conversations during narratives, personal accounts of the old days, medicinal songs, and jokes. My interlocutors highlighted these recordings as a favorite aspect of *A New Path*'s broadcasts. Such programming extended these popular genres to wider audiences, while remediating contexts where these interactions occurred.

Tuning In to Upper Napo Kichwa Media

In Napo, Kichwa radio is generally broadcast between the hours of four and six in the morning and after six in the evening, the hours when many Napo Runa are preparing to begin or end their day. From my room in Chaupishungo, I often awoke to the energetic sounds of Amazonian Kichwa music spilling from our neighbor's speakers. I then joined Serafina in her kitchen, alongside her daughters and young grandchildren. There, the gathered family drank guayusa tea and listened to the radio, either on their own small receiver or via the speakers of a close neighbor with the volume raised high. On mornings when her teenage foster son—the member of the household who most regularly turned the radio on—slept in, I would sit by the fire with Serafina as she told her life history. It was in these morning hours that I learned how the monthly live broadcast on *A New Path* sought to remediate and reanimate the familial routines of the wayusa upina. Many people see this time as central to the transmission of elders' knowledge, and thus social personhood and collective memory.

The wayusa upina is seen as increasingly endangered. Radio host Rita Tunay once argued that these practices are no longer carried out in most households, except for homes where a grandmother or grandfather still lives. In Chaupishungo, I found that in several extended families, several young adults had moved into town, returning to visit on weekends or holidays. This was a pattern I encountered across many of my interlocutors in Napo and Pastaza. Young parents and their children move into urban areas to be closer to work or school, returning on weekends to the countryside to visit with their relatives. As a result, daily relationships of intergenerational transmission between grandparents, elder caregivers, and young children have increasingly been reconfigured. Among families who had remained in the community, most adult children established their own homes near grandparents, but did not live communally. The grandchildren and foster children who lived in Mariano and Serafina's home had regular, near constant, access to their grandparents and the stories and conversations they shared in Kichwa with other adults. However, many within the grandchild generation spent most time at home with their own parents and siblings. Peer-based interactions among children were often in Spanish—their daily language at school—and caregivers frequently spoke to their children in Spanish. These children had less access to the intergenerational settings of Kichwa-language communication. Radio programming was one reliable source of Kichwa-language production in some of these households. Sometimes, adolescents sought these programs out, as they turned on the radio for their families in the morning.

In Napo, most radio stations are owned and directed by white-mestizo settlers. The ways these station managers imagine their Kichwa listeners both presupposes and reflects the listening habits of the Kichwa audience of radio media. Many families are at home and attentive to their radios in the early morning hours or in the evening, but many residents of rural communities have flexible schedules, determined by the variable daily labor of agricultural production. Listeners may be at home at various points of the day when Napo radio is shaped by Spanish talk and music. In the community of Chaupishungo, I often heard Spanish-language radio pouring out of people's homes during the day, as well as emerging from simple mobile phones as women worked in their manioc gardens.

Households with stereo systems capable of accepting flash drives would also play their own mixes of Kichwa, Spanish, and English music during the day. These listening practices suggest that Napo radio stations would find a receptive audience for Kichwa-language programming at times beyond the early morning and evening hours.

Most of the families in Chaupishungo had at least a battery-powered radio at home (figure 9). Three of fifteen households where I conducted reception studies did not have a radio. However, two of these families indicated that they would listen to the radio when they could hear it playing from a neighbor's house. Another son and neighbor did not have a radio, but the proximity of his home to those of his family members, and their propensity for high volumes, allowed his family to listen to local news or pray along with La Voz de Napo. The third family, meanwhile, reported that they used cell phones to tune in to local radio, a means for many to access the radio in the absence of a receiver.

Cell phones are another widely available communicative technology in Napo. Most families have at least one cell phone at home—I did not encounter anyone in Chaupishungo with a landline—and many peo-

FIGURE 9 Mariano Aguinda takes the family radio off the shelf for evening listening while his wife, Serafina Grefa, weaves. November 16, 2016. Photo by the author.

ple, especially young adults and teenagers, utilize personal touchscreen phones. Even elderly Serafina had a basic cell phone. Possessing a cell phone did not guarantee coverage or *saldo* (Sp. "credit") with which to use it. Most people I knew utilized low-cost, pay-as-you-go plans from the international telecommunication companies Claro and Movistar for their phones, purchasing limited packages of phone minutes, texts, or *megas* (Sp. "megabytes of Internet access"). These lasted anywhere from twenty-four hours to a week, depending on the quantity purchased and the terms of the package. Many people found themselves without saldo, and it was quite common for friends and family members to request a "loan" of saldo to make a phone call. I grew used to the request, "ushi Georgia, *kamba saldura mañachiwapay*" (daughter Georgia, please loan me your saldo). Smartphones were more accessible digital tools than expensive personal computers. Many of the people I knew recorded photos, video, and audio from live musical performances, beauty pageants, and other cultural and political events on their phones. They would later gather around the small screens to watch the clips with their family and friends. Social media platforms like Facebook and YouTube have emerged as popular channels to share Upper Napo Kichwa media. Kichwa-language media also circulates through a network of pirated-CD and -DVD stores (Floyd 2008) as well as the informal sharing of audio and video files via USB flash drives. These venues were also sites for the circulation of Highland Kichwa media, as well as Chicham- and Wao Tededo-language music and videos.

A few households in Chaupishungo had televisions. In their main sitting room, Serafina and Mariano had a twenty-inch tube television whose staticky picture was tinted green. Wood benches and stools were set around the edges of this room between doors that led to rooms shared by familial groups. During the afternoons and evenings, Serafina's adult children and young grandchildren would gather to watch Spanish-language news, movies, or telenovelas. Serafina sometimes joined them to watch before bed. These programs provided Serafina and her family members with information about significant differences between runa and mishu practices. For instance, when comparing the ways that women cry, Serafina contrasted the choked sobs she had seen from Spanish-speaking women on telenovelas with the tearful sung laments of Upper Napo Kichwa women. One of Serafina's sons had a television at home. When I would drop by in the evening, he and his family would sometimes be watching a comedy or action-adventure DVD, often a Chinese or Korean import dubbed in Spanish. I only encountered one other household in Chaupishungo with a functioning television during my fieldwork, in the home of Serafina's neighbor. When I visited, the television would often be tuned to the local public station AllyTV, which broadcast local news and informational programs, again predominantly in Spanish.

Television and film media in Napo are dominated by Spanish-language programming. The hour-long program entitled *Rayu Shinalla* (K. "Like the Lightening") was broadcast between five and six o'clock in the morning, focusing on local news and Kichwa music videos on AllyTV. Their other programming was in Spanish. I also collected DVDs (often pirated) of music videos by regional Kichwa groups, as well as community media, such as the Napo film *Kukama Runa* (P. Bermúdez and Uzendoski 2018). Although we first watched these videos together at my request, family members later asked to put on a DVD of videos by Los Playeros Kichwas or Los Jilgueritos to watch in the evening. As these videos portrayed significant regional stories and cultural practices, Serafina's children and grandchildren asked her for confirmation about what they saw on the screen. Similarly, they asked her for more information related to her experiences when they heard community recordings of traditional and personal narratives.

Media reception in Chaupishungo was most often a dialogic, group activity although it could be a solitary pursuit. Grandfather Mariano sometimes took the family's portable receiver into his bedroom to listen to the radio. Weaving alone, Serafina commented sometimes to herself on the radio she heard playing next door. Most often, however, groups listened together. Cell phone use was also communal, as young people collectively watched videos, browsed social media, or chatted with unknown others on WhatsApp and Facebook message groups to meet new friends. The residents of Chaupishungo consequently interacted with radio media as only one part of a much larger media ecology in Napo. But it was radio that was the regular channel to receive Kichwa-language programming. Residents had clear preferences among the Kichwa-language shows available to them.

In Chaupishungo, *A New Path* was of the most popular shows. One morning, listening to the radio with Serafina and her family I asked what programming they liked. Her daughter Corina offered that they preferred the program *Ali Ñambi*, while Serafina affirmed, "we most want to listen to *Ali Ñambi.*" When I asked why, she responded, "What is being spoken in Kichwa sounds good." Although the program is formally entitled *Mushuk Ñampi*, "A New Path," many called it *Ali Ñambi*, "A Good Path." This might reflect their positive evaluations of the program's content, or more broadly circulating discourses in Napo about following a "good path," whether actual or metaphorical. Serafina's daughter-in-law, Lucía, at the time in her mid-twenties added, "There is more local news, what is happening, and announcements about festivals, because it's from our town we understand more when we listen." The Pastaza station Radio Jatari was also popular in Chaupishungo, as it was the only dedicated Kichwa-language community-licensed station to reach the residents of Archidona. At hours when other regional stations were dominated by Spanish programming, Radio Jatari might have an automated mix featuring Kichwa music, though they often played national and international hits too.

Listeners scanned through radio stations when they grew tired of the content. They sometimes settled on *Antisuyu Ushay*. However, I found far fewer listeners of this program in the rural community of Chaupishungo, perhaps reflective of the host's greater orientation toward the Tena region, as well as the urban, bilingual public they imagined. Indeed, my observations suggest that listeners in Chaupishungo were much less interested in Spanish-language talk and interviews, often switching the station if there was too much talk in Spanish—including the long prerecorded informational segments with municipal staff and officials from the ministry of health often broadcast on *A New Path.*

Programming from La Voz de Napo was enjoyed in most households in Chaupishungo. Many people mentioned it as one of their preferred stations. The station was especially important for prayer. The daily rhythm of households in Chaupishungo was punctuated by Gloria Grefa's evening *risachina* (K. "to make pray" from Sp. *rezar*) from the *Devocionario Quichua*, which radio listeners faithfully repeated along with her. Upper Napo Kichwa radio media provided an intimate soundtrack to a family's daily activities. In many households, different hours of the morning corresponded to different shows. Many listeners would tune in to Radio Jatari's early morning talk and music show until four in the morning when *A New Path* came on the air. Between five and five thirty, listeners would then switch to La Voz de Napo for morning prayers, which, along with daybreak, signaled the end of that morning's wayusa upina.

Radio is such a significant channel for the reclamation of Upper Napo Kichwa linguistic and cultural practices because of its embedding in daily life. Napo's ecology of media has remediated many of the significant practices of verbal artistry used in face-to-face interactions in songs and entextualized narratives, reinforcing significant poetic and aesthetic practices. Radio media also reinforce face-to-face communicative networks, as messages between listeners and hosts circulate across various contexts and modalities of production. Such practices implicate named individuals, creating private spheres of interaction in public broadcasts. It is this entanglement with listeners' daily lives and communicative practices that makes radio such an effective grassroots strategy for linguistic and cultural reclamation. Aural radio media afford a more heterogeneous, multivocal use of language as a dynamic code than standardized text in formal education programs or as regimented toward Spanish-language institutional settings.

The Ecology of Print

Print literacy is sometimes treated as antithetical to the practices of primarily oral societies. Kichwa people in Ecuador, however, have sought out writing as an important social and political modality. In twentieth-century Ecuador, broad coalitions of Indigenous peoples, with the support of progressive missionaries and other activists, reshaped social and political life (Sawyer 2004; Becker 2008). In the Tena-Archidona region, FOIN, the Federation of Indigenous Organizations of Napo (Federación de Organizaciones Indígenas del Napo) played an important role in the formation of the CONFENIAE, Confederation of Indigenous Nationalities of the Ecuadorian Amazon (Confederación de Nacionalidades Indígenas de la Amazonía Ecuatoriana), in 1980 (Sawyer 2004; Macdonald 1999; Erazo 2013). Kichwa and Shuar leaders in CONFENIAE joined members of other Amazonian groups, including Waorani, Siona-Secoya, and Cofán communities, in a process of pan-Indigenous organizing. Their early congresses also included Highland-based organizations. These meetings led to the formation of the Confederación de Nacionalidades Indígenas del Ecuador (CONAIE—Confederation of Indigenous Nationalities of Ecuador). With demands centering on culture, education, health, and territorial rights (Sawyer 2004; Becker 2010), Indigenous activists have been successful in gaining more control of education and language planning. In this context, language standardization's influence on oral speech practices has been an unexpected outcome of Kichwa-language activism.

The remediation of print into oral broadcasts can have considerable effects on speech, particularly within the complicated ecologies of language and media in Napo. For Kichwa linguist Luis Montaluisa (2018, 302–3) many of the issues arising from the application of Unified Kichwa and bilingual education are related to corpus and status planning, or planning about the form of the language and its uses (McCarty 2018, 23). When primarily oral languages in an unstandardized linguistic ecology entered new regimes of value and contexts of use, the code's structures and sites of use became significant. Spanish-language literacy ideologies in Ecuador emphasize a transparent relationship between written form (grapheme) and meaningful sound (phoneme), as Spanish is treated as having a relatively "shallow" orthography with a "more precise match between letters and sounds" (Limerick 2017, 106). Such ideologies are transposed to literacy events and pedagogical materials for literacy in Kichwa.

Many of the language activists with whom I have spoken support language standardization at the written level, but most also expressed support for the maintenance of regional oral varieties. Nonetheless, pedagogical materials intended for bilingual educators are often ambiguous on how to present the relationship between oral and written forms of speech. The text *Method for the Intercultural Bilingual Education System* describes the purpose of the Academy of the Kichwa Language as "the consolidation of Kichwa at *oral* and written levels" (Ministerio de Educación del Ecuador 2013, 20, emphasis added), implying their concordance, in addition to an explicit goal of oral standardization. The *Methodological Manual for Language Teaching* asserts that "in the alphabets created more or less recently for some [I]ndigenous languages we find an unambiguous relationship between letter and sound, so that each form (sound) corresponds to one and only grapheme (letter)" (Ministerio de Educación del Ecuador 2010b, 52).

MEDIA ECOLOGY IN THE UPPER NAPO

This presentation of the relationship between letter and sound in teaching manuals implies their transparent correspondence, regardless of a student's regional variety. In the standardized orthography, regional phonological variations are essentially erased. Although the texts position Unified Kichwa as a *written* and not oral standard, they also create slippage between written and oral standardization, especially when combined with explicit calls for oral standardization. Such ideologies influence the relationship between oral and written forms for many of the people with whom I worked.

I encountered a great deal of opposition to the oral use of Unified Kichwa in radio media. Even Spanish-speaking station owners and managers in Tena were aware of the debates about the use of regional or standardized varieties. In interviews, many emphasized that their Kichwa-speaking audiences want *kichwa de aquí*, or "local Kichwa," that is, "from here." Like radio hosts, station managers often imagined their audiences as aligned with regional varieties of Kichwa.

The speech of radio hosts in Napo shows the complexity of literacy practices for Kichwa speakers. Radio hosts who incorporate Kichwa-language texts and messages into their programs generally read them aloud according to the orthography in which they are written. At the Voz de Napo station, Gloria Grefa read passages from a version of the *Devocionario Quichua* (Vicariato Apostólico de Napo 1995), which is written in a prior, Spanish-derived orthography and appears to mix morphemic and phonemic forms from several dialectal regions. Although other sections of the text are closer to the oral forms of Upper Napo Kichwa, the translation of "Gloria al Padre," for instance, includes the phrase *imashina carca callaricpi*, "as it was in the beginning," with the form *carca* (karka in Unified Kichwa), which in Upper Napo Kichwa would be realized aka. These differences are summarized in table 3.

TABLE 3 Comparison of past tense in different dialects

Devocionario text	Upper Napo	Pastaza	Lower Napo	Highland
<carca> [ka-rka]	a-ka	a-ra	ka-rka	ka-rka
BE-PA.3SG	BE-PA.3SG	BE-PA.3SG	BE-PA.3SG	BE-PA.3SG
"it was"	"it was"	"it was"	"it was"	"it was"

These variations result from loss of word-initial /k/ of *kana,* as well as elision of /r/ from the past tense marker *-rka* used in other dialects of Ecuadorian Kichwa. Pastaza Kichwa provides a further example of the phonological innovations of the southern and central Ecuadorian Amazon, as it also utilizes *ana* and its own unique past tense form, *-ra.* Both Lower Napo Kichwa and Highland Kichwa, in contrast, utilize the form found in the *Devocionario.*

Written forms can influence oral speech in the complex linguistic and media ecology of Napo. Although Gloria regularly used the copula ana, as well as forms using the past tense *-ka* of Upper Napo Kichwa on the air and in everyday speech, when reading from the *Devocionario* she pronounced it "karka." Radio listeners who prayed along at home similarly repeated the forms written in the book that were then pronounced on the air, even when in conflict with everyday patterns of regional speech. Likewise, on the radio program *A New Path,* the two cohosts regularly pronounced the name of the program [ɲampi], transposing the written grapheme <p> of Unified Kichwa, in contrast to the regularized postnasal voicing of [ɲambi] generally used by Upper Napo Kichwa speakers in everyday speech.

Several hosts acknowledged they are torn between appeasing audience members most comfortable with regional forms of speech and those aligned with linguistic unification. Despite the influence of orthography on their speech, many of the hosts of Kichwa-language programs broadcast from Tena and Archidona aligned with the use of regional varieties of Kichwa on the air. Hosts often imagined their audience as rural and elderly speakers, and thus claimed that listeners would not understand Unified Kichwa. Gloria sometimes received messages from listeners criticizing her speech. One listener wrote by text message—using an orthography that mixed standardized spellings and local realizations—to correct her description of a cell phone as *"celular muku"* (combining the Spanish for "cellular" with Kichwa for "junction/joint"). They suggested that she use the neologism *willilli.* This form, however, does not appear in the Unified Kichwa dictionary (Ministerio de Educación del Ecuador 2009). It is likely derived from the verb *willana,* "to tell, to inform"—a neologism reintroduced to replace the Spanish-derived *kwintana,* "to tell, to converse"— semantically extended to replace *celular.* Like Gloria, hosts of Kichwa-language programs faced regular dilemmas due to language choice.

MEDIA ECOLOGY IN THE UPPER NAPO

During reception of radio media, "other" varieties of Kichwa could be highly marked for listeners, even if they did not explicitly identify speakers to be using Unified Kichwa. Listeners in Archidona and Tena could pick up the signal from the Radio Jatari, a Kichwa-language, community-licensed radio station broadcast from Arajuno in neighboring Pastaza province. In contrast to some Napo radio programs, the hosts of Radio Jatari consistently utilized a broadcast register incorporating highly standardized forms in their programming (see Muniz 2022, 159–60). In turn, their speech often elicited commentary in the households where I studied uptake of radio shows. For instance, one morning, upon hearing the Radio Jatari announcer say *"aswakunata upyachinchi"* (we serve manioc beer to drink), my host Serafina repeated the phrase, *"'aswakunata upyachinchi' nin,"* "he says, 'we serve manioc beer to drink.'" When I queried her on its meaning, she emphasized that in her variety it is said differently. In the following transcript, the term in question—aswa or asa—is bolded and italicized, while morphemes that differ between varieties are bolded. The differing sounds are capitalized.

Serafina Grefa comments on dialectal difference, September 29, 2016

1 *as**Wa*** ni-nun, ñukanchi *asa* ni-nchi.
   aswa say-3PL 1PL *asa* say-1PL
   "They say *aswa*, we say *asa*."

2 *asa* **-Ra** upi-chi-ychi ni-nchi ñukanchi rima-nchi,
   asa -ACC drink-CAUS-2PL.IMP say-1PL 1PL speak-1PL
   "In our speech, we say 'serve *asa* to drink.'"

3 pay-guna-ga *as**Wa*-**Kuna**-**Ta*** upi-chi-ra-ychi ni-nun.
   3-PL-TOP aswa-PL-ACC drink-CAUS-do-2PL.IMP say-3PL
   "They, on the other hand, say 'serve *aswas* to drink.'"

Serafina's commentary points to several perceived differences between local speech and that of the host on Radio Jatari, though I am careful to note that she does not identify his speech as Unified Kichwa. Rather, she placed it into the regional variations of Arajuno. Nevertheless, she identified the speech as distinctly different from "our speech." Most salient seems to be his pronunciation of aswa, the drink known in Spanish as *chicha,* a fermented manioc brew that may range from mildly to strongly intoxicating, which is a staple product of many households. In Archidona, syncope of diphthongs is a common phonological process, yielding the form [asa], which contrasts with [aswa], bivalent with both Unified Kichwa and some local varieties of Kichwa.[6] Serafina demonstrates a high level of metalinguistic awareness about regional variations. She would similarly comment when she heard speakers on the radio using the form *yupaychani,* repeating "yupaychani nin," "s/he says yupaychani," which contrasted with her frequent use of *pagarachu* for "thank you." In everyday spaces of reception, the sounds of a standardized broadcast register remain marked for listeners, even when not explicitly identified as standardized. The markedness of these forms attunes us to some of the major debates surrounding language standardization and revitalization ongoing in Ecuador today.

Given levels of institutional and community support, alongside a still large population of fluent speakers, the situation of language shift in Ecuador might seem more hopeful than those of many minoritized languages around the world. It is important to highlight how many people continue to speak Kichwa in Napo, and how many more are recuperating it, given very recent discriminatory practices against speakers of Indigenous languages throughout Ecuador. Yet, ongoing patterns of language shift toward Spanish in Napo suggest it is also worth examining the effects that language revitalization projects are having on the ground. As Howard observed, "in Ecuador, the principle of a unified Quechua has been taken to the extreme, with its implementation somewhat forced onto the spoken and not only the written language" (Howard 2007, para. 327). Confirming other studies in the region (Wroblewski 2012; K. A. King 2001; Howard 2007), my research suggests that bilingual educators in Napo have helped develop a formal register, drawing upon features of

---

6. The form [aswa] is also in use in Archidona, and even Serafina may alternate between the two pronunciations, as she does in another transcript discussed later. Serafina's comments also point to perceived differences between the standardized plural marker -kuna and object marker -ta. For Serafina, plural marking appears to be non-obligatory, while the object marker is realized as -ra. An implicit contrast between the standardized pronunciation of the plural -kuna also emerges from her own voiced realization of the plural as [-guna] in "paygunaga."

Unified Kichwa and regional Upper Napo Kichwa, as well as forms that are bivalent (Woolard 1998b) between Unified Kichwa and neighboring varieties. There has also been a great deal of resistance by members of other publics, who align with regional forms of speech.

In attempting to establish a unified public of Kichwa speakers in Ecuador by standardizing the language's orthography, purifying it of Spanish loanwords, and transferring these norms to the spoken code, language planners and activists have largely normalized Highland varieties of Kichwa for the pan-Kichwa standard. These are further regimented for use in Spanish-language institutional settings, such as government and school, rather than the intimate familial spaces many contemporary speakers of Upper Napo Kichwa associated with language in use, deeply connected to what people call the "words our elders left behind." Ideologies of linguistic unification are tied to ideas about the relationship between a unified polity or nation and a unified, usually written, language (Silverstein 1996; Irvine 2006; Lippi-Green 2011). These may conflict with regional ideologies of social and linguistic belonging. For those without access to bilingual education and literacy programs, particularly women and elders with limited formal education, the written and spoken public established by linguistic unification and purification could also be experienced as exclusionary, with forms directed toward ratified participants, therein creating an exclusive or private sphere out of the public sphere. Further, for many, linguistic unification has violated ideologies about the connection between regional forms of speech and the reproduction of social personhood and cultural knowledge. Radio media and embodied performance afforded the remediation of the wayusa upina, considered by many to be integral to Kichwa linguistic and cultural socialization, in ways that classroom-based pedagogies and language standardization could not.

Conclusion

Studies of media ecology are often interested in the effects of different forms of mediation on human sociality and interaction. How do Kichwa-language media shape sociality and language reclamation in the Upper Napo? The goals of language-revitalization projects are frequently taken to be the creation of new speakers (Meek 2010; Grenoble and Whaley 2006; Fishman 1991). Napo community radio programs, however, do not directly produce new speakers, as the most frequent participants are usually already competent speakers of Upper Napo Kichwa. During my research, no one I knew became a fluent speaker of Kichwa solely by listening to the radio—nor did anyone try, to my knowledge. Such programs and their broader ecology of media still have effects among a diverse Upper Napo Kichwa community of practice.

Participants and producers in this ecology of media aim at what they call the *revalorization*—social, political, and economic—of Upper Napo Kichwa language and cultural practice. Such revalorization is taking place in the context of social, economic, and material pressures leading to shift toward Spanish-language and colonial lifeways, as well as ideologies of linguistic unification and standardization that shape many of the projects and discourses of Ecuador's pan-Kichwa and pan-Indigenous political organizations. In the face of shift toward Spanish and the institutional valorization of Unified Kichwa in bilingual education and much broadcast media, many producers of and participants in these projects attempted to reconfigure the regimes of value within which both traditional and contemporary regional cultural practices and forms of speech are positioned.

The interaction of media and people within a shared ecology can have identifiable effects on daily practices, as when Serafina recirculated the news about ukuy. Listeners of radio programs frequently comment on their content, extending conversations and narratives from the air. Participation in community media production also draws young media producers into greater dialogue with a wide range of social actors, sometimes leading to improvements in their own linguistic abilities. Cultural revalorization and tourism organizations bring together elders, adults, adolescents, and children, creating new sites of socialization into linguistic and cultural practices that are increasingly shifting.

The local ecology of Upper Napo Kichwa media has shifted the political economy of Kichwa use and reclamation in Napo. Several of the people I worked with earned money for work with Kichwa media. While some radio hosts earned a salary for their work, they were not the only beneficiaries of media production. The elder members and young apprentices of the Association of Kichwa Midwives of the Upper Napo also participate in cultural presentations for regional and international audiences, some of which include payments. Consequently, several young people have been recuperating Upper Napo Kichwa linguistic and cultural practices through their daily interactions with knowledgeable elders in media production. Emerging as a new form of labor, media production extends and amplifies the socioeconomic value of the traditional Upper Napo Kichwa domestic sphere within the overlay of a dominant settler colonial social system. Everyday habits, practices, and interactions are transformed into both a valued setting for public events and a site of economic opportunity.

Community media can serve as everyday sites of renewal for shifting sociocultural practices, linguistic and otherwise. They frequently allow language and culture to enter new regimes of economic and social value. Meanwhile, in Upper Napo Kichwa households and communities where *A New Path*'s daily morning programs are received, community radio programs reinvigorated communicative spaces and practices, providing culturally relevant and locally meaningful programming upon which listeners regularly reflect and comment, leading to further moments of storytelling and conversation within the home.

This overview of Napo's radio stations and programming highlights several features of the local media ecology. Radio media are inseparable from other forms of mediation and from the people who produce and consume it in Napo. Although I attend most closely to the production and reception of radio media in this account, both radio hosts and audiences interacted with a wide variety of media in relation to the radio and in their daily lives. All the programs intertextually incorporated written texts in some way, generally through announcements, news, or books. Hosts often found these sources online. Their programs circulated via the Internet and were intertwined with Meta products, as hosts received messages through their Facebook Messenger or WhatsApp accounts and searched for local news in their feeds. Kichwa-language programs also contained intertextual references to the broader Upper Napo Kichwa ecology of media, when radio hosts promoted local festivals, celebrations, and cultural events, further inviting local participants to speak about these projects on the air. Radio hosts were frequent MCs for these events. Radio listeners might become participants in community recordings or broadcasts, or further encounter radio production through the circulation of messages between listeners and hosts. The production of radio media was not only inseparable from other forms of mediation in Napo but also inseparable from relationships with radio's receptive audience. These various forms of media, genres of practice, and ideologies of mediation contribute to a complex, emergent ecology of media in the Upper Napo.

CHAPTER 3

Linguistic Natures and Revitalization Ideologies

Many speakers of Upper Napo Kichwa find themselves doubly marginalized. They first face Spanish-speaking settlers. Second, and perhaps unexpectedly, many find themselves marginalized by a well-intentioned regime of standard language. Rita Tunay, cohost of *A New Path*, linked the spread of Unified Kichwa to the government and educational system. She explained that many in Napo perceived it to be a government-mandated form, distinct from regional speech. According to Rita, "We began to abandon what is from here, in order to speak what is from there." She further suggested, "In these schools, in all of that, even children who don't speak learn [Unified Kichwa] in class." People like Rita described the top-down application of the standardized or "unified" variety in educational and institutional contexts as an imposition upon their own variety of runa shimi. Others echoed her comments, like the grandmother who argued that because the languages had been mixed, her grandson had learned "another" Kichwa in school.

Revitalization projects based on standard language literacy are seen by some to threaten local communicative norms. Such attitudes toward Unified Kichwa highlight the contradictions involved in language stan-

---

A version of this chapter originally appeared as "Linguistic Natures: Method, Media, and Language Reclamation in the Ecuadorian Amazon" (2020) in the *Journal of Linguistic Anthropology*. It has been modified slightly to fit within the structure of this book.

dardization, visible elsewhere (Gal 2006; K. A. King 2001; Jaffe 1999; Lane et al. 2018). Dialectal variation is frequently omitted from the concerns of language endangerment and revitalization (Wolfram and Schilling-Estes 1995). Language standardization, informed by ideologies of standard language, has been a significant strategy in language planning in the Andes and elsewhere (Haugen 1966; Hornberger and King 1998; Haboud and Limerick 2017; Lane et al. 2018; Grzech, Schwarz, and Ennis 2019). Although they were begun with the best of intentions, language revitalization projects in Ecuador have sometimes relied on hegemonic standard language ideologies, assuming the need for a singular language for a unified polity (Silverstein 1996; Anderson 1983). Institutional revitalization practices conflict with the practices of speakers of newly nonstandard, regional varieties of Ecuadorian Kichwa. Such methods for revitalization alone do not capture how Napo Runa think about linguistic and cultural transmission, where language is connected to place, personhood, and the transmission of the "words our elders left" across generations.

The assumptions of language standardization diverge from how many Napo Runa use and discuss language. Linguistic anthropologists have explored the tacit ideologies and ontologies of language embedded in standard language cultures (Gal 2006; Irvine and Gal 2000; Silverstein 1996). These include understandings of language as system, perception of its decontextualized and decontextualizable nature, and the connection between one language and one nation. Less understood is how these Euro-derived frameworks interface with Indigenous understandings of the nature of language in revitalization, particularly outside of North America (cf. Kroskrity 2009; Debenport 2015; High 2018). A growing body of scholarship (Davis 2017; Debenport 2015; De Korne and Leonard 2017; Perley 2012; Kroskrity and Field 2009; Meek 2010; Hill 2002) has shown how processes of language revitalization are not neutral but loaded with ideological commitments.

At stake in debates about language standardization in Napo are understandings of the nature of language and how it is connected to language socialization and social personhood. This chapter explores the ideological assemblages (Kroskrity 2018) and ontologies of language (Hauck and Heurich 2018; Ferguson 2019) shaping practices of and responses to linguistic planning. Elsewhere in the Amazon among Tukanoan speakers, language is understood as a "consubstantial, metaphysical product—a 'substance' in the development of the person" (Chernela 2018, 23). In Napo, language is a material inheritance that must be "grasped" by children as they mature. Speech and sociality are intimately connected in Napo. Upper Napo Kichwa stories describe how humans and other species shared an undifferentiated state, until moral failures led to divergent languages and outward forms (Swanson 2009). Language also helps to define ethnic groups, so as a Euro-American I am a speaker of *rancia shimi*, while *mishu shimi* is the language of Spanish-speaking white-mestizos. The lexeme *shimi* may refer to the mouth, words, and language. Spoken and sung language, through their connection to one's lifeforce (*ushay*) and breath (*samay*), are integral to medicinal and spiritual practices and daily sociality. Songs sung to absent children or lovers, or to the protective spirits of medicinal plants are known to sway the emotions of their targets, even over great distances (Uzendoski and Calapucha-Tapuy 2012; Seitz 1982).

Many of these ideas about the nature of language are drawn from interviews about individual and familial linguistic histories and beliefs, which provided opportunities for speakers to reflect on language use and learning. I have yet to explicitly ask "what is language?" This is a question that would likely be difficult for many to answer, as much of language falls below the level of metalinguistic awareness (Silverstein 1981). I complement interviews with observations and analyses of Upper Napo Kichwa narrative practice. Bringing these data together suggests that language has another nature among my interlocutors, one that is essentially connected with place of origin, embedded in specific interactional practices and participant structures, and emergent in listening and remembering.

Various ideological disjunctures (Meek 2010) can arise in language revitalization, underscoring the need for language ideological clarification (Dauenhauer and Dauenhauer 1998). Kroskrity defines this as "the process of identifying issues of language ideological contestation . . . , that can negatively impact community efforts to successfully engage in language maintenance and renewal" (2009, 73). We need not only ideological clarification but also *ontological* clarification in language revitalization. In linguistic renewal, advocates—external and otherwise—should consider how speakers understand the nature of language. Failing to recognize other assumptions about the nature(s) of language risks erasing the needs of community members set in language reclamation and the affordances of grassroots methods for renewal, more firmly grounded in community-internal norms for language socialization. The success of Maori "language nests" (J. King 2001) and "master-apprentice" models in Chickasaw language reclamation (Davis 2018) suggests the value of pedagogical models extending language learning beyond the classroom (Hinton 2013).

Aural media, particularly radio media, respond more effectively to the local emphasis on regional differentiation and intergenerational transmission than standard language practices. Interviews regarding linguistic differentiation and socialization, observations of language in use, and an analysis of interaction on radio programs, suggest that the nature of language for many speakers in Napo is in their embodied knowledge of "the words our elders left." Competency is connected to the proper reception and production of oral speech. Children demonstrate competency by listening and responding appropriately using regional speech, which conflicts with top-down methods of language revitalization based on standard language literacy.

Listening to "Our Language"

In Chaupishungo, elders, their speech, and the processes of socialization were ideologized in connection to "our language" or *ñukanchi shimi*. Serafina Grefa emphasized the importance of uninterrupted intergenerational transmission of language and knowledge. When I asked Serafina what language she wanted her children to speak, she described the ways her elders' speech was transmitted to her, noting that she does not want to "forget" (the bolded term, kungarina):

> **Serafina Grefa comments on intergenerational transmission, September 26, 2016**
>
> Ñawpamanda rukuguna sakishka shimira ama **kungaringak**, ama ichungak.[1] Ñukanchi, chima, payguna ima tunu nisha, kwinta-
>
> [I want] the language the elders from before left behind not to be **forgotten**, not to be thrown away.[1] There [by the fire], our elders

sha rukugunami shina rimasha, sakikuna aka ñukanchira.$_2$ "Kanguna mana **kungarina** changuichi. Ñukanchiga ñawpamanda rukumandami, kay shimira, ñukanchi apa yayaguna, achi yayagunami, kay shimira sakinuka" nishami kwintakuna aka ñuka mama, ñuka papa.$_3$ Shina rashami, ñukaga kasna kawsani.$_4$	told all kinds of things, speaking like that, they left [it] to us.$_2$ My mother, my father would tell [us], saying, "You all must not **forget**. Our grandfathers, the wise fathers, they left this language, from before, from the elders."$_3$ Doing it like that [not forgetting], I too live that way.$_4$

As she spoke line 2, Serafina gestured toward the fire, underscoring the importance of place in intergenerational language socialization. Her comments likely reference the socializing hours of the wayusa upina. In many homes, the demands of school, wage labor, and urban lifestyles have reshaped morning routines. Some say that these practices are being increasingly "forgotten." Like Serafina, many people in Napo describe cultural shift with the word kungarina, "to forget." Serafina, much like her parents, did not want her children to "forget" the words and language left by their elders. For her, language and speech are transmitted across generations through specific interactional routines. Beyond regional territories, language is essentially connected to the social relationships in which language—and knowledge—are shared.

Serafina provided further insight regarding the ways Kichwa people theorize communicative competence and the nature of language. One afternoon, I asked Serafina to explain a category used to describe children—that of the *shunguyuk wawa*, literally, "a child with a heart." I did not understand this term nor the related, *shunguyana*, "to become mature," but literally, "to become heartful." *Shungu* usually translates to "heart" (Sp. *corazón*). I was unsure what it might mean for a child to "have a heart." In Southern Peruvian Quechua, the related form *sunqu* can mean "essence," suggestive of the development of personhood or being.[1] Serafina emphasized the category's connection to language, and to "understanding" and "grasping" language.

---

1. Mannheim (personal communication, January 3, 2020) reports that in Southern Peruvian Quechua, the related form *sunqu* better translates to "essence."

Serafina Grefa comments on the concept of shunguyuk wawa, September 26, 2016

GE: Chita mana intindini <SG: mm> "shunguyuk wawa."₁

SG: Ali shunguyuk wawa, ali intindin rimangawa shimira.₂

Ari, ali iyayuk wawa ña umara apisha, ali kwintasha, kay ñukanchi shimira apisha ali kwintanun.₃

Nikpi payguna mana ali iyayuk wawaguna, payguna shuk castellanu shimillara yachasha, mana muna-sha tapushkawa, "kamba mamita mayma rika" nisha tapunchi.₄ Tapushkawa, "no sé, no sé" nin.₅

GE: I don't understand that [word] <SG: yes?> shunguyuk wawa.₁

SG: The mature child understands very well to speak language.₂ That's right, the intelligent child, once they develop their consciousness [lit. grasp the head], they converse well, they grasp this, our language, and they converse well.₃

[But] those called unintelligent children, they just know one Spanish language, and when we ask, "where did your mother go" they don't want [to respond].₄ When asked, [they] say [in Spanish] "I don't know, I don't know."₅

She contrasted this description with an imagined conversation in Kichwa with a respectful, intelligent child. Serafina's definition of *ali shunguyuk wawa* in line 2 contrasts with a dictionary translation (Orr and Wrisley 1981, 42) for *ali shunguyuj* to Spanish as *"amable, bondadosa"* or "kind, generous." Serafina's definition, which couples the term with the *ali iyayuk wawa* or the "intelligent child" in line 3, suggests central ideals about Upper Napo Kichwa personhood, and how children develop into competent members of society through embodied comportment and conversation. A younger, bilingual interlocutor explained that ali shunguyuk wawa translates to *"niño consciente o grande"*—an aware, mature child. To be "a mature child" is to understand and to "grasp" one's language. For Upper Napo Kichwa speakers, speaking *and* listening appropriately is evidence of understanding.

Serafina's comments reveal some of the ways Kichwa people might answer a significant question in the study of language—how to describe linguistic and communicative competence. A young person who is *"shun-*

guyuk" is recognized as a competent member of an Upper Napo Kichwa speech community because they have "grasped" their language and can respond appropriately. Chomsky's (1965, 4) suggestion that linguistic competence—or knowledge of grammar—is distinct from the performance of grammar in interaction betrays how disciplinary linguistics tends to theorize language. Linguistic anthropologists have reframed the issue as socialization into communicative competence, emphasizing what novices must learn to effectively make use of such grammatical knowledge in communication (Ochs and Schieffelin 1984; Ochs 1988; Briggs 1988). Serafina's comments suggest Kichwa people understand language as something agentively acquired (or "grasped"), but only evidenced in interaction. A father described that his toddler son's runa shimi had "yet to emerge," suggesting that it was an ability he had yet to express. One way that young Kichwa people acquire "our language" and demonstrate communicative competence is through listening.

The link between listening and communicative competence came to the fore when I asked the midwives of AMUPAKIN to drink wayusa together before dawn. Throughout research, I noted the importance of these early hours to Napo media and to conversations among the members of AMUPAKIN. Closely associated with the wayusa upina is a genre called kamachina, "to counsel, to advise, to scold," which is combined with embodied instruction and repetitive action. When remediated on the airwaves, such counseling sessions are usually one short segment among other kinds of verbal artistry and performance. The midwives used the intergenerational gathering to teach young women in attendance how the wayusa upina had been carried out in the past, and to transmit words of counsel (*kamachishka shimi*) of their elders, but without the programming constraints of a live broadcast.

Before four o'clock in the morning, the women of AMUPAKIN gathered in their organization's central building, a large structure with pounded bamboo slat walls. After drinking guayusa together, talk turned more explicitly to teaching and counseling. Inés Tanguila, a *malta mama* (young mother, an adult woman, roughly under sixty) called out for María Antonia Shiguango, a *ruku mama* (elder mother, generally over sixty) and founder of the organization, "Please do me the favor of counseling my daughter." For nearly ten minutes, María Antonia instructed Inés's daughter Kelly on what María Antonia identified as "our lifeways" (*ñukanchi kawsay*). Here, I only reproduce lines relevant to questions of the nature of language. In excerpt 1, her kamachina follows an established pattern for this and other narrative genres in Napo, which grounds her speech in her authority as an elder. In preceding lines, she also linked her speech to that of her mothers and grandmothers.

Excerpt 1 of María Antonia's kamachina counsel, June 10, 2017

MS: Shinakpiga, ushushi, kan, kanda, kamba mama mingachikpi ñukaga rimangaraushkani.[18] Ñuka munayga apisha imaras nisha rimangawa burla burla rimangawa mana ushashkani.[19] Ruku ashkamanda, ñuka ushashka tupuwara kanda iyayra chimbachingaraushkani.[20] Paya, **uyangui?**[21]

MS: So, daughter, you, as your mother has asked, I am going to speak to you.[18] Gathering my will, I wonder what to tell you, I cannot have spoken in jest.[19] As an elder, I am going to have transmitted what I can to your thought.[20] Girl, **do you hear?**[21]

Her phatic question in line 21, "girl, do you hear?" served to check the "channel" (Jakobson 1961) through which she would "transmit" (*chimbachina*) her speech to Kelly, who was kneeling in front of her. María Antonia continued, describing the wayusa upina in detail, explaining and demonstrating the tasks of a young daughter. After serving guayusa, María Antonia said, a daughter should sit beside the fire listening to her elders, who would discuss their dreams:

Excerpt 2 of María Antonia's kamachina counsel, June 10, 2017

MS: S'na rakpiga, maykan yayachu ima tunu muskuyras kwintangaraun.[48] Mamas muskuyras kwintangaraun.[49] Kanga chitaga ali pacha taripasha **uyana angui.**[50]

MS: Like that, what dreams the father is going to tell.[48] And the mother is going to tell her dreams too.[49] Now you **must listen** to all of that considering it carefully.[50]

LINGUISTIC NATURES AND REVITALIZATION IDEOLOGIES

At this moment in line 50, Kelly had sunk back on her heels, and was no longer listening with the upright attention expected of her. Her mother interrupted to tell her, "Daughter, listen closely!" María Antonia continued, as Kelly returned to kneel attentively before her. Listening is inseparable from embodied comportment.

Excerpt 3 of María Antonia's kamachina counsel, June 10, 2017

MS: Ali taripasha **uyasha** tiana angui.[51]
'Na rasha, 'na rasha **uyashami** chi **uyasha** tiasha kan kamba umayra tarpurin tukuy.[52]
[unintelligible sentence due to cross talk].[53]
Imara muskukuna, chitaga mana killkaybi iyarina an, umaybiga, kamba shungubi tarpushkarami.[54]

MS: You must sit, consider, and **listen.**[51]
When you do that, **listen**, sit and **listen**, everything grows inside your mind.[52...53]
What they dreamed, now that should not be remembered with writing, but in the mind, what is planted in your heart.[54]

In lines 51 and 52, María Antonia reminds Kelly that listening is central to understanding the speech of her elders. Writing is also not the correct modality for capturing their speech. Rather, it is the inscription of their words within the mind and the heart, as described in line 54.

María Antonia described the duties awaiting Kelly in the transition from daughter to wife and daughter-in-law. Crucially, if she listened to or obeyed the commands of her new family, she would mature (shunguyana) and become a *yuyak warmi*, a "knowledgeable woman." It would then be time for Kelly to transmit the counsel of her elders to her children. After counseling Kelly for more than five minutes, María Antonia concluded the first segment of her advice:

Excerpt 4 of María Antonia's kamachina counsel, June 10, 2017

MS: Shimi rimashkallara kambak shungubi tarpukbiga sumak ali payami tukungui.[87]
Paya, **uyanguichu** ñuka rimashkara.[88]

MS: Even though just spoken words, if they grow in your heart, you will certainly become a beautiful, good girl.[87]
Girl, do you **understand** what I have said to you?[88]

KH: Alimi **uyaunimi**, ruku mama.[89]
MS: Ari.[90]

KH: I am **understanding** well, grandmother.[89]
MS: Ok.[90]

After María Antonia checked the channel in line 88, she continued to counsel Kelly. She concluded this segment with another appeal to be heard:

Except 5 of María Antonia's kamachina counsel and response by Kelly, June 10, 2017

MS: 'Nakpi chishituwara **uyapangui**, rukuyasha kawsana punzhagama.[119] Chiwara kanda shimiwara pasachipani paya.[120]
KH: Ña mama ñuka **uyashkani** kamba rimashkara.[121]
MS: Mmhmm.[122]
KH: Gustu kushiwa kayta **uyani**, ashka pagarachu.[123]
MS: Ari.[124]
Ari, ama kungaringui ñukanchi kawsayra, chiwa rukuyangui, ña.[125]

MS: So, please **obey** just this little bit, as you get older and throughout your life.[119] With this, I politely pass a little speech to you, young one.[120]
KH: Ok, mother, I **have heard** what you have said.[121]
MS: Yes.[122]
KH: I have **heard** this happily and with pleasure, thank you very much.[123]
MS: Yes.[124]
Yes, don't forget our life, with it you become older, ok?[125]

The verb *uyana* translates as "to listen, to hear, to understand, and to obey" (Orr and Wrisley 1981, 91). These meanings emerge throughout the transcript. Adult caregivers ask children, "Are you listening?" If they don't respond, "*ari, uyauni*" or "*uyanimi*," (yes, I am listening), using "our language, from here," the adult very well might turn away in frustration.

The importance of listening in María Antonia's counsel draws attention to how Upper Napo Kichwa speakers conceive of language socialization as well as the broader role of listening in Indigenous language pedagogy. Meek (2007) details a similar ideology of the importance of listening and respecting elders among Northern Athapascan speakers of Kaska in the Yukon Territory. She notes that in the Yukon, discourses of respect "socialized children and other novices to engage passively with elders and other Kaska speakers during traditional Kaska activities" (2007, 33). These ideologies limited children's opportunity to practice speaking Kaska in ways that could encourage their shift away from Kaska, associated with generational differences in speech. Nevins describes that among White Mountain Apache speakers, a Southern Athapascan language, "discourse on language learning identifies language and listening with participation and fluency in practices constitutive of the family" (2004, 280). For White Mountain Apache, Nevins details how community-internal understandings conflicted with institutional understandings of classroom-based language pedagogy. The situation in Napo reflects elements of both cases. Napo Kichwa children are still being socialized to "grasp" Kichwa language through listening, modeling, and correction, but they also engage in a sociolinguistic world that encourages them to practice speaking in Spanish. Many children in Chaupishungo spoke Spanish more frequently among peers, and even when responding to caregivers. Yet, the assumptions of language standardization promulgated through institutional systems were controversial as a method to counter linguistic shift, because unification violated connections between local speech, familial inheritance, and personhood, representing a shift to "another" variety.

What is at stake today in Napo is that some children are not becoming shunguyuk wawa in the way their parents and grandparents expect. More than just complaints about "kids these days," elders are noticing ongoing forms of cultural and linguistic shift in Napo. These may be related to how children are socialized to listen to Kichwa but to speak Spanish in school and among their peers. Children and young adults may understand basic Kichwa, but many are most comfortable responding in Spanish, as Serafina suggested for the category of *mana ali iyayuk wawa*, which translates literally as the "child who does not possess good thought." Children who respond using "another" variety may be chastised by regional interlocutors. For many speakers of Upper Napo Kichwa, language is inseparable from the participant structures and forms of knowledge constituted by embodied intergenerational transmission, which contrasts markedly with the assumptions of language standardization.

Ideology and Ontology in Language Diversity and Unification

Since the 1970s, the educational activism and communicative needs of the pan-Kichwa and pan-Indigenous Confederation of Indigenous Nationalities of Ecuador (CONAIE) contributed to the development of Unified Kichwa (Montaluisa 2018, 294). Their efforts resulted in the National Directorate of Bilingual and Intercultural Education, which promoted Unified Kichwa (Montaluisa 2018). Unified Kichwa standardizes pronunciation and morphosyntax, while neologisms replace Spanish-derived loans.

Some tensions surrounding Unified Kichwa relate to preexisting regional differentiation within Napo's ecology of language. Highland and Lowland Kichwa are related, but their differences are salient to speakers and linguists. Regional lexicons, phonological and morphological forms, and syntactic patterns vary. Speakers report comprehension difficulties across the Lowland and Highland dialect continuum. The varieties of Kichwa spoken in Ecuador are best conceptualized as a relational field (Rumsey 2010), in which variations grade into each other, allowing speakers to differentiate among regions at various scales, while they suppress other differences (Irvine and Gal 2000). Speakers usually distinguish between varieties that they associate with named places. Unified Kichwa patterns closely with Highland dialects.

Speakers themselves have a historical (Muratorio 1991, 36) and contemporary preference (Grzech, Schwarz, and Ennis 2019) for making finer distinctions than linguists between regions based on forms in their own variety of runa shimi. Many people can produce examples of other varieties, which they describe that they have "grasped" (K. *apina*), similarly to how Serafina described a child "grasping" language. In Chaupishungo, words like *nda*, "yes," used in Pastaza (ari in other dialects), or the Loreto Kichwa form karka, "it was" (aka in Upper Napo Kichwa), were notable regional identifiers.

Even within Napo, speakers from neighboring communities distinguish between varieties. Around the township of Archidona, most speakers adhere to the form *yura*, "tree," while some communities are known to use the form *ruya*, a process of metathesis thought to distinguish Upper Napo and Pastaza Kichwa. Speakers are sensitive to and accepting of these microvariations in speech, referring to them as someone's "kind" of speech or describing it as the shimi (language/word) of a particular village. Languages, like people, are described using the ablative suffix *-manda*, indicating that they are from and of places. One woman in her fifties explained, "Language from elsewhere [*shuk partimanda shimi*] isn't like our language." Many emphasized the connection between "our language" and their place of origin. While the speech and language of others was described as inextricably linked to other places, my interlocutors indexically linked their own language to "here," suggesting an essential relationship (Mannheim 2017) between their natal territories and their sociolinguistic identities. The variety known as Unified Kichwa is similarly known to be from the Highlands.

María Antonia said her grandson had learned "another kind" of Kichwa in school. When a grandmother claims children are learning to speak another variety, she is making a statement laden with beliefs, rationalizations, and feelings about language, what linguistic anthropologists call ideologies of language (Silverstein 1979; Irvine 1989; Woolard 1998a; Kroskrity 2007). Analysts have considered how language ideologies are embedded in communicative practices and institutions (Kroskrity 2000) and how scholarly discourse reproduces such ideologies (Bauman and Briggs 2003; French 2003, 2010). Language ideologies are pervasive in social practice as they circulate through explanations of language and the social field, which articulate with broader political and economic formations (Gal and Irvine 2019). Language ideologies are also pervasive in language revitalization.

Young women like Rita are not the only ones who link Unified Kichwa to the Highlands. Such discourses circulate in many settings and media, from Facebook comments claiming that a TV presenter "sounds Highland" to the complaint that because the languages have been mixed, children have begun to speak like highlanders. Speakers make connections between the forms of Unified Kichwa and the Highlands largely because of how they already conceived of linguistic differentiation. Unified Kichwa entered a regional ecology of languages as "another variety," which many suggested, "sounded another way."

An assemblage of linguistic ideologies, what Kroskrity names "the interaction of clusters of ideologies that occur within or across linguistic communities" (2018, 134) are found in Napo. This assemblage emerges from the project of language revitalization. Such clusters of ideologies have been important in shaping the strategies and responses to revitalize and reclaim Kichwa. Ideologies of language revitalization espoused by advocates, Indigenous and otherwise, intersect with ideologies of language held by regional speakers. Not only do they conflict at the level of ideology but also they seem to come into conflict with community-internal ontologies of language.

In a decontextualized world of language as system, extracted from indexical meanings, phonological, morphological, or lexical forms may be interchangeable across dialects, but in the social world of some Napo Runa, one's variety is connected to one's personhood. Shift to Spanish is described as young people "becoming white-mestizos," mishu tukusha. Speaking with the voice of "another" variety can violate understandings of the relationship between self, place, family, and language. Community members' knowledge of what language is in the world and who they are through language shapes their responses to the use of different varieties, including those that might be seen as Lowland, Highland, or standardized.

Although related to language ideologies and assemblages of them, an ontological approach to language is not isomorphic with these concepts (Hauck and Heurich 2018; Ferguson 2019). As Hauck and Heurich suggest (2018, 2), ontologies of language highlight the multiple natures of language, without assuming what *language* is to our interlocutors. In inquiries into ontologies of language some debate remains between "strong" and "weak" approaches (Keane 2013). Ferguson (2019, 26–27) takes a "weak" approach to ontologies of language, dealing with the existential and spiritual nature of language. This conception of ontologies of language is closer to assemblages of linguistic ideologies, seen as inter-linked assumptions and propositions about the nature and the spiritual power of language in the world (Ferguson 2019, 27). An ontological approach emphasizes the subjective assumptions of the nature of language for the people with whom we work and decenters the taken-for-granted assumptions about language of linguists and anthropologists trained within our own epistemic traditions. Ideologies of language, particularly in assemblages, are sites in which ontologies of language become visible. What must the nature of language be for our interlocutors for their linguistic ideologies to make sense in, and make sense of, the world?

In trying to make sense of the ontological turn through Indigenous intellectual trajectories (Todd 2016), I turned to Vine Deloria Jr.'s development of an American Indian metaphysics, defined as "the set of first principles we must possess in order to make sense of the world in which we live" (2001, 2). The first principles of those enmeshed since birth in "standard language cultures" (Milroy 2001) can be quite different from those of Napo Kichwa speakers. Unlike contexts in which clarification has resulted in standardization and revitalization projects that emphasize compromise—as is reported to be the case in the unification of Inuit (Patrick, Murasugi, and Palluq-Cloutier 2018) or Basque (Urla 2012)—the standardization of Ecuadorian Kichwa has created major debate. The logics of language standardization, which conflict with other understandings of what language is and how it is used, motivate these debates.

A Voice from Somewhere

Although regional speakers often describe their language as a familial inheritance, language planners have sometimes treated regional languages as a problem to be overcome. Roberto Cerda, a local Kichwa politician who had worked in bilingual education in Napo for more than twenty years, explained to me that linguistic unification had two goals. The first was to remove Spanish loanwords from the language. According to Cerda, code-mixing between Kichwa and Spanish allowed Spanish speakers to understand conversations in Kichwa. The introduction of neologisms was intended to sharpen the boundaries between languages (Debenport 2015; Faudree 2013; Urla 2012).

Neologisms are of the most contested elements of Unified Kichwa. The neologism *yupaychana* ("to thank; to be grateful") used in political discourse and public speech continues to draw attention (Wroblewski 2012). Not all lexical elements of Unified Kichwa create the same ire. While some people still refer to Spanish-speaking white-mestizos as awallta (a regional pronunciation of awa llakta, "highlander") or blancu (from Spanish blanco, "white"), the neologism mishu is now in wide use (see Ministerio de Educación del Ecuador 2009, 100). Even Upper Napo Kichwa media hosts like Rita, most of whom align themselves with regional language, incorporate Unified neologisms, pronunciations, and morphological forms into their speech. Ideological boundaries between forms are porous in practice.

Cerda identified a second goal of linguistic unification during our interview: to establish an orthography despite the "issue" (llaki) of dialectal diversity. According to Cerda, representatives from the Lowlands and Highlands met with scholars at the Universidad Católica in Quito to discuss development of an orthography. As Cerda described, they gathered in 1980 to discuss the question of language diversity. He explained, "Limoncocha [provinces of Sucumbíos and Orellana] speaks one kind. Loreto [in Orellana province] speaks one kind. Tena [the capital of Napo] speaks one kind. Archidona [to the north of Tena] one kind, and then Punosuyo, highlanders (awallakta) from the sierra speak another kind." Faced with this diversity they asked, "What can be done?" The answer involved the intersection of multiple ideologies of language, which implied a distinct ontology to the one emphasizing an essential connection between language, place, and person.

Luis Montaluisa, one of unification's main architects, recounts that Unified Kichwa emerged through a long negotiation among Indigenous activists and educators, Ecuadorian scholars, state institutions, foreign missionaries and linguists, and international NGOs (2018, 289–300). At stake in Montaluisa's account are beliefs regarding the necessity of a single language for a single polity, and the role of experts in consolidating a standard. At the early standardization meetings, proponents of linguistic unification argued that "the Indigenous peoples of [Ecuador] faced shared problems, and that unification of all was necessary to confront these problems, [and] proposed orthographic unification and literacy methods" to meet this goal (Montaluisa 2018, 294). Montaluisa credits nationalist Basque revitalization of Euskera through standardization based on linguistic history as a major inspiration for the unification of Ecuadorian Kichwa (2018, 288). He is particularly drawn to the use of diachronic and etymological studies to construct a standard on the basis of shared linguistic history (2018, 312, 288). The orthographic and grammatical norms of Unified Kichwa are grounded in a linguistic reconstruction, initially based on a small dialectal survey of the Highlands by linguists at the Pontifical Catholic University of Ecuador (Montaluisa 2018, 291).

Some contemporary varieties are closer to the standard than others. As Montaluisa describes, the central Highlands and the Amazonian regions differ most from a reconstruction of proto-Quechua (2018, 317–18). Many speakers of regional varieties in the Amazon experience the standard as an imposition, because written norms closer to the speech of the Highlands are the model for new oral registers. For many people in Napo, the standard does not serve as an authoritative, anonymous "voice from nowhere," (Gal and Woolard 2001) because of the way that it is articulated for them as a voice from somewhere. That somewhere is the sierra, whose iconic forms it most closely approximates. This language, however, was never intended to have a voice at all and was first positioned as a written language (K. A. King 2001, 42).

In Napo and other regions, slippage between written and oral standardization has resulted in the transference of written norms to speech (Wroblewski 2012; K. A. King 2001; Howard 2007). Although Unified Kichwa was intended as a written standard, attitudes toward standardization have varied. Pedagogical materials for bilingual educators are sometimes ambiguous regarding oral and written forms. Unified Kichwa standardizes phonology and morphology through a "deep orthography" in which numerous regional variations in pronunciation are attached to a single grapheme (Limerick 2017). As discussed in the previous chapter, Spanish-derived literacy ideologies also treat the relationship between symbol and sound as transparent. When Kichwa speakers read Kichwa, they usually pronounce words as written, rather than according to regional phonological and morphological forms. The assemblage of these ideologies facilitates oral standardization based upon the written standard.

Lack of ideological clarification, prescriptive attitudes, and Spanish literacy norms have resulted in the enregisterment of an oral code of Unified Kichwa in many institutional contexts. Enregisterment reflects a semiotic process described by Asif Agha (2005), in which particular signs become linked to recognizable social personae or figures of personhood. Unified Kichwa has become the expected code for politics, education, and much mass media, associated with social figures like bilingual educators and Kichwa cultural pageant contestants (Wroblewski 2014). This code has engendered anxiety among speakers who do not control the norms of the standard and has spurred discourses of purity and authenticity around regional and standardized forms (Hornberger and King 1998; Gal and Woolard 2001; Wroblewski 2014; Grzech, Schwarz, and

Ennis 2019). Resistance to slippage between written and oral unification is rooted in understandings of the nature of language, personhood, and relationality. These contrast with linguistic unification's assembled ideologies of linguistic nationalism, scientific rationality, and linguistic prescriptivism, which imply a decontextualized nature of language.

For many in Napo, adopting new forms of speech violates the connection between language, family, and self, discussed as "the language our elders left," *ñukanchi rukuguna sakishka shimi*. Fabian, a father in his late thirties, told me, "We must not forget runa shimi. The language left by our elders should only be forgotten upon one's death." For Fabian, one way for young people to remember these stories is by recording them. Recording has become a central method for reclamation on community radio programs in Napo. Through broadcast media, speakers of Upper Napo Kichwa have spoken back to the assumptions of top-down language standardization, using media focused on language-in-use and social interaction. Tuning in to Napo Kichwa radio reveals the importance of familial interactional routines and community-internal language practices in grassroots reclamation media.

Finding A New Path

Upper Napo Kichwa radio media programs frequently remediated the wayusa hours to extend and amplify a time deeply associated with linguistic and cultural socialization. Host Rita Tunay explicitly identified the wayusa upina as the time when she developed her skills in Kichwa. "When I was about to start kindergarten," Rita explained, "my mother used to punish me for speaking Kichwa. She told me, 'You must speak Spanish [mishu shimi; literally, "the mestizo language"]." Rita's mother spoke limited Spanish and hoped the language would open new opportunities for Rita. Rita often spent time with her grandparents, who had moved into town. They cared for her while her parents were living and working on their agricultural lands a few hours away. In Rita's estimation, children who spend time with their grandparents have the greatest abilities in Kichwa. But now, she said, while parents are at work, children spend time at daycare or school, rather than in their grandparents' homes. Rita's parents were ultimately very glad that she had maintained Kichwa. In Rita's childhood memories, as for others, the wayusa upina was one of the most important times for elders to transmit their knowledge and their language. On radio shows, linguistic and cultural transmission were inseparable, as regional speakers described childhood routines shaped by the practices, narratives, and counsel of their elders. Their stories came to life during live broadcasts, suggesting new modalities for linguistic and cultural revitalization in Napo, grounded in local ontologies of language as the interactional practices and forms of knowledge transmitted between elders and children.

Each morning from four to six o'clock, *A New Path* focused on the revalorization of contemporary and historical cultural practices. Local and national news complemented their cultural programming, alongside regional shout-outs, announcements, public health campaigns, economic development projects, and live and prerecorded music. *A New Path*'s program was also one of the most popular in Napo. Tuning into their program revealed the centrality of regional voices to the production of revitalization media in Napo. It also showed the significance of embodied interactional routines of listening to and remembering what people called "the words our elders left," and the possibilities of oral and aural media to respond to the multiple ideological assemblages in which language-in-use is enmeshed. It exemplified the use of broadcast media as a method for cultural and linguistic revalorization—the goal set by the show's producers for revitalization, responsive to many of the ontologies and ideological assemblages of language found elsewhere in Napo.

Radio media is consumed daily in many Kichwa households around Napo and provides a powerful channel for revitalization projects. Kichwa-language radio programming is largely limited to the early morning hours before dawn and in the evening, when Spanish-speaking station owners imagine their audiences to be home and attentive to the radio. These early morning hours provide a central trope to many programs, as hosts exhort listeners to awaken and drink guayusa. The interactional routines and forms of knowledge transmitted during the wayusa upina were especially important for the programming of *A New Path*.

The program is framed in terms of an early morning conversation among family. Before dawn, Rita and James welcomed listeners, calling out to the members of an extended family—mothers, fathers, children, grandparents—to get up and to drink guayusa. They often referred to each other as *pani* (sister of male ego) and *turi* (brother of female ego), positioning themselves as a brother-sister team, speaking to their listening ayllu (family) around the morning fire. The wayusa upina also informed a popular feature of the program—the archive of community-sourced recordings focused on the kinds of talk that occurs during the wayusa upina, including elder speakers' auto-biographical counseling, local histories, and other narratives. Augosto Grefa from Kashayacu framed a recording by saying, "I am going to tell . . . what my father told. Sitting [us] by the fire, when the pot of wayusa was being brewed, when wayusa was drunk, he would begin to talk about the time before. . . ." These interactional frames animate many of the recordings in the archive. Speakers recount stories and speech from their elders, interweaving the voices of other times and spaces.

The programming on *A New Path* was also informed by an ideology of the essential connection between speech, identity, and place, transmitted through familial interaction. As Mayor Shiguango told me, he "disagreed" with the practice of linguistic unification. As he explained, "With this program *A New Path*, the desire is to enter finally into communities that actually have their own language, let's say, their own way of speaking." One way the program entered these communities with their distinctive styles of speech was through their archive of community recordings. During weekly visits to villages and neighborhoods around the township of Archidona, Rita and James recorded local histories, personal narratives, jokes, and songs with a focus on elder and adult speakers (figure 10). These recordings were very popular segments in the households where I studied radio reception. Conversations would be paused to listen and to comment on community-sourced narratives and music. Where standardized phrases like yupaychani, "I am thankful," drew critical comments on form from listeners in Chaupishungo, the local voices in these stories often elicited evaluative comments on their content.

The program reconnected with the knowledge and skills of the residents of rural communities through monthly live broadcasts, hosted by villages and organizations around Archidona. These programs focused even more than their daily counterparts on the host of socialization practices associated with guayusa tea drinking. *A New Path*'s live wayusa broadcasts sought to recreate the family home on the air, thereby extending its interactional frameworks to a wider public.

FIGURE 10 Rita Tunay and James Yumbo interview Mario Yumbo for the radio archive. June 9, 2016. Photo by author.

Even though the physical space of live broadcasts was accessible only to a relatively small co-present audience, these monthly radio programs focused on detailed realizations of embodied practices (Ennis 2019a). As community participants moved through waking, drinking wayusa, and telling stories together, hosts Rita and James helped to reanimate a lively space of intergenerational interaction for listening audiences. These programs transposed elements from historical narratives and from the contemporary homes of listeners. On the air, the interactional routines that emerged between elder María Antonia; young Kelly; and her mother, Inés, were repeated with other women and children.

The importance of interactional routines based in listening are evident in a wayusa upina broadcast from the community of Santa Rita on September 13, 2016. As the show began, participants in the program lay under blankets beside a central fire. Rita introduced the setting to her cohost, proclaiming, "This morning, our grandfathers and grandmothers before just this way carried out all the parts of the wayusa upina, and they continued teaching their children, James." She continued, "However, now today we have forgotten a little, we didn't value every kind." Rita echoes the concern of many people that the material practices of their elders are being "forgotten," linking this amnesia to a lack of appreciation. However, she suggested, "Even though it's that way, this morning we will find how it is in the community of Santa Rita." The antidote to forgetting is to experience how the wayusa upina is, or was, practiced in the community of Santa Rita.

As at AMUPAKIN, counseling was an important element of wayusa upina programming. Over the next two hours, Rita and James followed along with their listening audience as residents of Santa Rita participated in a wayusa upina, guided by community members, including a woman named Mama Olga. After the family had brewed, served, and drunk guayusa, they watched live musical performances and storytelling sessions. About an hour into the broadcast, the program turned to explicit instruction of young people into local material practices, including the production of baskets and net bags. Rita began by asking Mama Olga, "What did [your] grandfathers and grandmothers counsel when the dawn was breaking?" Olga's response embeds her elders' advice into the interactional frame of the wayusa upina, when they taught her to weave net shigra bags:

Excerpt 1 of *A New Path*, "Santa Rita Wayusa Upina," September 13, 2016

Olga: Kay ñawpa punda, ña waysara upikanchi.$_2$ Ña chiwasha, kay ñukanchi ruku mamauna ñawpa kasna rasha, shigrara awasha, mashti, katusha ganana anmi nisha kamachikuna anmi.$_3$	**Olga**: First, we drank guayusa.$_2$ Then after that, our female elders counsel us, saying "first doing it like this, weaving shigra, um, selling [them], [you] have to earn [money]."$_3$

Olga then switches the interactional frame from voicing the authoritative speech of her female elders to directly addressing two young girls. As she does so in line 4, she refashions and expands the instructions of her elders voiced in line 3.

LINGUISTIC NATURES AND REVITALIZATION IDEOLOGIES   135

Excerpt 2 of *A New Path*, "Santa Rita Wayusa Upina," September 13, 2016

Olga: Shinakpi payauna **uyanguichi**, kasna rasha, awasha, mastisha, katuna, mashti kulkira ikuna, chimanda mana killa wawa tukuna, shigrara awana, ishinga awana, mashti manga llutana awana, chiguna mashti, mashti anmi.₄ Uyanguichi.₅ Kuna ña chillarami rimani ñuka₆ **Uyapanguichi** payauna₇

Olga: So, girls **listen**, doing it like this, weaving, um, to sell, like this you'll get money, then, you must not turn into lazy children, [but must] weave shigra, weave ishinga nets, um, craft earthen pots. **Listen**.₅ Now that's all I have to say.₆ **Please listen** girls.₇

As she begins and ends this turn of talk in lines 4 and 7, she asks the two young girls to listen to her. Unlike María Antonia's speech, this counsel was brief. Rita prompted her to continue, asking about the bags and their use. Olga further explained how they are woven, as well as how the fibers are produced, but she remained within the framework of a lesson, telling the young girls to look and to listen. As Olga concluded her lesson about weaving, she grounded her authority in the discourse of the past, and again asked the daughters to listen.

Excerpt 3 of *A New Path*, "Santa Rita Wayusa Upina," September 13, 2016

Olga: Paya rikuy, rikuychi.₂₇ Kasnami, kasna rashami, kangunaga shigrara awashaga kangunawak valirina.₂₈ Imas maykan, maykanbas katusha ganana tukunchi kaywa.₂₉ Payauna **uyanguichi**.₃₀ Ñuka ima tunus, ruku tunumi rimauni, ruku mama ashkamanda, kangunawak valiringawa.₃₁ **Uyanguichichu** payauna?₃₂

Olga: Girl look, look [plural].₂₇ Like this, doing it like this, now you all weaving the shigra must value what is yours.₂₈ Whatever we sell, we end up earning with this.₂₉ Girls **listen**.₃₀ I am speaking in the way of the elders, from being a ruku mama, in order to value what is yours.₃₁ **Are you listening** girls?₃₂

Despite Olga's impassioned plea using her authority as an elder, this interactional routine nearly met the infelicitous fate of others between elders and young people, who often fail to respond to the phatic question, "Are you listening?" The two girls were silent until Rita quietly prompted them to speak in line 33:

Excerpt 4 of *A New Path*, "Santa Rita Wayusa Upina," September 13, 2016

Rita: Rimay, rimay. $_{33}$ **Rita**: Speak, speak. $_{33}$

"Paya": Ari, **uyanchimi.**$_{34}$ **"Paya"**: Yes, we are **really listening.**$_{34}$

During *A New Path*'s production of the wayusa upina, families sleep side by side. Children rise alongside their elders, to be counseled into the interactional routines and social practices that sustained the transmission of Napo Runa lifeways rooted in material conditions of the Ecuadorian Amazon. Participants in these exchanges bring a social world to life where children respond appropriately to elders. Aided by Rita's voice as the *animadora* (Sp. "announcer, MC"; literally, "animator"), participants reconnect with routines central to the transmission of cultural and linguistic knowledge. Such routines may be planted in their hearts for later remembrance.

A New Path's monthly live programs addressed a broader preference in Napo for reclaiming language, not as a decontextualized code but through contexts of use and interaction where that code has meaning. These programs were ways that the spoken words and practices of "the words our elders left" were remembered among participants and co-present and listening audiences. Such programming highlights the importance of intergenerational transmission and embodied interaction in community-led efforts to revalorize and reclaim linguistic and cultural practices.

Conclusion: The Role of Linguistic Diversity in Language Reclamation

Well-intentioned processes of language revitalization place once-unstandardized languages into complex ideological assemblages, bringing together distinct ontologies of language. Linguistic documentation—developing an orthography, dictionary, and grammar—often provides the basis for language revitalization projects (Grenoble and Whaley 2006; Nettle and Romaine 2000). Standardization and formal education remain significant strategies recommended by scholars (Lane et al. 2018). Such practices erase the precarious situations of many regional varieties (Wolfram and Schilling-Estes 1995), which become nonstandard. For some speakers of Upper Napo Kichwa, the decontextualized and decontextualizable nature of language assumed by language standardization contrasts with their understanding of language as essentially connected to places and people.

One of the primary advantages of broadcast media for Napo Kichwa language reclamation is the recontextualization of socialization routines in new settings. There are contradictions to these methods, as there are with the introduction of any new form of mediation. *A New Path's* community-sourced recordings extend knowledge to a wider public (cf. Debenport 2015), while removing many of the narratives from the close familial relationships where they were once transmitted, often as confidential sources of knowledge and authority for medicinal practices. While radio makes the stories accessible to wider audiences, changes in "channel" (Jakobson 1961) may reshape the ways novices come to interact with this knowledge. Yet, like language standardization, these strategies are now being advocated by many community members.

The development of a standard remains a goal of many Kichwa language activists, politicians, and community members, underscoring its importance within other communities of practice in Ecuador. Unified Kichwa plays an important role as a language of government and education, legitimizing the language for speakers of various backgrounds and abilities. As Qui'chi Patlan (Martinez 2019) has suggested for the Highlands, Unified Kichwa also continues to develop as a literary language and may be the preferred oral code of speakers who have reclaimed Kichwa later in life. As a code, it provides another voice with which to articulate contemporary Kichwa sovereignty in Ecuador, which is as meaningful to its speakers as regional registers of Kichwa utilized by many of my interlocutors in their daily lives.

There is still a significant contradiction in how Unified Kichwa has been applied as a hegemonic standard in state-sponsored education and institutional contexts and how many Kichwa speakers in Napo utilize language. For many people, language and linguistic practice are not decontextualizable but essentially connected to place of origin. Languages, like people, are from known places. One's language is not transmitted in authoritative, anonymous relationships or embedded within books, as standard languages so often are. Rather, language is transmitted through familial practice, discussed in relation to something that one's elders left behind in interactions grounded in speaking and listening, which is expected to emerge in the socially competent child or ali shunguyuk wawa.

At issue today is that runa shimi does not always emerge as expected from young people and children, some of whom may be socialized to listen more in Kichwa at home but to speak in Spanish at school and among their peers. Yet, the situation in Napo shows that language shift is not irrevocable. We have met several people in prior chapters who are reclaiming Kichwa as adults. The presence of young and middle-aged adults who have reclaimed spoken Kichwa later in life among my interlocutors suggests that listening is a significant aspect of language socialization, which may "plant" the "words of the elders" in the heart and minds of their receptive audience for later growth.

As speakers of different ideological and ontological commitments come into contact, it is perhaps inevitable that conflicts will emerge. They are not insurmountable. My interlocutors' acceptance of dialectal differences as part of the fabric of social life suggests that there is a way for multiple forms of Kichwa to co-exist, including regional and standardized varieties. Greater ideological and ontological clarification are needed regarding the forms used in always complex settings of linguistic revitalization. Ontological clarification is a process of identifying issues related to the multiple natures of language that may emerge during language planning. In collaborative approaches to language reclamation between communities and external scholars, this might involve asking our interlocutors to think in possibly new ways about the nature of language. To develop media and methods for reclamation grounded in how language matters to the communities scholars seek to serve, we must ask ourselves to take seriously the natures of language our interlocutors may teach us to understand.

Tuning in to Upper Napo Kichwa radio media demonstrates the importance of alternative modalities for language revitalization and attunes us to the ways that linguistic transmission matters to the communities most affected by language shift and planning. By allowing for the transmission of a wide range of voices and fashions of speaking, Upper Napo Kichwa broadcast media establish a public in which regional and standardized forms find space together. As Mayor Shiguango said to me once, "What must be done is value what we have and show it to the public, so that they know it." These radio programs contribute to the development of a robust, heterogeneous Indigenous public sphere that reverberates in Napo and beyond. In doing so, they contribute to animating and reanimating Kichwa in daily practice, demonstrating a powerful methodology through which community media extend and amplify the contemporary voices of Indigenous languages and their speakers.

CHAPTER 4

Reanimating Kichwa in Napo's Media Ecology

Young women's speech was a central preoccupation during preparations for the cultural pageant Sumak Ñusta Chunta Warmi (Miss Peach Palm Princess). Pageant organizers—Kichwa and white-mestizo members of Mayor Jaime Shiguango's staff—emphasized that contestants should emulate their elders' speech. In one preparatory meeting, the non-Kichwa director of tourism advised young pageant participants to "speak like their grandparents," while "limit[ing] Unificado." Mayor Shiguango advised the candidates, all in their late teens and early twenties, to speak with elder family members about local Kichwa. The Unified neologism yupaychani ("thank you; I am thankful") was singled out. Contestants were advised to use the locally recognizable form pagarachu.[1] Why were they so concerned with young women's speech during a beauty pageant? In regimenting the young women's speech, organizers were attempting to recalibrate the expected ways of speaking in Kichwa pageantry, to align local cultural and environmental practices with local language varieties.

---

1. The term "pagarachu" (thank you) and related forms like *"pagarachuni"* (I am thankful) are likely derived from the Spanish phrase *"que Dios le pague"* (may God bless you) using the Spanish verb *pagar*. The final -chu may represent the purposive -chun (see Nuckolls and Swanson 2020, 232 for an analysis of this morpheme), which is sometimes realized as [-chu] in Napo due to elision of the final nasal consonant; see Wroblewski 2022, 76 for an alternative analysis. These terms may also be pronounced "pagrachu."

The cultural pageant Sumak Ñusta Chunta Warmi was part of a well-developed genre of Kichwa live performance, closely related to radio within Napo's broader ecology of media. Radio host Rita Tunay was a former pageant contestant. She was regularly chosen as the Kichwa MC for local pageants, sometimes alongside her radio cohost, James Yumbo. Radio and pageantry further overlapped, as audio from regional pageants like Archidona's Ñusta Chunta Warmi, Tena's Ñusta Wayusa Warmi (Miss Wayusa Princess), or the provincial Ñusta Napu Marka (Miss Napo) were simultaneously broadcast on local radio. Parish- and community-level pageants provided contestants for the glitzy cantonal, provincial, and—sometimes—national or international events. Pageantry coincides with and supports political organization. Pageant winners regularly attend local political events, opening opportunities for some young women to enter politics (Erazo and Benitez 2022). Pageant contestants are guests on radio shows and media outlets to publicize the events. Cultural pageantry and performance are complex practices within Napo's ecology of media, in which younger and elder Kichwa women learn relatively new forms of public participation.

Bilingual educators in Napo have used pageants featuring young women to glamorize Kichwa cultural practices and promote a formal speech register heavily influenced by Unified Kichwa. This chapter explores the role of embodied performance in cultural revitalization. Producers and participants sought to animate and reanimate—or semiotically bring to life—language alongside different forms of cultural practice. By comparing two cultural events in the township of Archidona sponsored by the administration of Mayor Jaime Shiguango—the yearly cultural-beauty pageant held during the annual Festival Intercultural de la Chonta (Intercultural Peach Palm Festival) and the municipality's monthly wayusa upina performance—I show how producers and hosts recalibrated cultural performance to include voices they thought had been ignored—those of rural audiences and elder speakers. Cultural performance and broadcast media are a multimodal method of reclamation, affording the development of a polyphonic public sphere. They are also sites where expectations about gender, ethnicity, memory, and history are negotiated and regimented.

In the Ecuadorian Amazon, scholars have approached many of these forms of public culture through the lens of cultural performance (Rogers

1998; Wroblewski 2014), often leading to questions of authenticity and essentialization. Other scholars have explored how these pageants contribute to regional environmental practices (Perreault 2005) and women's political formation (Erazo and Benitez 2022). As Graham and Penny (2014, 4) suggest, Indigenous peoples "achieve, accomplish, and even improvise indigeneity through performance and performative acts." Indigeneity is not a timeless category. It is one that emerges from particular historical formations and relationships. Like other dimensions of identity—gender, class, race, ethnicity—it is constructed through the repetition of embodied actions and discourse (Butler 1993; Taylor 2003; Canessa 2012). These iterations are performative in Austin's (1962) sense—as actions that not only describe but create the social world. As some scholars note, "performance" may imply an exaggerated sense of agency, that one can take off and put on an identity at will (Canessa 2012, 26–27). Identities are intersubjective (Bucholtz and Hall 2005), emerging from interactions with other social actors and norms. Anthropologists have explored how Indigenous Amazonians negotiate external expectations (Graham and Penny 2014; Conklin 1997; Conklin and Graham 1995; Turner 1991), particularly regarding what Bernard Perley (2014) has called "charismatic Indigeneity." Napo Kichwa performers are aware of internal and external norms, which they reproduce and challenge in their acts.

Cultural pageantry and performance, and the media ecology of which they are part, are ways for Napo Runa activists to remediate and reanimate—bring back to life—the world of their elders' past within the present for ongoing circulation in the future. The analytic of animation draws attention to the techniques and semiotic modes through which a group of participants project "qualities perceived as human—life, power, agency, will, personality, and so on—outside of the self and into the sensory environment" (Silvio 2010, 247). Moving beyond notions of animation as tied to a particular medium—as hand-drawn or computer-generated—the anthropology of animation deals with what Silvio (2010, 427) calls "the comparative study of the technes of animation," referring to the ways characters and interactional environments are brought to life. Within performance spaces, groups of various ideological and ontological commitments debate the voice—as a techne of animation—which Napo Kichwa communities will animate (Goffman 1981a), not just now, but in the past and the future.

Mayor Shiguango once told me that linguistic unification "has made us lose our own cultural identity, our own language," and worried that "what is ours" was being lost because of it. Cultural pageantry in Napo has been closely linked to language unification and bilingual education (Wroblewski 2014; Rogers 1998). Archidona's programming provided an alternative to language revitalization based on the use of Unified Kichwa in well-intentioned bilingual education programs. Through Indigenous beauty pageants and public storytelling exhibitions, largely directed at an urban, bilingual audience, educators from the Provincial Directorate of Bilingual and Intercultural Education in Napo (DIPEIB-N) enregistered what Wroblewski describes as an "intercultural code" (2014, 66), a regionalized Unified Kichwa. This code was used alongside well-established icons of Amazonian practice based on swidden agriculture and forest-based subsistence (Perreault 2005). Despite Archidona organizers' suggestion to contestants that they speak "like their grandparents," how participants took this advice varied considerably, depending on the prior experiences and beliefs they and their families held.

Alternative reclamation projects like *A New Path*'s multimodal radio programming allowed for the recalibration of performance routines to establish indexical links to the voices of elder figures, utilizing regional varieties of Kichwa. These programs were oriented toward a local counterpublic (Warner 2002), who felt ignored by revitalization practices based around bilingual education, language standardization, and literacy. Through repeated public instantiations of their elders' words and worlds, the participants in these radio programs sought to reanimate and revalorize what they defined as their history of linguistic and cultural practices in the context of social, economic, and environmental changes spurring shift at multiple levels.

Cultural Pageantry in Napo

Spectators densely packed the arena on the night of Archidona's 2017 Ñusta Chunta Warmi pageant. Rows of chairs flanked the floor of the indoor sports arena hosting the festivities, while the stands were full of the contestants' supporters. In the standing-room-only crowd, the group of midwives from AMUPAKIN became separated. Part of our group was seated near the front by the stage, among other invited guests and local politicians. The glitzy event seemed far removed from the muddy soccer field where one contestant had been elected to represent her community several months before. The crowd then had also been large and boisterous.

Indigenous pageantry in Napo dates to the 1970s and 1980s.[2] Cultural activists created what has become a major site of cultural production in the area—the crowning (*akllana*, "selection, election") of a *ñusta*, an Indigenous princess, in elaborate cultural pageants. As elsewhere in Latin America and around the globe (Cohen, Wilk, and Stoeltje 1995; Pequeño 2013; Rasch 2020), such pageants were partly modeled on beauty pageants in the United States. Beauty pageants in Ecuador began in 1930 but excluded Indigenous and Afro-Ecuadorian contestants in favor of white-mestiza candidates from Quito and Guayaquil (Pequeño 2013, 115). Indigenous peoples in Ecuador, as elsewhere, carved out alternative pageant spaces that parallel and expand the format of white-mestizo pageantry (Rogers 1998; Konefal 2009).

According to Roberto Cerda, regional educator and politician, local activists demanded space to produce Indigenous or Kichwa pageants because they wanted to highlight the beauty of their own culture. He explained, "We were ignored. There was only one culture: settler [*colona*], white [*blanca*], Hispanic [*hispana*], whatever you want to call it, culture. And ours?" These public events, according to Cerda, were opportunities to "value" the beauty of Kichwa women and culture, which had been "ignored" by the dominant colonial society. Over several decades, such pageants have become a popular feature of the Upper Napo Kichwa media ecology, although they are not without contradictions and critics.

Nadino Calapucha—a full-blown Amazonian Kichwa popstar from the province of Pastaza who leads the band Kambak (Yours)—performs

---

2. It is somewhat unclear when these pageants were first organized in Napo. My interlocutor Roberto Cerda suggested 1980 for Tena. This coincides with a claim by Andrea Pequeño, citing interviews with anthropologist Blanca Muratorio, that "Indigenous beauty pageants began to take place around the 1980s" (Pequeño 2007, 97, n5). Rogers (1998, 62) suggests that Archidona's pageant began in the 1970s, when Archidona's municipality sponsored an agricultural festival to celebrate the chonta harvest in 1972.

regularly at ñusta pageants. He proposed that the pageants sometimes turn women into "adornments," but they are among the only urban spaces in places like Tena where Kichwa people can make their cultural practices visible. His comments address a tension in considerations of global beauty pageants. Critics tend to define such events as objectifying, essentializing, and exploitative of women and children. More sympathetic scholars have pointed to the need to understand the local meanings of such events (Cohen, Wilk, and Stoeltje 1995; Balogun 2012, 2020). In Guatemala, Indigenous pageantry has been a site of political expression for young women, who have used the space to contest state repression of Indigenous communities during the civil war (Konefal 2009) and contemporary male domination in social movements (Schackt 2005).

Upper Napo Kichwa pageantry is likewise a complex enterprise, with social, political, and economic implications for women. Recent analyses stress that participation in Indigenous pageants can afford young women greater political and community participation from Alaska (Williams 2019) to the Amazon (Erazo and Benitez 2022). This is a significant political change for young Indigenous women in the Amazon and elsewhere in Ecuador. Several elder, predominately monolingual Kichwa women—born in the 1950s—reported that their families did not send them to school to protect them from outsiders and because less value was placed on educating girls in colonial schools. Members of AMUPAKIN have discussed the disapproval they faced from some male relatives regarding their participation in the organization, which is a cultural and political center, as well as health cooperative. Political scientist Manuela Picq (2018) emphasizes Indigenous women's contributions to Ecuadorian politics, despite the challenges they face, ranging from the erasure of their activism to sexual assault. In the 1990s, Blanca Muratorio reported that "nationally and within the Amazon region, [Indigenous political] organizations have been almost exclusively led by men" (1998, 410). This situation has changed since the institution of a new elections law in 2000, which required at least 30 percent of political candidates on a party list to be women (Erazo 2013, 185). Women had once been functionally excluded from acquiring the norms of political discourse through their exclusion from politics. Kichwa political organizations found themselves in need of women prepared to engage in the political sphere, a need pageant participants could meet.

Pageant participation is not required for women to work in politics or media, but it does increase a young woman's profile, experience with public speaking, and political networks. Gabriela Cerda, for instance, was elected to the Ecuadorian National Assembly between 2017 and 2021. Cerda was formerly a reporter for Napo television channel AllyTV and pageant contestant. Rita Tunay, former cohost of *A New Path*, entered regional politics in 2019 as the running mate for the non-Indigenous candidate of the Pachakutik Party, Dr. Edison Chavez. After less than a year in office, Chavez died following complications from surgery, leaving Tunay to assume the prefecture (Erazo and Benitez 2022, 162). The existence of multiple female Kichwa media personalities in Napo is somewhat unusual, as Muniz reports that in neighboring Pastaza, "the presence of female hosts is scarce on the radios" (2022, 151).

Indigenous pageantry and performance also contribute to the production, transmission, and transformation of community identities (Rasch 2020). The emphasis on embodied transmission of knowledge in performance likely contributes to its popularity for cultural and linguistic reclamation in Napo. Live performances convey what Taylor calls an "embodied repertoire" of knowledge regarding practices, habitus, and spoken language (2003, 16, 19). Live performances address a preference for the experiential transmission of knowledge, encapsulated by the Kichwa verb *riksina*, "to know (by experience)." Participation in live performances can allow participants to learn and practice embodied forms of knowledge. It may also allow them to reclaim some of the "words of their elders," though the role of spoken language in cultural pageants is complex. The demonstrations performed on stage often brought young people into closer contact with significant cultural practices and knowledge. One contestant, following family advice, constructed a scene in which she entered a mountain, communed with its spiritual owners, and emerged as a *yachak warmi*, a female shaman. This is a striking example, as women have often hidden shamanic knowledge and practices to avoid accusations of witchcraft (Muratorio 1995).

Cultural pageants remain popular among Kichwa publics in Napo. Across scales—from rural communities to large coliseums—pageants draw crowds of various ages, who clamor for their preferred contestants. There is no singular format for pageants in Napo, though large and small events follow similar structures, related to the norms of *reina* beauty pageants for non-Indigenous groups.[3] Larger pageants usually include non-Indigenous producers, who may have experience in non-Indigenous pageantry. However, smaller community pageants are often Napo Runa spaces, in which local aesthetic preferences, knowledge, and traditions are foregrounded. As pageants move through the community, parish, cantonal, and provincial levels they become more highly produced and amplified. The largest events take place in coliseums with elaborate lighting and sound production. Smaller competitions might take place outside in communal gathering places like covered soccer fields, drawing crowds of several hundred people. Many events are free to the public, though there may be a cover charge to attend the larger pageants. Most Napo pageants feature three scored performances in addition to a final question-and-answer segment. The performances roughly correlate to three specific outfits, defined as traditional by participants and organizers.

In Napo, Kichwa pageants typically proceed in the following manner: Most are held on a weekend evening as part of a multi-day community festival. They begin around eight or nine in the evening, often lasting until the early morning hours. In addition to contestants, pageants feature performances by regional Kichwa dance groups and musicians, furthering their connection to the local ecology of media. Larger provincial pageants like Chunta Warmi and Wayusa Warmi may be "intercultural," combining the Indigenous and mestizo pageants into one event performed and judged simultaneously. Such was the case in Archidona in 2016 and 2017, when government austerity necessitated combining the pageants. Sometimes the events are held separately.

Contestants are introduced in an initial choreographed dance, wearing contemporary versions of traditional dress like the one-shouldered *pacha*. At many pageants, this means pacha in bright colors like hot pink or using faux animal skins, satin, or velvet textures, and embellishments of gold ricrac trim, rhinestones, and feathers. The pacha is a one-shouldered dress, usually made of dark blue fabric, referencing

---

3. Generally, the non-Indigenous pageants in Napo featured exclusively white-mestiza contestants drawn from the urban middle and upper classes of Tena and Archidona; more recently, Afro-Ecuadorian contestants have also entered these pageants.

historical forms of dress. During the 2017 intercultural Chunta Warmi pageant, Kichwa contestants wore blue sequined dresses that mirrored the white cocktail dresses worn by their non-Indigenous counterparts competing for Queen of Archidona. While the aesthetics of these events are often related to the past, they also clearly take place in the present. After this initial dance, ñusta contestants briefly introduce themselves to the audience in Kichwa.

The scored portion of the pageant begins with individual performances in traditional pacha dress, which roughly coincides with the "talent" portion of non-Indigenous pageants and allows contestants to demonstrate knowledge of significant Kichwa skills and practices. At one event, MCs Rita and James emphasized that these were presentations of "ruku kawsay" or traditional cultural practices—literally, the old way of life. Contestants may include their family and friends. Popular choices for presentations include performances of the wayusa upina and counseling between an elder and the young contestant; harvest and preparation of significant plants such as chunda (peach palm), guayusa leaves, or the fiber pita; scenes of hunting, fishing, and food preparation; the disciplining and strengthening application of hot pepper to the eyes known as *uchu churana*; medicinal practices such as steam baths or cleansings; and more. Some participants include these practices while they portray contemporary community tourism or agricultural activities, serving as guides to local cultures and ecologies for foreign visitors.

Many of these activities have long been indicative of women's knowledge and strength. Blanca Muratorio describes that for elder women terms such as "*allihuarmi* (beautiful woman)" and "*sabiruhuarmi* (wise woman)" are given to women "in whom knowledge, skill, and physical beauty complement each other as expressed in her everyday practices" (1998, 414). Muratorio also notes that pan-Indigenous political discourses tend to "[naturalize] women's identities, most commonly by stereotypical female identification with Mother Earth" (1998, 411). Pageants often emphasize women's environmental knowledge. Yet, these are feminine practices that feature in elder women's nostalgic memories, and in their critiques of young women's behavior. In these settings, young women not only bring to life traditional practices but also show themselves to be capable guides and entrepreneurs. Pageantry can be a launching board for a further career in politics and media. I also know several women who went on to become the *chagra mamaguna* (garden mothers) they depicted on stage—wives and mothers who utilize their skills and knowledge to feed their families through agroforestry and the cultivation of manioc.

Young women and their supporters negotiate, accommodate, and challenge internal and external expectations of Indigenous women through these pageants. The next segment is called *traje de muyu*, or "seed outfit," replacing the swimsuit segment of non-Indigenous pageants. This seems to be a more recent innovation of Napo pageantry, as Rogers (1998, 66–67) reports that in the early 1990s, bikini-style outfits were disfavored for violating norms of modesty, while evening gowns were common. During my research on pageants in 2015, 2016, and 2017, the seed ensemble was an unsurprising feature of all pageants, but evening gowns were almost entirely absent. Beaded outfits are sometimes justified as ways women dressed in the historical past prior to missionization (see also Erazo and Benitez 2022, 159). This is a way of imagining a past in which women are scantily clad but still dressed—a significant way in which Kichwa define themselves in opposition to other Amazonian groups like the Waorani (Muratorio 1991, 151). Some contestants push their imagination of the past beyond the comfort of pageant organizers. In 2016, the contestant from Archidona for Ñusta Napu Marka surprised the crowd by appearing on stage hidden behind a large leaf, which, when lowered, revealed that was she was wearing only black body paint (likely representing designs painted with *wituk* dye), seed necklaces, and a black bikini bottom. Municipal organizers admonished the next year's contestants in Archidona to avoid "exhibitionism." The 2016 contestant, however, went on to win the title of Miss Napo. She has remained active in regional media production. These performances also include representations of contemporary practices. Another contestant (figure 11) demonstrated producing and selling the fruit *naranjilla* to a colonist during her presentation, then danced with the money "earned" in the transaction.

The final segment is known as *makikutuna* in reference to an outfit consisting of a long-sleeved blouse with square neckline and a straight wrapped skirt (*anaku*), fastened with a woven belt (*chumbi*), further adorned by a woven shigra bag and a necklace of rainbow beads known as a *wallka*. This segment corresponds to the evening gown segment in

FIGURE 11 A contestant wearing "traje de muyu" dances during the cultural pageant in San Pablo de Ushpayaku. April 6, 2017. Photo by the author.

other pageants, semiotically elevating historical Kichwa dress to the level of formality held by ball gowns. Members of AMUPAKIN were concerned with whether young women had adorned themselves with wallka during pageants. The midwives explained the importance of the wallka in terms of the environmental meanings of the different colors of beads. The makikutuna segment is where young women demonstrate their skills in traditional dance. Elder women frequently discuss how their female elders danced and sang while serving aswa, moving their long black hair with the rhythm of the music (Muratorio 1998, 416). These practices come to life again in pageantry. Although Kichwa pageants feature both electronic and acoustic Kichwa music, the makikutuna dance is typically performed to an older, non-amplified song.

As public events, pageants and other performances in Napo address multiple audiences. These pageants may activate specific memories and forms of knowledge for Kichwa people that are not immediately evident or may appear stereotypical to outside audiences. As in all forms of semiotic practice, the signs deployed in such pageants will have distinct semiotic grounds for different audience members. For some, these pageants stress forms of environmental knowledge about forest-based subsistence undergoing shift in many communities, in ways that have reinforced the value and persistence of chagra garden systems and food products (Perreault 2005). For others, the signs recruited in such pageants are essentialized icons of feminine Amazonian indigeneity. Through the lens of cultural performance and representation (Rogers 1998, 1996; Wroblewski 2014), participants don historical and imagined forms of dress of the past, representing social figures that are more "ideal" than "real."

Among many Upper Napo Kichwa community radio producers, media consumers, and cultural organizations, public media events become ways of reanimating, or bringing back to life, figures from the past in the present. Many of the signs treated in prior analyses as essentialized icons or as "play acting" of native rituals are often interpreted contiguously with contemporary homes by cultural producers, participants, and many audience members, as well as with how they remember and imagine the past. In these programs, participants define and reconnect to interactional practices, lifeways, and material forms that have been increasingly ruptured in the contemporary context of settler colonialism. Not just some spurious "invented tradition" or mimetic performance of "real" culture, these programs create opportunities through which cultural practices—such as the wayusa upina—can be remediated across contexts and reanimated across sites of production and generations.

From Cultural Performance to Reanimation

The first live wayusa upina program on *A New Path* took place in early March 2016 at AMUPAKIN, a few months after I began observations with the program. The municipal communications staff installed a mobile internet link, bringing along mixing boards and microphones, to transmit the broadcast to local radio partners. The broadcast took place in the building that served as AMUPAKIN's kitchen, a large rectangular building of wooden posts and bamboo slats. In one corner, the midwives arranged a bamboo *gaytu* (sleeping platform) and two tripod-like stone *tullpa* (hearths) nearby to brew wayusa. Several midwives, two of their husbands, and a few grandchildren participated in the performance, with most wearing traditional dress like the makikutuna for women and the dark blue *kushma* and short pants for men. Several baskets, bundles of plants, and traditional handicrafts completed the scene. As the program began, the participants acted out slumbering by the fire. One of the members imitated the call of the *kukupa* owl, the sign to awaken before dawn and begin preparations for the day. An elder man called out to his wife and family to prepare wayusa. Over the next two hours, the members of AMUPAKIN participated in bringing to life the practice of the wayusa upina, using the familiar sounds of Upper Napo Kichwa.

The program sought to reconnect audiences to contemporary and historical practices that continue in many homes, but which are no longer materially possible in many others. These programs attempted to create a historically grounded, collective memory of what they called "our own" language and culture, authenticated through mass media, as a communal site of remembering in the face of "forgetting" or cultural shift. Rita and James repeated on air that their wayusa upina existed "so that we don't forget our elders' lifeways," *ñukanchi ruku kawsayra ama kungaringak.* Discursive genres including interviews, narratives, musical performances, and interactions between elders and young people combined with signs like bird calls and acoustic instrumentation to reanimate a past home on the air.

Sound, however, was just one modality for memory in these performances. Though produced for the radio, the programs were accompanied by often-elaborate live reenactments of the morning hours. These productions were incomplete without the material reanimation of the familial hearth and home for their live audiences. Yet, the complex multimodal scenes framing the show were largely undescribed and inaccessible to the listening audience. After the first wayusa upina at AMUPAKIN, I asked Rita why the hosts mostly did not describe or narrate the events taking place, instead letting the action unfold on air. She answered that members of their audience would be able to imagine what was occurring. *A New Path*'s programs relied on the experiential connections of their various audience members to bring them fully to life. In person, these productions must be fully embodied reanimations of elders' narrative chronotopes (Bakhtin 1981b) of the past to be considered successful. The loss of the other semiotic modes on the air, however, is a constraint of radio media (Goffman 1981b).

The emphasis on cultural pageantry and performance in Napo indicates a preference for transmitting history "in front of the eyes" and for experiential learning, as the "words of the elders" are reanimated on stage and on air. Anthropologist Margarita Huayhua (2020) describes that in Peru, Quechua villagers have similar preferences for bringing the past to life in the present. For Southern Peruvian Quechua communities, she explains, the past is not contained "in a third-person narrative that looks like a history book or even a courtroom testimony." Rather, her interlocutors prefer to "[bring] the past into the living present—it is *ñawpaqniykipi*, in front of your eyes or in front of the eyes" (Huayhua 2020). Huayhua's interlocutors were concerned with bringing the past to life through community film telling their history, from their perspective. In Southern Peruvian Quechua and Amazonian Kichwa, the word *ñawpa* refers to the front of one's body and the past, while Amazonian Kichwa refers to the future as *washa*, one's back. Canessa observes that Aymara speakers follow similar spatial and temporal patterns, and "the future is thus behind, unknowable and invisible, and the past is in front, visible through personal knowledge but also through communication with the ancestors" (Canessa 2012, 32).

For many of the elder members of AMUPAKIN, their participation in programs like the live wayusa upina staged on *A New Path* were not about performing a character. Rather, these women described themselves as bringing to life temporally displaced social figures and practices—those of their past selves, as well as mothers, aunts, and grandmothers. Diverse media forms, including speech, clothing, face paint, crafts, and staple foods, among others, on and around their contemporary bodies served as technes of animation. Explorations of "animation" as an alternative to "performance" in linguistic anthropology emphasize how agents bring variously mediated characters—such as cartoons, digital avatars, and puppets—to life (Silvio 2010; Manning and Gershon 2013; Nozawa 2013, 2016; Gershon 2015). At stake are the ways that a diversity of media and agents, human and nonhuman alike, are drawn together to create "the effect of a unified living character" (Manning and Gershon 2013, 109). Think of how social figures or characters are brought to life in cosplay. In their performances, Napo Kichwa communities utilize signs drawn from their memories of the historical past, more distant oral history, and from people's imagination of the pre-conquest world. They are also familiar with widely circulating expectations of indigeneity and incorporate these strategically into their presentations.

María Antonia Shiguango, the founder AMUPAKIN, explained members wear the clothing of ruku kawsay (old lifeways) to honor their mothers and fathers when participating in cultural presentations and media productions. Contemporary elder women remember being taught to paint their faces with bold red *manduru* (achiote) fruit before planting manioc, a sign of blood and the maternal relationship between a woman and the tubers. Others remember their parents adorning themselves with manduru and feathered crowns, and many styles of dress—the blue, one-shouldered pacha, or the purple kushma gathered and pinned at each shoulder—that are commonly worn in Upper Napo Kichwa performance media. For many, they or their parents were of the generations discouraged from such practices by an encroaching and discriminatory settler society.

On the programs, participants shift from narratively animating the lessons of their elders to using bodies as a medium to reanimate their stories. These programs are sites where narrative lessons from elders are recontextualized and reanimated for new audiences. Excerpts are drawn from the wayusa upina broadcast in the community of Santa Rita on September 13, 2016, introduced in chapter 3. Mama Olga's description, which grounds the practices of the wayusa upina in her elders' knowledge and practices, shows how narrative testimonies of elders' practices are reanimated on the air. When Rita asks Olga "what did [your] grandfathers and grandmothers counsel?" Olga discursively reanimated the scene as it occurred in her childhood, before she voiced the speech of counsel (kamachina) of her female relatives, directly embedding their words into her story using the verb *nina* or "to say."

"Santa Rita Wayusa Upina," kamachina excerpt 1.1–1, September 13, 2016

Rita: Imara kamachinuk akai ruku yaya**Kuna** ruku mama**Kuna** kay punzhayana**Kunai**, Mama Olga yallichipay ña?[1]

Olga: Kay ñawpa punda, ña waysara upikanchi.[2] Ña chiwasha, kay ñukanchi ruku mamauna ñawpa kasna rasha, shigrara awasha, mashti, katusha ganana anmi **nisha kamachikuna** anmi.[3]

Rita: What did [your] grandfathers and grandmothers counsel [you] when the dawn was breaking, Mama Olga please demonstrate, ok?[1]

Olga: First, we drank guayusa.[2] Then after that, our female elders **counsel us, saying** "first doing it like this, weaving shigra, um, selling [them], [you] have to earn [money]."[3]

There are several interesting features of the speech in this excerpt, bolded in excerpt 1.1–1. In line 1, for instance, Rita seems to utilize some pronunciations associated with Unified Kichwa, such as the plural form [kuna] rather than [guna] or [una] associated with Upper Napo Kichwa. Olga, however, uses a distinctly regional register. Further, in this excerpt of line 3, the grammar leads Olga to voice the speech of her grandmothers and mark it with the quotative phrase using *nisha*:

(3)

nisha kamachikuna anmi

ni -sha kamachi -k -una a -n-mi

say-SS counsel -AG -PL COP-3-EPST[4]

"they (would) counsel us, saying . . ."

Olga switches from the past tense in line 2 to the present tense in line 3 as she describes the counsel of her elders, with the grammar suggesting their contemporaneity.

Speakers of Upper Napo Kichwa describe themselves as "not forgetting" (*mana kungarina*) their elders and their knowledge by "living" (*kawsana*) their words and practices in daily life. They are *animators* in Goffman's sense (1981a) for the words of others, who may be projected as *figures* of the interaction (see also Manning and Gershon 2013; Irvine 1996). These roles and figures may "leak" across contexts and frames of interaction (Irvine 1996), allowing the past to slip into the present through the inclusion of its voices. These interactional roles are particularly important in Upper Napo Kichwa narrative practices, in which tellers transmit words and knowledge passed down through oral tradition, marking the speech of others with the verb *nina*, "to say," therein reanimating figures of their elders through their speech (Nuckolls 2008, 76). The grammatically direct reporting of elders' speech is one strategy to "remember" their knowledge and practices in the present.

Bodies are another modality to bring the past into the present, as gesture and embodied forms bring the narrated event to life. The members

---

4. I follow Karolina Grzech's analysis that the enclitic -*mi* in Tena Kichwa is a marker of "epistemic primacy," defined as "the relative right to know or claim" (Grzech 2016, 89).

REANIMATING KICHWA IN NAPO'S MEDIA ECOLOGY

of AMUPAKIN once complained about young women who wore shoes during a cultural parade, when elder members of their organization usually went barefoot, even when walking on public streets. For them, walking barefoot indexed the embodied habits of their mothers, who had walked barefoot through the forest before the introduction of rubber boots. Media production and other cultural events, then, create spaces in which these practices can be lived and remember, even temporarily, in public.

In this second excerpt from the program, Rita talks with Mama Olga, and together they discursively animate for the listening audience the social figures of *paya*, an affection term for female kin, which can be applied to sisters, aunts, cousins, and friends, as well as young girls. In this exchange, Rita and Olga use speech to bring these women to life on the air. Meanwhile, the female figures projected by their speech and by community residents moved to serve guayusa to the family gathered by the fireside, as well as to the larger co-present audience.

"Santa Rita Wayusa Upina," preparing guayusa, September 13, 2016

Rita: Alimi, shinakpi kayma kikindalla kuna maykan payagunara kumbirangaraunchi kay waysa yakura yanungak?$_{23}$

Olga: Kay payauna, kimsa payaunami tianun.$_{24}$

Rita: Ña shutira rimapay.$_{25}$

Olga: Lourdes Alvarado, Gloria Andi, y mashti, como se llama? *ay*! y . . . [asina] Denise Chimbo.$_{26}$

Rita: Ña payna yanungaranun.$_{27}$ Kuna payna imasnara rashara yananuk akai?$_{28}$ [xxx] panga mayllasha, shinakpi chayta kwintapay.$_{29}$

Olga: Shu mangawara apisha, waysa pangara sumakta mayllasha, kiwichisha mangai churasha

Rita: Very good, so, here like this now who are the sisters we will invite to brew this infusion of waysa?$_{23}$

Olga: These sisters, there are three sisters.$_{24}$

Rita: Now tell us their names please.$_{25}$

Olga: Lourdes Alvarado, Gloria Andi, and um [Sp. what's her name?] ay! and . . . [audience laughter] Denise Chimbo.$_{26}$

Rita: Ok, they're going to prepare it.$_{27}$ Now how would they used to have prepared it?$_{28}$ [unintelligible] washing the leaves, so tell us about that please.$_{29}$

Olga: To serve [wayusa] you have to take a little pot, wash the

yanusha upichina anmi.[30]	waysa leaves very well, twist
Shina, shina rasha ñawpa-	them up, put them in the pot,
mandas shina rikuchikuna	and brew them.[30] Doing it
anmi ñukanchi ruku mam-	like that from before too our
auna.[31] Chitami kuna chita	grandmothers have shown
paktachingaranun payguna.[32]	us.[31] That's what they are
	going to carry out now.[32]

In this excerpt, Rita and Olga link the social figures of *payaguna*, "daughters," to the women serving guayusa, connecting their actions to the way their grandmothers showed them how to do things "from before," as described in line 31. Throughout this segment, material practices and nondiscursive signs are co-enregistered with regional forms of speech, as both Olga and Rita utilize a regional register of Upper Napo Kichwa to describe them. In this section of the transcript there are no forms indicative of Unified Kichwa. Participants regularly use the form *waysa*, the casual, regionally inflected pronunciation heard around hearths in Archidona, as women call out "waysa, waysa" into the darkness of the early hours before dawn.

The analytic of animation shifts attention from presumed gaps between performers and their roles to how social characters are co-constructed by their animators, audiences, and media forms. Animation draws attention to the lamination of various modalities to construct a character (Silvio 2010, 429). These laminations are evident in puppetry (Barker 2019a, 2019b) in which various communicative modes and media forms—the puppet itself, the staging, and actors' voices—create a character or figure from their confluence. In embodied animations, such as *A New Path*'s wayusa upina broadcasts or ñusta pageants, participants breathe life into social figures and interactional spaces, assembled in collaboration with a team of producers. These figures are further animated through their reception by co-present and listening audiences, who intersubjectively imbue them with various meanings and values.

Upper Napo Kichwa productions—though primarily directed toward Kichwa speakers in the canton of Archidona and other regions in Napo— are part of a larger process of branding of Indigenous culture, carried out by local and national government, as well as NGOs and community tourism groups. Archidona's director of tourism explained that municipal support for the ñusta and reina pageants was intended to develop the canton's potential as a tourist destination, partly by highlighting the physical beauty of local women, as well as the area's cultural richness. As Erazo and Benitez have noted (2022, 158), beauty pageants contribute to developing tourism projects in Napo, which involve the overt sexualization of women. *A New Path*'s live broadcasts were also framed as a potential tourist attraction, though with less sexual overtones. The concept of animation further speaks to a moment in which content creation and branding are becoming some of the dominant modes of engaging in the "new economy." As Silvio suggests, social actors now see "the brand as the primary repository of value and branding as a precondition for action in the world" (Silvio 2010, 431). Audience members may invest these social figures and worlds with different kinds of life, imaginatively co-constructing a particular social figure from the different semiotic modalities that cohere in bodies and scenes.

In radio broadcasts and live pageants, my interlocutors sought to remediate and reanimate both their elders' lifeways and their contemporary present on air. These productions inscribed a mass-mediated version of embodied history, arising to interact with the present. Yet, these programs are often polyphonic, as the oral and aural affordances of radio media allowed a range of contemporary voices and codes to emerge on the air. Embodied media affords ongoing processes of accommodation and adjustment among regional and standardized forms, creating space for multiple fashions of speaking to coincide together.

What Should a Kichwa Woman Sound Like?

Napo pageantry regiments the practices, aesthetics, and behavior of Kichwa women in several ways, including language. Wroblewski (2014) notes that beauty pageants have been tied to language unification through an "intercultural code" in which limited, highly marked features of Unified Kichwa are mixed with regional dialect forms. Yet, Archidona's pageants were a site of debate about the voice with which young Indigenous women speak as representatives of their communities and families, reflecting larger issues in Indigenous communities about how to represent themselves through language to each other and to outsiders

(Graham 2002). As Mayor Shiguango said, he "opposed" the practices of language unification. I have observed several pageants in Napo at various stages of production, and language practices are complex.

Contestants generally have two opportunities to speak in the pageants—in their initial introductions and in the final question-and-answer segment. Both sections present challenges to young speakers to demonstrate mastery of a genre of public, political speech once more difficult for women to acquire (Rogers 1998, 68). Women were once less likely to be bilingual in Spanish and Kichwa than men, and many of the elder and adult women with whom I work still prefer Kichwa. Indigenous women in the Andes are frequently seen as *more* Indigenous than their male counterparts, partly because of their perceived lack of proficiency in Spanish (Canessa 2012, 271; De la Cadena 2000). Regional scholars suggest that Indigenous women have frequently been excluded in politics (Picq 2018; Muratorio 1998), as well as from the forms of speech used in them (Harvey 1994; Harris 1980). Harvey (1994, 46) identifies several features of Spanish political speechmaking used in Bolivia, which include long, complex utterances; specialized vocabulary; reference to names and dates; use of proverbs and clichés; and particular intonation patterns. Limerick (2020) notes standardized greetings in Unified Kichwa are used in public meetings and political spaces, which calque the conventions of Spanish greetings into Kichwa. Such greetings make Kichwa commensurate with Spanish, but usually only frame events, as speakers switch into Spanish.

In ñusta events, standardized greetings like *ali tuta*, "good evening," are mobilized by young women, who attempt to command a standardized register for public speaking. In the excerpts of self-introductions by Contestants 1 and 3, speakers utilize several forms suggestive of language standardization, including the de-voiced [k]. Morphology utilizing Unified forms is underlined and bolded, while regionally unexpected sounds are capitalized for emphasis (following Wroblewski 2014). For example, the form -**manTa** shows that the speaker has used the Unified morpheme -*manta*, usually realized with the voiced consonant -*manDa* in Napo. For speakers of English dialects this might be somewhat akin to whether one pronounces the "tt" of *butter* as a "t" or a "d" sound. While seemingly minor, listeners notice these differences.

Self-introduction by Pitak Waska Ñusta Contestant 1, June 17, 2016

Ali tuta nisha, **alichani**.₁ Ñuka shut-imi **Kan** [Ñusta 1].₂ Gustu kushiwa shamuni San Rafael ayllu llakta-**manTa**.₃ Ashka**Ta yupaychani!**₄

I greet [you] by saying "good evening".₁ My name is [Contestant 1].₂ I come with the greatest joy from the community of San Rafael.₃ Thank you very much!₄

Self-introduction by Pitak Waska Ñusta Contestant 3, June 17, 2016

Ali tuta nisha **alichani** tukuy apu**Kuna**ra, ayllu**Kuna**ra, mashi-**Kuna**ra.₁₄ Ñuka shutimi **Kan** [Ñusta 3].₁₅ Shamuni kay **kiti** llakta Chaka Rumi ayllu llakta**manTa**.₁₆ Ashka**Ta** pagarachuni.₁₇

Saying 'good evening' I greet all the leaders, family, and friends.₁₄ My name is [Contestant 3].₁₅ I come from this community of Chaka Rumi, a family commu-nity.₁₆ Thank you very much!₁₇

Interestingly, Contestant 3 blends the use of more regional direct object marker [-ra] in line 14, while she uses the pronunciation [-ta] in final line 17. Moreover, in line 17 she also utilizes the regional form pagarachuni, rather than the yupaychani of her competitor. Despite individual variations, these introductions follow a formula common in public events, in which speakers introduce themselves, where they are from, and greet their listening audience (Limerick 2020, 211). Emphasis on the speaker's positive affect and emphatic intonation further shape the conventions of this register.

The makikutuna dance presentation usually leads into the final question-and-answer portion of the competition. Many pageants once included bilingual question-and-answer sessions in which candidates had to respond in both Spanish and Kichwa (Rogers 1998, 69; Erazo 2013, 184). In most pageants I observed, the question was asked and answered in Kichwa, though the original written questions given to hosts and con-testants were likely in Spanish. It is an open secret that contestants pre-viously receive these questions, allowing them to attempt to memorize prepared responses in Kichwa. Some did so in consultation with more fluent relatives and elders. This is one way that educators and activists have sought to move young students from the ideological role of listener discussed in the prior chapter, to a role of speaker by encouraging their participation in public life. Like the broader transformation of women's public participation, this is also a relatively new practice for Kichwa communities, who generally equate authority with age and life experience (Erazo and Benitez 2022, 162; Mezzenzana 2020). However, many of the questions posed in pageants ask young participants to speak about significant political, cultural, and economic issues in the region.

The first examples (table 4) are drawn from the 2016 election of the Pitak Waska Ñusta (Princess of Pita) in the Union of Kichwa Communities of Amarun Rumi (UCKAR). This event was themed around the local product pita (also spelled *pitak* or *pitaj*).[5] Pita was extracted from Kichwa people as tribute during the colonial period (Oberem 1980, 94). It is still used to weave shigra bags and other implements. To my knowledge, participants in this event did not receive instructions to speak "local Kichwa." Rita hosted the evening competition with James.

Rita's and contestants' speech from this pageant demonstrate more standardized forms than at the Chunta Warmi pageant held in 2017. I have provided a rough estimate of the proportion of speech suggesting some degree of influence from the standard by counting the total number of *words* in each utterance, and dividing these by the total number of *morphemes* that evidence a likely standardized phonological or morphological structure; some words have more than one standardized feature. This is not intended to provide an exact measurement of Unified Kichwa but to give a general sense of how seemingly standardized features are deployed in public speech.

The speech deployed in this pageant closely fits Wroblewski's (2014) analysis of the "intercultural code," in which a few highly salient features of Unified Kichwa are mixed with regional forms of speech. Contestant 1, a young woman named Karen Pizango, incorporated eleven tokens representative of Unified Kichwa within forty-nine words, approximately 22.4 percent of her speech. Most notable is the plural marker

---

5. The most frequent pronunciation of this term is [pita] though the word is often written as "pitak" and sometimes as "pitaj." This may be a case of orthographic hypercorrection related to Unified Kichwa norms. In Napo Kichwa the interrogative "who" is realized as "pita," while Unified Kichwa prescribes the spelling "pitak" (Ministerio de Educación del Ecuador 2009, 38). There may be transference from this norm, which is then refracted through prior orthographies in which the <k> of Unified Kichwa in word final position was written as <j>.

TABLE 4 Pitak Waska Ñusta, Q&A with winner Karen Pizango, June 17, 2016

Speaker	Kichwa	English free translation	Morphemes/ Words
Rita:	Tapungaraushkanchi, kan ñusta warmi tuku**shPa** kay UCKAR organización uku**manTa**, imasna rashara yanapangaraungui ñukanchi kikin allpayuk sumaktalla tarpusha awayachisha apangak kay UCKAR llakta**Pi**?₁	We will have asked you: if you become Miss Princess of Pita of UCKAR, how are you going to help our landholders to improve the valuable agriculture with the community of UCKAR?₁	3/22 (13.6%)
#1:	Kan rimashkara kutipasha.₂ UCKAR**Pi** wangurishka ayllugunara, imasna tarpuk muyu**Kuna**ra, wiwa**Kuna**ra sumakta tarpusha mirachisha ali katina anga.₃ UCKAR apu**Kun**-**a**wa yanaparisha, pay**Kuna**wa kikin allpamanda apu**Kuna**ra mañasha tarpuk muyu**Kuna**ra, wiwa**Kuna**ra, sumakta tarpunara, mirachinara yachangak.₄ Chasna rurashami ali, kay cacao, cafia, waysa inzhik, sara, **atallPa**, aychawa.₅ Chasna rashami awama apana anga.₆ Ashka**Ta yupaychani**!₇	I will respond to your question.₂ For the families of the organization UCKAR, how must we continue planting and raising the animals well?₃ With the support of the leaders of UCKAR, we will ask the leaders of our own land for seeds to plant, for animals, to know how to plant and raise them well.₄ Doing it in that way, [with] this cacao, coffee, guayusa, peanut, corn, chicken, and fish.₅ In that way, we will advance.₆ Thank you very much!₇	11/49 (22.4%)

-*kuna*, more commonly pronounced as -*guna* or even with elision and dipthongization, as in [mamauna] or [mamawna], "mothers," in Napo. Similarly, she and other contestants use the forms -pi for the locative, often voiced as [-bi] or a diphthongized [-j] in Napo, sounding more like "llaktay" than "llaktapi." In line 5, she likewise used a [p] sound in the word *atallpa* (chicken), a pronunciation that causes consternation for some grandmothers. Pizango evidenced the most Unified Kichwa in her speech, though she was closely followed by the runner-up, who used sixteen Unified tokens within seventy-five words, or roughly 21.3 percent of her speech. The third-place contestant likewise incorporated standardized forms, but struggled to produce her speech, receiving jeers from the crowd. Pizango was crowned Pitak Waska Ñusta. She went on to participate in the 2017 Chunta Warmi competition as the representative of UCKAR.

When hosts and participants received explicit instructions to utilize "local Kichwa" like their elders, the forms used were somewhat different. Compare Rita's speech while hosting the 2016 pageant to the examples in table 4 from the 2017 Chunta Warmi pageant, which emphasized local speech. In 2016, Rita's turns of talk incorporated 10–30 percent Unified Kichwa features during the Q&A segment. However, in 2017, only two of her utterances in this Q&A segment included markedly Unified forms.[6] Rita can adeptly shift the codes she uses, from a more Unified, "intercultural" form to a more regionalized form, depending on audience, interlocutor, and setting, skills which she honed as a host of the radio program *A New Path*. In lines 1–6 of the excerpt from 2017 (table 5), Rita demonstrates more switches to Spanish (marked in italics) than to standardized forms. Compared to Rita's speech in 2016, several standardized features are absent, including the morpheme *-shpa*. Notably, Rita does use the verb *yallichina* (roughly "to advance, move ahead") which interlocutors in Napo have identified as a Unified neologism.

Despite instructions from pageant organizers and Rita's modeling of local dialect, several of the contestants in the Chunta Warmi pageant spoke with Unified features. Consider the examples from Contestant 1 and Contestant 4 in tables 6 and 7, in which more than approximately 25 percent of the utterances are influenced by Unified forms.

Despite the presence of Unified Kichwa forms and Spanish syntax in the first contestant's speech, several of the midwives had overall positive evaluations of both the content and the fluidity with which it was delivered. Ultimately, Contestant 1 received third place in the competition, suggesting that the presence of Unified morphology and phonology was

---

6. In this chapter, I have not marked the word *chay* (that) as a Unified form due to its bivalency with regional dialects of Amazonian Kichwa, though the more expected form in Napo in these contexts would usually be *chi*. In Napo, chay can mean "that, over there," but it is also the form of the demonstrative mandated by Unified Kichwa. The transcriptionists I worked with did not comment specifically on this term. Due to the elision of names, some word counts vary slightly between these transcripts and the analyzed transcripts.

TABLE 5 Chunta Warmi Ñusta, Q&A for Contestant 1, April 21, 2017

Speaker	Kichwa	English free translation	Morphemes/ Words
Rita	Kuna kay ratuway kangunara kikindalla mañauni chay ña sumaktalla chunlla asha uyangak.[1] Payguna ñuka tapushkara kutipasha **yallichi**ngaraunun.[2]	I now request that you all are very quiet to listen.[1] They will now take us forward by responding to my questions.[2]	1/17 (5.8%)
	Chaywa kumbirana munani . . . chaywa kumbirana munani ñukanchi ñawpa punda *candidata representante de la parroquía Cotundo*, [Ñusta 1].[3]	With that I want to invite . . . with that I want to invite our first *candidate, representative of Cotundo parish*, [Contestant 1].[3]	0/19
Rita	<<Tiaukguna: wooooooow!>> Mañaunchi sumaktalla uyangak.[4]	<<Audience: wooooooow!>> We are asking you to all listen well.[4]	0/3
Rita	[Ñusta 1], *municipio* wasi *rutas turisticas* nishkara **yallichi**shka ima sami pishku, *cacao y chocolate, petroglifos.*[5] Kay iyarisha, imara munaringui yanapangak?[6]	[Contestant 1], the *municipality* has developed what's called the *"Tourist Route"* about birds, *cacao and chocolate*, and petroglyphs.[5] Considering this, what would you want to help?[6]	1/19 (5.2%)

not a complete disqualifier in Archidona. As seen in table 7, Contestant 4 made a shorter speech containing thirteen Unified tokens within thirty-two words. Unlike Contestant 1, the speech was more halting and obviously memorized, and elicited boos from the audience.

The midwives evaluated that Contestant 4 had made "mistakes" in her speech, though they were hesitant to identify them. However, the word yupaychani detracted from several speeches that my interlocutors otherwise enjoyed. It was also somewhat unusual for her to refer to the language as "Kichwa" rather than "runa shimi" in line 37.

While I was seated in the audience with AMUPAKIN's founder, María Antonia Shiguango, she commented that she thought the contestants from UCKAR and San Pablo would take the top two spots. Her predic-

TABLE 6 Chunta Warmi Ñusta, Q&A, response by Contestant 1, April 21, 2017

Speaker	Kichwa	English free translation	Morphemes/ Words
#1	Kay ñukanchi Archiruna **kiti**, Cotundo **kiti** charin sumak kallari pacha**KunamanTa**.[7] Killkashka rumi**Kuna** charin San Augustin.[8] Cavernas Jumandi, Boa Loma, Rumi Ñawi, Awayakupi, shinalla**Ta** charin yachak rumi**Kuna**, pacha**Kuna**, sacha ukuk**Kuna**, shinalla**Ta** kucha**Kuna**.[9] Kay**Kuna**mi mana killkashkachu **Kan**.[10] Chay**man-Ta**mi yanapayta mañanchi kay apu**KunaTa** kaychu killkashka achu chaybi charinchi.[11] Kay shinalla**Ta** mañani kay killkachu kaybi.[12] Ecuador mama llakta**Pi** chaybimi ushanchi kay ñukanchi**Ka** alilla rasha apa**ngaPak**.[13] Shinalla**Ta** kumbiranga ushanchi shuk laya [wangurishka] aylluguna**Ta**.[14] [Pay**Kuna**mi kay ayllu llakta**Ta** apamusha sumakta rasha apinuka].[15][a] Paygunami shinalla**Ta** ñukanchira yanapanuka kay [kulki**KunaTa**] mirachisha.[16] Chaywami ñukanchi Archiruna **kiti** sumakta alilla awama ringak.[17] **YUPAYCHANI!**[18]	Our canton Archidona, our [parish] Cotundo has beautiful [things] from the beginning times.[7] San Augustin has petroglyphs.[8] Cavernas Jumandi, Boa Loma, Rumi Ñawi, and Awayaku likewise have the powerful stones of the *yachak*, waterfalls, deep forest, and likewise lakes.[9] These are not written down.[10] That's why we request help from the authorities so that these places we have here are written down.[11] This is what I ask to be written down here.[12] In the country of Ecuador, there we can carry on by doing well.[13] Likewise we can invite families [grouped] of a different kind.[14] [They brought this family community, and doing well, received].[15][a] That's how they helped us by increasing our money.[16] With this, our canton of Archidona [can] go beautifully upward.[17] THANK YOU![18]	29/92 (31.5%)

[a] This translation proved challenging for the transcriptionists with whom I work. This speaker's syntax suggests influence of Spanish, such as in line 9, in which a SVO (subject-verb-object) structure is utilized, without regular object marking. This contrasts with the subject-object-verb syntax of Kichwa. As such, not all the speaker's meanings were evident to my consultants or me upon review, particularly in line 15. One consultant suggested that the contestant likely wanted to express the idea that "they had been organizing this community or town in a good way, and that is how they received it."

TABLE 7 Chunta Warmi Ñusta, Q&A, response by Contestant 4, April 21, 2017

Speaker	Kichwa	English free translation	Morphemes/ Words
#4	**Kiti kitilli** kawsak runa**KunawaN** wamburisha rina nisha ñukanchi kawsay**KunaTa** mana kungarinami **Kanchi.**$_{36}$ Tukuy**Kuna** washama sakikpi kay ñukanchi <u>kichwa</u> shimi**Pi** mana, mana kungarina **Kanchi.**$_{37}$ Chitaga . . . chitaga, sumak kushiwa pakllana apana **Kanchi.**$_{38}$ Ashka**Ta yupaychani!**$_{39}$	Uniting with the people who live in this parish, we should not forget our lifeways.$_{36}$ [Even] if we leave everything behind, this our Kichwa language, we must not forget.$_{37}$ This . . . this we should openly carry forward with happiness.$_{38}$ Thank you so much!$_{39}$	13/32 (40.6%)

tion following their speeches was correct. Ñusta Pitak Warmi of UCKAR Karen Pizango (Contestant 6) ultimately won the title of Chunta Warmi 2017. Her 2017 speech (table 8) had less influence from Unified Kichwa than her speech in 2016 (table 4), as it included only six tokens within thirty-three words, or approximately 18 percent.[7]

Her competitor, Contestant 2 from San Pablo, earned second place with a speech (table 9) that included only two noticeably Unified tokens in thirty-four words. This was even fewer than the winning speech, with only approximately 6 percent of the utterance suggesting standardized influence.

Contestant 2's speech was well received by the audience, but the midwives noted her mistake of saying "yupaychani," rather than "pagarachu" or "pagarachuni." Where other pageants may have rewarded the greater facility with Unified forms demonstrated by Contestant 1, it was the two young women who most closely approximated local Kichwa who achieved the greatest success in Archidona's 2017 pageant. This is part of a larger attempt in Napo to realign the embodied repertoire (Taylor

---

7. In line 55, I have not marked the -*ta* object marker of "yanapayta" as standardized influence, as [ta] is the expected form following diphthongs in Napo. "Mishu" is also a standardized neologism, though it is widely accepted in Napo.

TABLE 8 Chunta Warmi Ñusta, Q&A, winning response by Contestant 6, April 21, 2017

Speaker	Kichwa	English free translation	Morphemes/ Words
Rita	[Ñusta 6], imara urzagunara tian ñukanchi llaktai, payta shinzhiyasha ringak?[53]	[Contestant 6], what forces are there in our community to continue strengthening itself?[53]	0/9
#6	Ñukanchi llaktara shinzhichingak, astawnba awama apangak sumak mu-skurisha, sumak yuyay**KunaTa** charingak, ama killa, ama llulla, ama shuwa.[54] Shinallara tukuy apugunawa rimari-sha yanapayta mañangak runa**Kuna**wa, **mishuKuna**wa tandarisha sumakta llanga-sha, ñukanchi llaktara awama apangak.[55] **YUPAYCHANI!**[56]	To strengthen our community, as well as to carry it upward, [we] dream well and have good thoughts, [like] "do not be idle, do not lie, do not steal."[54] Like this, speaking with all of the leaders to ask for their support, bringing together Indigenous people and *mishu* people, working together well, to carry our community higher.[55] THANK YOU![56]	6/33 (18.2%)

2003) of performance with the sounds of regional speakers in both the present and their remembrances of the past.

Mediating Linguistic Diversity

Although Mayor Shiguango opposed linguistic unification, *A New Path*'s broadcasts accepted a range of social actors. While most explicitly oriented toward members of a regional public, participants included politicians, bilingual educators, and other proponents of linguistic unification, making space for many fashions of speaking to emerge on the air. Radio's affordances allowed their shows to be interdiscursive and polyphonic. The past reanimated on the air was largely determined by its participants, making room for contestation and creativity in production. During *A New Path*'s programs, a variety of social figures could emerge—rural elders and adults, intercultural educators, as well as bilingual, bidialectal youth.

TABLE 9 Chunta Warmi Ñusta, Q&A, response by runner-up Contestant 2, April 21, 2017

Speaker	Kichwa	English free translation	Morphemes/Words
Rita	[Ñusta 2], runa shimira malta wanraguna kungarisha ri-nushka.[20] Kan iyarisha, imara ruranguima kayta **Hawayachi-sha** apangak?[21]	[Contestant 2], young people have been forgetting runa shimi.[20] Reflecting on this, what would you do to elevate this [our language]?[21]	1/14 (7%)
#2	Jumandi, Wami, Beto shinzhi makanushka washa yachachisha sakishkara mana kungarinami anchi.[22] Chaymanda ñusta warmi tukusha kangunara rinrichini, ima shina wasibi runa shimii rimanuzhu, killkagu-nai runa shimii killkanuzhu.[23] Chasna rashami ñukanchi shimi**Ta** mana chingachinanga.[24] **YUPAYCHANI!**[25]	We must not forget the lessons left by Jumandi, Wami, and Beto after their fierce struggle [with the Spaniards].[22] If I become Ñusta, I will counsel you how to speak runa shimi at home and how to write in runa shimi in text.[23] If we do this our language will not be made to disappear.[24] THANK YOU![25]	2/34 (5.8%)

Like ñusta pageants, radio broadcasts are sites where women become public speakers. Significantly, during the Santa Rita broadcast, Mama Olga utilized a familiar regional register, while navigating a formal register of regional Kichwa. This is evident from the moment she is introduced:

"Santa Rita Wayusa Upina," Mama Olga discusses wayusa upina, September 13, 2016

Rita: Ña shinami, Mama Olga, imasnara tuparingui?[20]

Olga: Ali punzha, kay ayllu llakta-manda tiaukguna, chimanda, shuk mashti, ñukanchi apuma, apuunara saludani kay punzhai.[21] 'Nakpi ñukanchi ñawpa, ñawpa timpu mam-auna kasna rasha, yanusha,

Rita: Ok, so, Mama Olga, how are you?[20]

Olga: Good day, to all the people here from this community, and also, one, uh, our leader, to our leaders I greet you to-day.[21] So, our grandmothers in the time before, doing it like this, brewing, getting up and

atarisha yanusha upikunami.	brewing they would drink. So
Abisba, machakuy ama	that snakes and bees wouldn't
kaningawa, tukuy ama killa,	bite, to keep from being lazy,
killangawa, sumak traban-	to work hard, that's all I have
gawa, chillami rimani.[22]	to say.[22]

Mama Olga's speech is distinctly marked by the regional variations of Upper Napo Kichwa. She consistently voices stops and affricates following nasals, as in [manda] and [pundʒa]. She also elides several sounds in ways that mark the speech of Upper Napo Kichwa. Like most others in the Archidona-Tena region, she reduces the durative realized in other regions as [ku] or [hu] to -u realized as [w] in [tiawxguna] and makes a fricative of the agentive -k in "those who are being here" in line 21. Similarly, she elides the [g] of the plural [guna], pronouncing [apu:na], and further marking it with the regional accusative -ra in line 21. In terms of lexicon, her Spanish-derived verb *saludana*, "to greet," contrasts with the neologism *alichana*, sometimes used in public discourse and radio media. In such segments, significant cultural icons like wayusa are reenregistered alongside the voices of regional speakers, linked to the authority of their elders in the past.

Olga's response demonstrates a familiarity, albeit halting, with the conventions of political discourse in Upper Napo Kichwa. The phrases *ayllu llakta* (familial settlement) and *apu* (leader) are part of the discourse of Indigenous politics in Napo, while ali punzha (good day) is a calque of Spanish *buenos días* widely used to frame intercultural political events (Limerick 2020). Andronis suggests that this is a form that was introduced into the Amazon through contact with Highland speakers, or which is at least ideologized as a Highland or Unified form (2004, 267). Contrasting these Spanish-derived greetings, some elders remember other interactional routines in the past. They call for people to greet each other by lightly touching their open palms together while loudly exclaiming *"chis!"*

Beyond the inclusion of women in public performance and politics, the public sphere of Napo's media ecology emphasizes remediation of women's domestic, intimate spaces. Public spaces have become popular sites of kamachina, narrative counseling, between elders and novices. Elders use the words left by their elders—familial history—and narratives of personal experience to advise young people on how to live. These sessions are often gendered. Counseling sessions generally occur organically during the wayusa upina of day-to-day interaction, as grandmothers, mothers, and daughters gather to weave shigra and drink guayusa. Counseling is remediated across sites of production, serving as a socialization routine on programs like *A New Path*. There has been a major shift in the genres of interaction in which women engage, and how their social histories are remediated and made public. *A New Path* shows the domestic sphere to be a central site of cultural revalorization and reclamation.

A New Path's programs play a complex role in the mediation of regional diversity. The affordances of oral and aural broadcast media allow multiple voices to emerge on air. Such programming extends media production to populations—particularly rural elders and adults—who are the audience, not the producers, of media. Mama Olga utilized regional patterns throughout her speech. The program's archive of community recordings is likewise shaped by the cadences of local speech. Speakers of more standardized varieties are still given space. When Grandfather Efraín, for instance, introduced the wayusa upina in Santa Rita, several of the forms he used suggested the norms of Unified Kichwa.

"Santa Rita Wayusa Upina," Grandfather Efraín awakens, September 13, 2016

Efraín: Ña shinakpi, mama**Kuna Ha-tariy**chi, churi**Kuna Hatariy**-chi, ña waysa upina pachami tukunchi atariychi, shamiy-chi, ña ruku kawsaunimi.[16]

Efraín: Ok with this, **mothers get up, sons get up**, we have come to the time to drink waysa, get up, come here, the old man is awake now![16]

Like many pageant contestants, Efraín utilized the plural morpheme [kuna] in *mamakuna* and *churikuna*, "mothers" and "sons." Mama Olga instead pronounced "mothers" as [mamawna] in her counsel. Efraín also utilized the Unified form [hatarina], though the initial consonant is generally elided to [atarina] in Napo, as it is almost immediately after in line 16. In many ways, his speech is also consistent with the regional cadences of the Upper Napo.

Kichwa speakers in Napo navigate a complex assemblage of language ideologies about different varieties of Kichwa. Where linguistic unification, at least in its most extreme form, prescribes one voice with which to write *and* to speak, the flexibility provided by the aural and oral affordances of radio media responds to multiple ways of using language. Broadcast media may transmit standardized forms, depending on the ideological commitments of the speaker. However, use of the intercultural code does not always mean support for this code. Mayor Shiguango explained, "Sometimes, so I don't come off poorly in other institutional spaces, I say 'yupaychani,' since it can be necessary to be neither too left-wing nor right-wing, right? It's better to keep joining together, right? But demanding what is fair, that we can't lose our own culture, our own language, what we speak." Although he "disagreed" with language unification, he also accommodated some of the norms of Unified Kichwa.

It is problematic to approach standardized forms—or forms that appear to be so—in broadcast media as support for the enregisterment of an oral standard. Though there are strong indexical connections between the forms employed in these transcripts and standardized forms of speech, individual speech practices are very complex. Many forms used in Unified Kichwa are bivalent with forms used in other regional varieties. For instance, cohost of *A New Path* James Yumbo often used "kana" for the copula, rather than "ana." At first this seems like the influence of Unified Kichwa, and it could be. But it also results from his familial linguistic history—his mother is a speaker of Coca Kichwa where the copula is kana, while his father is from Archidona, where it is ana. This bivalency may also make speakers—and listeners—more accepting of mixing.

In the ideologically fraught world of cultural revitalization, as Mayor Shiguango suggested, it is better to choose a middle path, while still "maintaining what is ours." Although several of the participants in this exchange incorporated some Unified variants, their use likely represents situational code-switching (Gumperz 1989), or perhaps register shifting, in response to the perceived linguistic stances of their conversational partners. While Rita and James mark themselves as familiar with the Unified "power code" (Wroblewski 2014; Hill and Hill 1986), it is a minor adjustment in their speech, which is for the most part consistent with the familiar register of Upper Napo Kichwa. In many interactions, speakers seem to choose a middle path between the norms of fully standardized language, while simultaneously maintaining "what is ours." These radio programs offer an alternative model of cultural and linguistic reclamation, one grounded in embodied interaction, which remembers the voices that many worry are being forgotten with the shift toward Spanish and Unified Kichwa.

Conclusion

Anthropologists of the Ecuadorian Amazon have largely described these forms of cultural pageantry as "performances," and as folkloric "representations" of culture. However, as Charles Briggs has written, "Folkloric performances are not simply repetitions of time-worn traditions; they rather provide common ground between a shared textual tradition and host of unique human encounters, thus preserving the vitality and dynamism of the past as they endeavor to make sense of the present" (1988, xv). An emphasis on performance has led past analysts to focus on the intertextual gaps between performer and role, between lived and performed reality, between the text and its context (Bauman and Briggs 1990). Rogers, in writing about "representation" in Archidona argues that "when social reality is consciously re-presented it undergoes a semiotic transformation that introduces a slippage between the representation and that which is represented" (1996, 77). Such slippage emerges in the infelicitous performance of Kichwa discourse by pageant contestants or in Olga forgetting the names of her fellow performers. These slippages introduce elements of the "uncanny" of animation (Silvio 2010) into these programs. Characterological figures are not always entirely lifelike, reminding viewers and listeners that these are not simply the intimate familial practices of their memories or their homes, but their public remediation and reconstitution in a new medium.

A New Path's remediation and reanimation of the wayusa upina, and the broader category of cultural pageantry of which it is part, are an iterative form of cultural practice, not just a performance of some preexisting reality. Mannheim (2018a) distinguishes between two notions of representation, which help to disentangle some of the analytical difference between performance and animation. In the first, what he calls "representation$_1$," language and cultural forms "stand for" an objective social reality. Here, ethnographers and other scholars decode the symbolic material of culture. Performance-oriented analyses of media productions, then, are akin to decoding a "representation$_1$" of the objective reality of cultural life. However, Mannheim's second form of representation, "representation$_2$," refers to the "essential properties" of an expression, as used in math, linguistics, and cognitive science. It is in this view of representation$_2$ that Mannheim finds the possibility of an ontological approach, or "an ethnographic view of language and culture as actively engaged in making the world we take for granted, rather than representing it" (2018a, 241–42). The concept of animation speaks to the ways in which a meaningful world is brought to life by participants. The live-broadcast wayusa upina is not just the familial event it remediates and reanimates from daily experience. It is its own contemporary practice—an emergent vitality (Perley 2013) on air and a way participants can continue to "remember" their elders' lifeways as mediated communities of practice.

Viewed through an analytic of reanimation, events like *A New Path*'s wayusa upina become sites in which language and culture are engaged in making the social world. Repeated instantiations of these productions contribute to the enregisterment of a range of signs—linguistic, visual, durable objects, activities and lifestyle practices—in a multimodal register (Ennis 2019a; Agha 2011, 2005), through which participants project figures of their elders. By reanimating contexts of interaction and figures of social personhood, both remembered and imagined, in the present, radio producers and participants make and remake, their social world. These productions are not meant to be "real," but hyperreal in the sense advocated by Biddle and Lea (2018, 6 original emphasis), referring to "art at work to make the real *more* real, when the real is itself what is at risk, at stake: namely, Indigenous history, language, presence, silence, denied, ignored." They are events attempting to remake a reality that has been ruptured by the social and material changes engendered by colonial policies and external regimes of value within which Napo Runa communities find themselves. Many confront a world in which they experience their culture and language as deeply threatened, as indicated by the decision of Carlos Alvarado—influential Upper Napo Kichwa musician and cultural activist—to entitle a book *Historia de una Cultura a la que se Quiere Matar* (The History of a Culture which They Want to Kill; 1994). Not just a "representation$_1$" or "play acting" of culture, these events are a site of cultural production, a new way of living culture in the present—a form of survivance (Vizenor 1994) in the face of ongoing threats to Napo's social and material world.

CHAPTER 5

Affective Technologies and Intimate Publics

Entering the kitchen around four in the morning, I found Serafina weaving by the fire with her family. Her adopted teenage son held a portable radio in his lap. He occasionally adjusted the volume, raising it for recordings of community stories to ascend above the ongoing conversation. A couple of Serafina's adult daughters were there with their toddlers, as were a daughter-in-law and an adolescent granddaughter. Serafina and her daughters were chatting in Kichwa about a locally recorded clip broadcast on *A New Path* (*Mushuk Ñampi*). That morning, *A New Path* was the wayusa hours' main accompaniment. The program became a point of discussion while people listened. Later in the day, listeners recirculated the stories, songs, news, and other speech they had heard on the air.

The ways Napo Runa communities produce, circulate, and react to local media show that radio and related media are significant means to encourage cultural maintenance and reclamation. The Napo ecology of media allows for the remediation of significant genres of Kichwa speech, verbal artistry, and action on air—including the wayusa upina and associated discourse genres. Media production is an effective and affective technology to create "emergent vitalities" (Perley 2011), new contexts and domains of use developing from reclamation projects. In the case of

---

Portions of this chapter first appeared in the article "Affective Technologies: Kichwa Women's Media Activism in the Ecuadorian Amazon." *Resonance* 1 (4): 376–93. https://doi.org/10.1525/res.2020.1.4.376.

Maliseet, Bernard Perley describes how new media serve as an emergent vitality as "the Internet and television make Maliseet discourses available to anyone who decides to access those discourses" (2011, 191). Linguist Joshua Fishman once questioned the possibilities of mass media for language revitalization, arguing that they "are insufficiently interpersonal, child oriented, affect suffused, societally binding to attain cumulative intergenerational mother tongue transmission" (1991, 374). This evaluation of media misses many of the ways that community media are produced and circulated in Napo, which can evoke affective responses and intergenerational interaction. Although media may not simulate the immersive socialization of "mother tongue transmission," they can be an important extension to face-to-face interactions.

In households like that of Serafina and Mariano, radio extended and amplified the knowledge and speech of elders, reinforcing it among their families. Like the Internet and television, radio makes discourse in Indigenous languages more accessible to wider audiences. The circulation of significant poetic forms and genres across contexts creates societal cohesion. Media contribute to the formation of collective memories (Taylor 2003; French 2012). They also create publics (Warner 2002; Papacharissi 2015), who are hailed by the culturally intimate (Herzfeld 2016) content of the local ecology of media. Mass media alone may not create new speakers through intergenerational transmission, but they can strengthen existing communities of practice and extend membership within them to new audiences. My abilities in Kichwa benefited from hours spent recording and transcribing radio programs and from participation in production events. My understanding of Kichwa further benefited from accompanying listeners as they commented upon programs. It was in these moments with listeners that I was introduced to the meaning of much of the media for the audiences that it addressed. It was also where I became familiar with contemporary genres of Kichwa verbal art and their conventions.

This chapter presents three genres of Kichwa verbal artistry to explore their remediation and ongoing circulation through Napo's ecology of media: laments, jokes, and local histories. These genres' circulation create what Zizi Papacharissi (2016) has called an "affective public," but one that responds to the remediated poetics (Jakobson 1968, 1961) of Kichwa media rather than the referential content of hashtags Papacharissi discusses. For Papacharissi, affective publics are "networked publics that are mobilized and connected, identified, and potentially disconnected through expressions of sentiment" (2016, 311). Napo's affective public is at least partly predicated on cultural intimacy, to use Michael Herzfeld's (2016 [1997]) term, in which shared recognition of potentially embarrassing or hidden practices nonetheless provides the basis for group cohesion. Unlike the anonymous, stranger sociality associated with Warner's formulation of publics (2002), this is an idea of the public grounded in intimacy and social recognition (Debenport 2017). Such intimacy shapes *wakana*, or songs of lament, principally performed by women. These laments are sung at funerals and in other intimate moments, as well as at public celebrations and reclamation events. In Napo, and across the Amazon, songs are an important technology for influencing the emotions and actions of others, while they establish interpersonal relationships between people, and between people and their environments (Swanson and Reddekop 2023; Swanson 2009; Uzendoski and Calapucha-Tapuy 2012; Brown 2007; Harrison 1989). I explore the affective poetics of this genre and its resonances with Kichwa women's musical artistry in Napo.

Songs of lament create conviviality (Overing and Passes 2000) through the evocation of compassion and empathy. Upper Napo Kichwa speakers also emphasize laughter and joking in daily relationships. I further explore the circulation of "spicy" jokes between face-to-face and radio mediation, which constructs a Napo Runa media public hailed by culturally intimate forms. Narrative jokes belong to the genre of *kachu* (from Spanish *cacho*, joke), which contrast with the genre of *kwintu* (from Spanish *cuentos*, stories) that elders have left behind. Radio media became an important way to circulate elders' stories and the knowledge they contain but also transformed how this knowledge might be perceived. Attention to actual spaces of production and reception highlight that community media are suffused with affect, evoke interpersonal and intergenerational interactions, and contribute to the formation of an intimate community of shared practices that centers on Napo, but has resonances beyond.

Remediating Affect on the Airwaves

"We realized that in the times before there were many singers," Rita explained as she discussed the programming on *A New Path*, "when they sang, they would tell stories, the elders would tell stories of how their elders had lived in their songs." This was the impetus for the program to record not only stories but songs of local musical groups. Napo bands who perform *runa paju* music, which Uzendoski and Calapucha-Tapuy translate as "indigenous magic" (see also Uzendoski and Calapucha-Tapuy 2012, 72–77), are a point of vitality for Kichwa in many communities. In Amazonian Kichwa, *paju* can mean an ability or gift—a magical touch—transmitted intergenerationally. These abilities are often transmitted by grasping and cracking the knuckles of a knowledgeable elder. Such gifts may be agricultural, like the gift of growing corn, *sara paju*, or medicinal, such as the ability to cure an illness. Paju also means "illness" in Amazonian Kichwa, such that the idea of illness and the ability to cure it are intimately bound together. Such abilities may also involve musicality, including songs for plants and trees to encourage their growth or to harvest their medicine.

The Kichwa-language music recorded in Napo ranged from acoustic songs performed with a violin, guitar, flute, or drums, and fast-paced, amplified tunes featuring full "orchestras," with electronic keyboards, electric and bass guitar, drum kits, violins, and a range of other instruments. Such songs are frequent accompaniments to Kichwa celebrations and are popular for dancing. Many of these amplified songs feature animal and plant metaphors and discuss the social life of Kichwa communities. Acoustic songs more directly remediate traditional Kichwa music.

Rita continued, "When our listeners from Tena heard those songs, they said, 'we remember our fathers and mothers, those that had died long ago!' They told us, 'When we hear those songs, it makes us sad.' . . . They wrote messages to us saying that they were just remembering, crying [when they heard them]." Rita explained this was the case for listeners from Napo, and the neighboring provinces of Orellana, Sucumbíos, and Pastaza. Rita's comments point to the importance of music and musicality for verbal artistry, daily communication, and sociality in Napo and more widely in the Amazon. They also speak to the daily experience of listening to the radio in Napo, where radio media elicited strong responses from listeners. My fieldnotes of reception studies in Chaupishungo are filled with hopeful examples of children and adolescents singing along to songs heard on the radio or listening attentively to community recordings. They also contain examples of elderly Serafina and her daughters commenting sadly on songs about the death of a beloved mother, or even breaking down into tears when listening to such music.

Song is an especially affective medium for speakers of Amazonian Kichwa, making it an ideal mode for maintaining and reclaiming Kichwa linguistic and cultural practices. Music is an important means of eliciting emotional, empathetic responses and mediating relationships among Amazonian Kichwa communities (Swanson and Reddekop 2023; Swanson 2009; Uzendoski and Calapucha-Tapuy 2012; Harrison 1989). This is likely tied to a broader preference in the Amazon for utilizing music and musicality to shape convivial relationships. Anthropologist Michael Brown (2007) described music as "a technology of sentiment" for the Chicham-speaking Awajún of the western Peruvian Amazon. It is a practice through which people relate to and influence the environment and each other. Swanson and Reddekop (2023) suggest that Amazonian Kichwa singers influence social relationships by eliciting compassion and empathy (*llakichina*) within listeners, in ways that tie together an ayllu or relational family network that includes people, plants, animals, and the land they inhabit.

Women are especially potent mediators of sociality through song, although the Napo recording industry is largely dominated by male musicians and groups. Women may sing about their individual and family histories and accomplishments in musical narratives (Muratorio 1995, 412). Their songs mediate relationships between singers and more-than-human beings, evident when a Kichwa woman sings to her manioc crops to encourage them to grow (Guzmán Gallegos 1997, 77) or to a tree to ask permission to gather its medicine. Uzendoski and Calapucha-Tapuy analyze the power associated with women's song to influence plants, crops, and interpersonal relationships as a form of feminine shamanism, as "songs are social action, acts that *attract* energy, qualities, people, and power" (2012, 81, original emphasis). Women's songs can also mediate more intimate relationships between the singer and her family members, including absent partners and children (Seitz 1982). Songs further mediate relationships with the dead. In

Napo, as well as the Ecuadorian Highlands (Corr 2010), Kichwa women sing as they cry at funerals and when remembering the dead. Some of these forms are described as llakichina, which means to evoke both love and sorrow (Swanson and Reddekop 2023; Seitz 1982), as the songs sway the emotional states of the recipient, even when that person or being is absent.

The feeling of llaki is a central emotional category described in Quechuan languages.[1] In Amazonian Ecuador, its dual senses of love and sadness are inseparable (Harrison 1989, 147; Swanson 2009; Orr and Wrisley 1981). While the noun *llaki* can describe sadness, a tragedy, or love, the verb *llakina* generally describes love and empathy for another person. Once, when discussing a mutual friend with a sometimes-difficult character, Serafina remarked, nevertheless, "I care for her a great deal" (*payta ashka llakini*). Similarly, radio hosts address their audiences "with great love" (*ashka llakishkawa*). However, when the reflexive suffix *-ri* is added, turning the action back on the speaker, the resulting verb *llakirina* means "to be sad," though it can also connote longing. The addition of the causative suffix *-chi* extends the action to another person, evoking in them the feelings of llaki. The form of singing described by academics as llakichina has more to do with the emotional effects of the songs than with a strict metalinguistic categorization of genre. Harrison, for instance, writes that the songs she catalogued "are not categorized and labeled with any one term; however, the motive of singing was attributed to llakichina" (1989, 147). The affective, interpersonal power of women's often private songs are reembedded, or remediated, through the ecology of Napo Kichwa media.

Women's Affect and Song in Napo

One genre of song especially associated with the effect of llakichina is that of wakana or lament. I first experienced this genre when attending the wake for an elder Kichwa man. I was accompanying Serafina, who knelt before the coffin, crying, and who tearfully addressed the deceased,

---

1. See Mannheim (1998, 269) for a discussion of the pairing of *llakiy* (to be sad, to feel sorrow) and *waqay* in Southern Peruvian Quechua.

her godson, with song. When I mentioned this to a friend in his late thirties, he explained that in Napo, women "cry singing," a sentiment repeated by several other interlocutors. The verb wakana most literally means to cry in Amazonian Kichwa (Orr and Wrisley 1981, 23). Mannheim identifies a broader semantic range for Southern Peruvian Quechua, in which waqay is translated as "to cry, crow, or bray, to sound (for a musical instrument), to suffer, to feel sorrow" (1998, 269). This more extended sense is also present in Napo Kichwa, where the songs of birds can be described with wakana (Ennis 2019b, 264).

The women with whom I worked regularly sang wakana, and I became intimately acquainted with the genre across settings. These ranged from political events to private farewells. Singers mobilized laments to produce affective and empathetic bonds with their listeners. María Antonia Shiguango, founder of AMUPAKIN, broke into a tearful song at an anniversary celebration as she recounted the struggles of the organization during their history. Serafina frequently broke into lament when she remembered her deceased relatives—especially her own mother. She performed lament when a relative or acquaintance died, both upon hearing the news and when attending a funeral. She further used lament to establish affective, empathetic bonds with me, her rancia ushi, or white-European daughter. When I was about to return to the United States, she sang, asking me not to forget her, a woman for whom I had become "like her own daughter." It would eventually become a genre in which I would myself cry and sing, as I expressed my grief for Serafina's death several years later. I had no idea of how important wakana would become to me and my research when one morning Serafina drew my attention to a song that was playing on the radio.

"Listen," Serafina said one November morning in 2016, "we're listening to a lament." The song "Yapa Wakak Mama/Llanto y cariño de mama" (The Crying Mother/A Mother's Lament and Love) by the performance troupe Los Jilgueritos (Sp. The Goldfinches) was playing. As the song continued, she paused and shook her head wistfully, "When I hear that it really makes me want to cry, poor thing." I nodded, and she took the invitation to explain, "She's singing about how her mother cared for her." Returning to her weaving, Serafina wiped her eyes. The mournful refrain of the song played on in the background:

Exert of "Yapa Wakak Mama" by Los Jilgueritos

Llullugu ashkaiga,	When I was very young,
changawaimi sirikani mamita	I lay in your lap, dear mother.
Rigrawai markashaka,	And carrying me in your arms,
shimiwai mucharkangui,[2]	you kissed me,
Ñuka mamitawalla	My dearest mother
Ñuka mamitawalla	My dearest mother
Ñuka mamitawalla	My dearest mother
Parijumi kawsashun	Let us live together always,
nishachu yuyarkangui	must be what you thought.
Kan wañushka punzhaka	But the day that you die,
Imara tukusharí	what will become of me?
Ñuka mamitawalla	My dearest mother
Ñuka mamitawalla	My dearest mother
Ñuka mamitawalla	My dearest mother

As the verse ended, Serafina began crying her own song, singing for the loss of her mother with a sadness elicited by the song on the radio, which drew upon similar understandings of the poetics of lament. Even after the radio changed to an upbeat tune, Serafina sang for her mother, using melodies and images that resonated with the mournful lament heard on the radio.

In Napo, the idea that women cry by singing is one of the defining features of feminine comportment. Despite the regularity with which elderly Serafina would cry while she sang, few of her adult daughters engaged in the practice, nor did any of her granddaughters appear to cry in this way. Young women may come to adopt the practice later in life, as they become elders themselves, but it certainly seems to be one that is undergoing shift (See also Harrison 1989; Seitz 1982). Laments are increasingly circulated in public through recordings and live performances, which extends their audiences and contexts of use, and creates emergent

---

2. This transcript differs slightly from versions I have previously published. Upon repeated listening, I have more recently noted the use of the past tense -rka- and several other features of this song suggestive of language unification, alongside more regional forms like the -ra object marker.

AFFECTIVE TECHNOLOGIES AND INTIMATE PUBLICS

vitalities for the genre. The circulation of such songs also shapes an affective public, who respond, as Serafina did, to the remediation of culturally intimate forms on the air.

Cultural reclamation in Napo implicated both elders and young people. As a member of AMUPAKIN, Serafina sometimes performed lament at public events and contributed to the circulation of the genre. AMUPAKIN was also an important site of linguistic and cultural reclamation. As Serafina explained, she had "forgotten" some of what her own elders had practiced in the past in their absence. Instead, she said, the founder of AMUPAKIN counseled the members to sing and to tell stories, and in doing so, to focus on remembering.

Serafina told me that before a performance she asked herself, "What should I sing?" The answer came, she said, when she realized that she wanted to sing "how my mother cried, how my mother sang." However, the performance of lament was inseparable from the affect produced by it. Serafina continued, "It really makes us feel like crying, even when we cry just for show." She then demonstrated a song for me, which provoked her to truly lament. Her song shows correspondences between the prerecorded song on the radio, and her own laments, both those performed in public and those performed in more spontaneous, intimate settings.

Serafina performs a lament at home, November 25, 2016

Ñuka mamitawalla,$_1$
kan rikuchisha sakishka shimira,$_2$
kunaga mana kungarisha.$_3$

My dear little mother,$_1$
the speech that you showed and left me,$_2$
now, I will never forget.$_3$

Kan mama,$_4$
kan yachachishka pajugunara apisha,$_5$
kay tukuyra turminduriniga mama.$_6$
Ñuka kay tukuy turmindarisha purikpis,$_7$
mana pagawanunga mama.$_8$

You, mother,$_4$
grasping your gifts [paju] that you taught,$_5$
I am suffering from all of this, mother.$_6$
And as I go on suffering all of this,$_7$
they don't pay me, mother.$_8$

Imara angata yachachisha saki-
wakangui ñuka mama.$_9$

What could it be that you left behind to me in your teaching, my mother?$_9$

| Kasna ñukara, kan yachachisha sakikpi,[10] | You taught me like this and when you left,[10] |
| kay turmindu, kay castigora tupanchi mama.[11] | we find this suffering, this punishment, mother.[11] |

Both the lament on the radio and the song Serafina sung that day resonate with similar poetics, from their shared address to "my dear little mother," to their emphasis on interaction and loss. As she sang, Serafina became overwhelmed by emotion and placed her head in her hands. Attempting to collect herself, she told me, "When I really remember, I feel like crying."

The Cultural Intimacy of Lament

What do people like Serafina and her family hear when they interact with an on-air lament? What forms of cultural intimacy are involved? Tears are more accepted among speakers of Upper Napo Kichwa, especially among women, than they are for many speakers of American English, where intense public displays of emotion are discouraged. Consider the entry for *wakay siki* provided by Nuckolls and Swanson (2020, 268), which suggests a cultural norm for women to be sensitive and prone to tears:

> *Wakay siki* [cry baby] (when said of a child; when said of a woman it means a sensitive woman prone to tears; lit.: 'cry-butt').

Although people might be teased for being a wakay siki, it is a recognized social category, ideologically linked to women, to motherhood, and to memory. These ideas intersect in the Kichwa and Spanish title for the song "Yapa Wakak Mama / Llanto y cariño de mama" by Los Jilgueritos, which roughly translates as "The Crying Mother / A Mother's Lament and Love." Swanson and Reddekop (2023, 13) describe a similar song performed at Mother's Day celebrations, suggesting it belongs to a broader genre in Napo. Media in Napo are suffused with affect in ways that encourage interpersonal interaction and amplify the intergenerational transmission of affective verbal artistry, like songs that result in llaki, or shared empathy.

Crying is not only enregistered as a gendered practice in Napo but one linked to ethnicity, so that different ways of expressing sadness through tears are seen as indexical of not only femininity, but Napo Runa femininity. Serafina once imitated how she had seen Spanish-speaking women cry in telenovelas. For Serafina, the way mishu women cried amounted to pitiful sobs and heavy breathing. Instead, she explained, Napo Runa women cry singing, talking to the person that has gone and describing their suffering at being left alone. I was told repeatedly that women sing wakana. Initially, I only observed women singing wakana, even at the first funeral I attended with Serafina and her daughters.

The remediation of songs of lament address not just women. Although women cried often, I rarely saw Kichwa men cry in Napo. The major exception has been at funerals. In 2017, Serafina's elderly sister-in-law died. Serafina was unsurprisingly moved to tears and song. It was at the wake, however, that I saw men cry and lament around the coffin. Serafina's nephew embraced his aunt while he cried for his mother.[3] Men's songs of lament are also remediated on air. Serafina and her daughters commented sadly on a man who sang, "My mother has died/she has drowned in the Hollín river." As her daughter repeated the line about the mother's death, Serafina responded, "Yes, that's what they're singing about, poor thing, 'a buzzard ate her,' he says." The circulation of these songs reinforces their poetics among their receptive publics. It also reminds listeners of the intimate moments when they may be moved to song through the inevitability of grief.

During her sister-in-law's wake, Serafina took my hand and led me to view her body through a window in the wooden coffin. She sang, crying, reminding us that she would someday be lying there. Serafina's prediction came true in November of 2020, when she passed away after several months of illness. I was unable to attend her funeral due to the COVID-19 pandemic, but I was present via a Facebook Messenger video call, arranged by a member of AMUPAKIN. I had rarely seen Serafina's

---

3. Blanca Muratorio (1998, 415, 418) suggests that there is a difference between the wailing performed by men and women at wakes and the everyday expressions of grief and remembrance that might take place in women's other songs. This distinction between realizations or kinds of wakana, however, was not one that emerged among my interlocutors.

daughters perform wakana, but several cried laments for their mother during the funeral. Gathered around Serafina's coffin, some of her male relatives sang laments. Although the most salient indirect index (Ochs 1992) of wakana is to women, it is also a way to index affective stances and express grief, accessed by both men and women, at least in some settings. In July 2023, I returned to Napo to sing my own lament for Serafina, my voice hesitant, but bolstered by the piercing songs of her daughters. Kneeling beside Serafina's grave, their voices moved me to sing and cry for the mother we had lost. For those who have been socialized into this genre, laments demand an emotional response from the listener.

The poetics of such songs reverberate in their remediation through radio and other media. They draw listeners into a mediated community of practice emerging around radio reception. The power of the mediated voice to elicit emotions from listeners helps to give shape to Upper Napo Kichwa speakers as a receptive community for local radio media programming. This power transforms them into an affective public, organized by their recognition of and emotive response to the culturally intimate poetics embedded within local radio media. This is one of the main reasons that music and radio media have proved so well-suited for Upper Napo Kichwa language maintenance and reclamation, as the spoken and sung voice circulates and imbues rural and urban homes with the affective sounds of intimate expressive and interactional practices (see also Faudree 2013). This affective public, however, was held together by more than just lament.

"Spicy Speech" and Culturally Intimate Publics

A New Path was so popular in Napo partly because listeners heard themselves and their meaningful forms of speech on air. As Dario Lopez, the white-mestizo director of *A New Path* described, one of the main goals of the program was to "give voice" to a public "who had not had a voice." Soon after their second anniversary, Dario reflected on the program. "Part of the strategy of *A New Path* was to visit the communities ourselves," he explained, "so that they would tell us a little of their history, how the community was created, how many people there are, a little of their legends, their myths, and their nicknames." Nicknames, better called "joking names," (burla shuti) are widely used in Kichwa communities, often referencing humorous anecdotes. The popularity of nickname stories was surprising to Dario, who—as a monolingual Spanish speaker—relied on the Kichwa members of the communications department to help develop the content of the radio programs. He continued, "When my team suggested we produce a segment of jokes, truthfully, I told them I wasn't so interested in it." For Dario, as a director of a "serious program," he thought that "those kinds of features had nothing to do with the program." Dario did not want to "discourage" the young cohosts and ultimately assented.

Although Dario was unsure about jokes on *A New Path*, their receptive public was not. "When people came to talk with the team, I asked them what they like most about *A New Path*," Dario continued, "and almost everyone agreed on the jokes and nicknames." As Dario suggested, "the idiosyncrasies of mestizos are not the same as the idiosyncrasies of Kichwas," implying that the content that hailed a Kichwa public might not make sense for another. Humor became a central part of *A New Path*, which responded to its importance in daily interactions.

Like some other Amazonian peoples (Overing 2000), humor is central to daily social interactions in Napo Runa communities. Speakers of Upper Napo Kichwa emphasize the ability to tell a good joke (asichina), as well as how one laughs (*asina*). Speakers ideologize the appropriate way for an Amazonian Runa woman to laugh, a lilting hoot rising in pitch (see also Nuckolls and Swanson 2020, 20–21). Most men receive a burla shuti, often a humorous allusion to their personality, a male relative, or to something that happened during their marriage ceremony. Jokes comparing people to animals are common, maintaining the circulation of some forms of environmental knowledge. Serafina sometimes joked that her daughter, mother to twins, was a *chikallu warmi* when she carried one son strapped to her front and the other to her back, because she said a *chikallu* is a kind of animal who carries her babies while nursing them. Some jokes rely on punning or intertextual reference, but many take the form of extended narratives. Both men and women tell jokes.

The genre called uchu shimi, literally "spicy speech," is one category of humor ideologized as a male genre, at least among elders. The members of AMUPAKIN, who delighted in joking and laughing together, introduced me to uchu shimi. The younger members, in their mid to late thirties and forties, regularly made ribald, sexual jokes to each other, about each other, and about people they knew—including me. Participating in such joking was an important part of building rapport with them. As anthropologist Edward Hall suggested, joking is a form of a play (1990, 75), which is itself a complex phenomenon in which meanings may be inverted or temporarily suspended (Bateson 1972). Gaining facility with a community's humor means one has gained "control of nearly everything else" (Hall 1990, 75). Elder members of AMUPAKIN, women in their sixties, disapprovingly described such jokes as the way men talked.

Like men's use of wakana in situations of heightened emotion, women access uchu shimi to create communicative effects. While the more salient index of uchu shimi is toward men, it might also index conviviality and good humor in ways attractive to younger women. The use of uchu shimi may allow younger women to distinguish themselves from their mothers and grandmothers. Amazonian Kichwa speakers generally talk openly about the body and its processes. There still are degrees of vulgarity and politeness associated with different words and topics of conversation. The artful use of euphemism and double entendre indicates an especially skilled—and funny—iteration of uchu shimi. As in all communities of practice, tolerance for different jokes varied widely, as I learned while listening to the radio with Serafina's family.

Elder women like Serafina often identified uchu shimi as an indirect index of men or masculine communication. Consider her evaluation of an extended joke-narrative told by a woman we heard on the radio. Lasting several minutes, it centered on a husband and wife. Fearful that their children had discovered their sexual activity, the couple told them that the house was shaking because of an earthquake (*allpa kuyana*). The children were awoken by the nightly shaking of their house and prayed to God to make the earthquake stop. As Serafina listened to the joke on the radio, she laughed and then commented under her breath "*karishina warmi*," literally a "woman who is like a man." This was an evaluation she repeated as I asked her about the joke, which she directly connected to men's way of speaking:

AFFECTIVE TECHNOLOGIES AND INTIMATE PUBLICS

Serafina Grefa comments on a radio-broadcast joke; excerpt 1.1, April 18, 2017

GE: Chi ichilla kachuwara kwintaka.[1]

SG: Ari, ichilla kachura kwintan mama, karishina mamaga.[2]

GE: Imai?[3]

SG: Karishina mamami kwintaun.[4]

GE: Ah, karishina mama.[5]

SG: Ari, karishina mama, ruku mama asha kwintan chi.[6]

. . .

SG: Asichingawa, pay kariunawa kwintashkarami kwintaun, kariuna kwintashkara.[12]

GE: Kariguna kwintashkara, chi uchu shimi. . . . [13]

SG: Uchu shimi, chitami kwintan.[14] Chita ama uyangak piñasha tiani.[15] <asin>

GE: [She] told that little joke.[1]

SG: Yes, the lady told a little joke, a *karishina* [like a man/inept] lady.[2]

GE: What?[3]

SG: A karishina lady was talking![4]

GE: Oh, a karishina lady.[5]

SG: Yes, a karishina lady, [even though] she's an old lady told that.[6]

. . .

SG: To make [others] laugh, she told what the men say, what the men speak.[12]

GE: [She told] men's speech, that spicy talk. . . . [13]

SG: Spicy talk, that's what she told.[14] I'm here, being annoyed, [wishing] not to hear such [talk].[15] <laughs>

Although I identified the story as uchu shimi, Serafina quickly agreed with this categorization, which matched her evaluation that the story was men's speech. Surprisingly, Serafina's musings on the concept of allpa kuyana (earthquake) led her to reflect on her own experiences with earthquakes. These included lessons that her mother had shared when Serafina was young about earthquakes as signs of spatiotemporal transformation. It is difficult to predict the memories media may evoke in their circulation, thus contributing to language maintenance and reclamation in unexpected ways.

Serafina was struck by uchu shimi she had heard on the radio or among the midwives. Despite her claims to be "annoyed" when she heard such humor, she would retell these jokes, carefully attributing them to a named source and distancing herself from the content (Irvine 1993) using embedded discourse. An example emerged as she explained the joke to me:

Serafina Grefa comments on a radio-broadcast joke; excerpt 1.2, April 18, 2017

GE: Imai?[19]

SG: Payguna shina tuta kwin-tashka riparanushka **nin**, payguna kariwa warmiwas mishkichishkara.[20]

GE: What?[19]

SG: They [the children] realized what was told at night, **she says**, when they—the husband with the wife too—"made it sweet."[20]

Serafina often seemed a bit shocked when she arrived at the punchline of jokes she was retelling and would laugh heartily, sometimes shouting "*amay!*," an exclamation akin to "well, I never!" Serafina's insistence that she disliked these jokes and her displacement for responsibility for such talk onto other speakers suggests that such humor is a site of cultural intimacy—as a practice that is disclaimed—for speakers of Upper Napo Kichwa.

Although some people receive uchu shimi with reservation or embarrassment, it is a genre other speakers and listeners enjoy. Kichwa humor is a site for commentary upon social anxieties and antihegemonic inversions of the social order (Calhoun 2019; Bermúdez 2020). A popular joke told repeatedly on *A New Path* concerned a runa girl and her foreign boyfriend. The identity of the partner varied in each telling from mestizo to gringo. What didn't change was his linguistic ineptitude in Kichwa. Only understanding Spanish, the joke goes, the would-be lover becomes confused when his Kichwa-speaking partner tells him that there is "*turu*" (mud) on the ground, mishearing it as Spanish "*toro*" (bull) and running away. When she calls out in Kichwa, "*Tigriy, tigriy*" (return, return), he runs faster, sure he is being chased by a tiger, similarly pronounced "*tigre*" in Spanish. For Kichwa listeners, this joke partly inverts the discrimination they may face from Spanish speakers, while it comments upon social and sexual relationships in the Amazon. Jokes are playful forms. What is communicated does not always denote the meaning that might emerge if they were interpreted as serious (Bateson 1972). Linguistic anthropologist Keith Basso (1979) suggests that jokes about the "Whiteman" among the Western Apache depend on the "danger" of the joke. These jokes provide commentary on both social relationships between participants and the cultural meanings associated with images of the other. The jokes were also subtle critiques. Their danger emerged from the fact that they carried the potential to disrupt relationships between jokers and their

AFFECTIVE TECHNOLOGIES AND INTIMATE PUBLICS

audiences if not interpreted as forms of appropriate play. Although Dario initially saw joking as an unserious form of speech, it is one requiring deep cultural knowledge and intimacy to be "in on" the joke.

The Circulation of Spicy Speech

Jokes were a popular feature of both studio and live broadcasts of *A New Path*. As Herzfeld has written, "Cultural intimacy, though associated with secrecy and embarrassment, may erupt into public life and collective self-representation" (2016 [1997], 7). This was sometimes the case on *A New Path*. Within the small sample of recordings collected from *A New Path*'s archive, several were labeled (in Spanish) "PIKANTE," likely referencing their status as "uchu shimi." Guests on live programs would occasionally tell spicy jokes, usually against the explicit instructions of the program's cohosts.

In November 2016, *A New Path* hosted a live broadcast of the wayusa upina dedicated to Jumandi Yuyay, or the "Wisdom of Jumandi," known as a "national hero and symbol of anticolonial resistance," for his leadership in an uprising against the Spaniards in 1578 (Oberem 1980, 88–90; Uzendoski 2005, 145). Prior to the event, Rita instructed participants to avoid spicy jokes. One guest, however, allowed the cultural intimacy of uchu shimi to "erupt" during jokes about Jumandi. The first joke was a narrative about Jumandi being served wayusa by his daughters, which received hearty laughs from the crowd. Looking out over the audience, which included the members of AMUPAKIN, he then remarked, "Seeing those women reminds me [of another one], as Jumandi's wife had powerful gifts." He then recounted how a young woman had sought to apprentice herself as a midwife to Jumandi's wife. Interpreting the joke required understandings of medicinal practices and the transmission of knowledge, such as the transmission of paju between elders and novices:

Excerpt from *A New Path* "Jumandi Yuyay," November 16, 2016

Shinakpiga ruku mama kayashka shami ushushi nisha,[40] kandami tukuy pajura kungarauni nisha,[41] makira apisha kurush, kurush, kurush pajura kushka.[42]	So, the old lady called out to her and said, "come here, daughter.[40] She said, "I'm going to give to you all my gifts."[41] She took her hand and going *kurush*, *kurush*, *kurush*, she gave her the gift.[42]

This segment embeds and discursively animates a scene of the transmission of powers between an elder and a young person. The repeated ideophone (Nuckolls 1996) *kurush* indicates the sound of popping knuckle joints, which accompanies the transmission of power from one hand to another. These joking narratives remediate significant forms of verbal artistry and cultural knowledge, albeit through humor.

The crux of the joke included a critique of elder women that carried the danger of misunderstanding if it was not "received in the right spirit," as Perley (2011, 154) suggests in his analysis of humor. After transmitting her paju, the speaker continued, the elder midwife got drunk while she and her apprentice were attending a birth, leaving the young attendant in charge. The elder midwife advised she would be able to feel the baby's head emerging from the mother, after which she would guide the child out. The young apprentice attempted this, but while she "pulled and pulled," the baby did not come. The young midwife said, "No, grandmother, I can't do it," adding, "try it your old self." The midwife felt around and said, "in vain you have been pulling on her pubic hair [*raka ilma*], not the baby!" Although he utilized the word *raka*, an often-avoided term referencing female anatomy, the crowd, including the midwives of AMUPAKIN, burst into laughter when it was revealed that the inexperienced midwife had mistaken the mother's pubic hair for the baby's head. Live broadcasts are always unpredictable. Relistening to the joke several years later with members of AMUPAKIN provoked further laughter. One listener commented that the speaker was her cousin. On *A New Path*, listeners in Napo heard not only culturally intimate forms of speech, but their own social intimates on the air.

This joke made an impression on elderly Serafina, who was in the audience that morning as a participant of the wayusa upina. A few hours later, at home, Serafina accompanied her youngest son and her eldest grandson as they harvested palm grubs from a downed tree. Their conversation turned to the wayusa upina that Serafina had attended that morning, and Serafina interjected, "Awful people! Did you hear what those people were saying?"

Her grandson responded, "What? We didn't hear anything." Her son added, "I enjoyed listening to what they said about Jumandi's wisdom. What did you see?"

Serafina told a compressed version of the joke, first avoiding the more vulgar term raka in favor of the euphemistic phrase, "*pay charishka ilma*," or "the hair she has (down there)." After she finished, her son asked, "That's what you heard?"

She responded, "They really make [people] laugh when they say that, but I say, no way!" Although Serafina repeated that she disliked the story, she told it again, but this time she included the punchline about "raka ilma" and added a final detail that it was "really curly," before breaking into a lilting laugh, "hoo-hoo-ha-hay!" Her audience laughed along with her. Although Serafina claimed she disliked such speech, she sometimes retold lightly bawdy jokes. Perhaps this was because Kichwa speakers in the Upper Napo use humor to foster conviviality, even when it veers into the realm of the culturally intimate, the embarrassing, and the hidden.

The importance of humor to radio programming in Napo further illustrates how media may be suffused with affect and implicated in unpredictable forms of interaction. Radio-mediated speech had a life extending beyond the initial broadcast as listeners recounted and commented upon what they had heard. Such media also transformed significant genres of face-to-face interaction as it remediated them on the air.

The Words of the Elders on the Air

My interlocutors in Napo often classified jokes as kachu, which they contrasted with the genre of kwintu, stories transmitted intergenerationally. Kachu were unlikely to be true, told for entertainment, while kwintu were likely to be understood as true stories, seen as sources of knowledge. These narratives were of the most popular segments from *A New Path*'s archive. Such programming made knowledgeable, often elderly, speakers available to listeners for dialogic commentary, frequently leading to new narrative events, grounded in the personal knowledge of a present elder or adult. The aural reception of Upper Napo Kichwa radio programs both shaped and reinvigorated the wayusa hours in Chaupishungo.

One morning when a community recording came on *A New Path*, Serafina paused to repeat a line from the story heard in the background, "He said, '[the man] became a boa.'" Turning to her grandson, she directed, "Listen, he's speaking."

The recording of that morning is difficult, as it includes the daily sonic textures of the home—multiple conversations, roosters crowing, pots clanking, and other sounds. Talk came to a lull as the speaker on the radio narrated a story involving a mother boa and her child, who made a distinctive sound as it called out in line 8.

Dialogic radio reception, Chaupishungo; excerpt 1.1, November 17, 2016

Radio: Chi wawa, umaymanda
    chi-ii-yaw, chi-ii-aw,
    chiaw chiaw. [8]
    {Chimanda mamaga. . . . [9]
SG: {Ña *chiaw.* [10]

Radio: That child, from [its] head
    "*chi-ii-yaw, chi-ii-aw,*
    chiaw chiaw." [8]
    {Then the mother . . . [9]
SG: {Ah, *chiaw.* [10]

In line 8, the radio speaker introduced an ideophone used to voice the boa child, *chiaw*, which became a focus of the family's discussion. Nuckolls (1996) describes ideophones as "sound symbolic expressions" that poetically mark grammatical aspect. In line 10, Serafina quickly repeats the ideophone *chiaw*, overlapping the radio. During this period, the family is largely attentive to the story, except for Serafina's young grandson, Michael, who commented on one of the cats and continued to talk to himself after receiving no response.

However, in line 18, Michael spontaneously shouted "chiaw!" mimicking the ideophone earlier used on the radio. Repeated by Serafina and then by Michael, the sound symbolic chiaw became a feature of the conversation surrounding the behavior of snakes with Serafina, her daughter Marcia, and her grandson Michael.

Dialogic radio reception, Chaupishungo; excerpt 1.2, November 17, 2016

Michael: *Chiaaaaw!* [18]
    Chiaaaw! Chiiaaw! [19]
Marcia: Shinara wakan amarun. [20]
Michael: *Chiaaww!* [21]
Serafina: Amarun, shina wakan kay
    amarun. [22]
    Shina wakan yaku kuchama
    ikungarausha *yaaaw chiaw*
    wakasha, chi yaku kuchama
    ikusha kay amarun. [23]

Michael: *Chiaaaaw!* [18]
    Chiaaaw! Chiiaaw! [19]
Marcia: Like how the boa cries out. [20]
Michael: *Chiaaww!* [21]
Serafina: The boa, that's how that
    boa cries out. [22]
    That's how it cries out when
    it's entering the deep pool,
    crying out "*yaaaw chiaw*,"
    when it's entering the deep
    pool, that boa. [23]

Serafina further used the ideophone *TU-PUun!* to animate the sound of the boa diving into the pool of water in line 50 (see Nuckolls 1996, 103).

Dialogic radio reception, Chaupishungo, excerpt 1.3, November 17, 2016

Serafina: Yaku amarun shina kaparianunmi. [49]	**Serafina**: The river boas call out like that. [49]
Kaparisha, kaparisha ukumandami, awamanda, kasna yura patai tiashkamanda *TU-PUun!* yakui ikunun. [50]	Calling out, calling out from inside, from above, like that perched in a tree, going *TU-PUun!* they enter the water. [50]
Awai mikiy pasasha, playai sirisha, kiknasha, sirishka ukumanda saltasha [xxx] manda yakuma. [51]	Above, after eating, laying on the shore regurgitating, it would have laid, diving from [xxx] into the water. [51]
Michael: {*Tum!* [52]	**Michael**: {*Tum!* [52]

In Chaupishungo, *amarun* and the places where they are said to live were regular topics of conversation. When foraging in the nearby river for small, armored catfish and freshwater shellfish, Serafina and her family moved quietly and cautiously past the deep bend known to be an *amarun wasi*—a home for the boa and their owners, the *yaku runa*, "river beings." Serafina further described the various *sasi*, "prohibitions," associated with killing boas—abstinence from sex, salt, and spice—as well as the dire consequences—madness and rage—awaiting those who fail to observe them. Like other media circulated on the radio, this story's reception enlivened the conversation and extended listeners' knowledge. It also extended the circulation of a significant form of Amazonian Kichwa verbal artistry—the use of sound symbolic ideophones like kurush, chiaw, and tupun—to younger audiences.

Speakers employed ideophones in the story and the face-to-face narrative event that emerged from it. Nuckolls suggests sound symbolic words are an important poetic and grammatical feature of Amazonian Kichwa conversational narrative, as "sound-symbolic images allow the Pastaza Quichua to share moments of focused attention on the salient qualities of an action, event, or process as it unfolds in time" (1996, 101). Despite their centrality in Amazonian Kichwa verbal artistry, sound symbolic expressions are vulnerable to language shift and ideological change. Nuckolls indicates that speakers associated ideophones with both a regionally authentic register and women's speech (1996, 102), a confluence of linguistic and gender ideologies not uncommon in contexts of linguistic and cultural shift (French 2010; Weismantel 2001; Hill and Hill 1986). Changes to these poetic practices due to language shift and linguistic unification represent not merely the loss of a distinctive grammatical practice and local identity, but the loss of a form of social engagement with other people and with the natural world. The continued oral transmission of such aurally evocative linguistic practices is one of the significant affordances of radio media. Yet the circulation of traditional narratives on air also transformed them.

Narrative Transformations

"The language of our elders should only be erased [forgotten] by death," My *compadre* Fabian, a father and farmer in his late thirties, told me. According to Fabian, "Each community has those kinds of old stories," which they must safeguard. He continued, "When they're told, the young people [should] understand, record, and grasp [them], so that when the elders die, the words they spoke will not be forgotten." Fabian said young people should "record" (Sp. *grabar*) and "grasp" (K. apina) the words of their elders. It was unclear whether Fabian meant electronic or metaphorical recording "within the heart," but his comments indicate the importance of narratives in Napo.

Intergenerational transmission is an important way a collective memory of the past is authenticated among speakers of Upper Napo Kichwa. My interlocutors often referenced "the words our elders left" as guidance for their everyday animation of Runa lifeways in Napo, as well as their performative reanimations of the past. Radio programs like *A New Path* amplified and extended the reach of familial knowledge, making it available to listeners who might not have access to such narratives or embodied interactions within their families. Serafina and her family used radio narratives as a dialogic point of departure to discuss their knowledge and experiences, accompanied by children who listened quietly. Contemporary elders, meanwhile, recount similarly listening to assembled groups of elders in their own youths.

AFFECTIVE TECHNOLOGIES AND INTIMATE PUBLICS

Radio media may remove the authoritative intergenerational framing of elders' narratives. Serafina responded with skepticism about the validity of stories she had heard on the radio. Later in the morning, when most of the family was preparing for school or work, I asked her what she thought of these kinds of stories. We had just finished listening to another community narrative, introduced by the female storyteller as a narrative her grandfather had shared about the importance of being generous with food and avoiding stinginess. Serafina's reply indicates the complexities involved in the remediation of these stories on the radio. Although Serafina and others have emphasized the truth of the stories they have told me, she was less sure about the stories she heard on the air. Like the other transcript from that morning, the audio from this segment has been difficult to analyze and transcribe due to the ongoing activity of the morning household.

Dialogic radio reception, Chaupishungo excerpt 2.1, November 17, 2016

GE: Chi kwintana . . . imara ningui?$_1$

SG: [Chi shungumanda], chi wañushka kasnara kwintashka, payguna chi kwinturami kwintanchi nisha kwintanun.$_2$

Payguna ñawpa timpumi kwintakuna aka nisha,$_3$ chitami kwintarianun.$_4$

Chiga, payguna yanga imasna rimashkara uyakuna [xxx].$_5$ Chi kwintura apinchi nisha apinun shina.$_6$

GE: That story . . . what do you think?$_1$

SG: [That from the heart], that deceased person told stories like this, they tell stories saying, "we're telling those stories [told by our elders]."$_2$

They say, "they would tell those stories in the time before."$_3$ That's what they're telling.$_4$

But then, they (could have) heard all kinds of baseless talk [xxx].$_5$ They receive those stories like that, saying "we receive that story."$_6$

Unlike stories transmitted by her elders, Serafina seemed skeptical of what she heard on the radio. Serafina was often proud of the way that she "remembered" the speech and practices of her elders, though she admitted to "forgetting" some of what she had heard as a child. This forgetting limited her ability to determine the veracity of many of the stories she heard on the radio. She attributed her forgetting to the loss of the social settings where such narratives were told and retold. In the excerpt below, I asked Serafina if she liked the stories. Her reply emphasized not the stories that she had heard on the radio but their connection to the relationships and settings where they were transmitted:

Dialogic radio reception, Chaupishungo, excerpt 2.2, November 17, 2016

SG: Ñawpakmandak urasgunara, ñuka mama kwintashkarami kungarini nini, mana kasna kwintanusha tiasha.$_{25}$
Ñawpaunaga, ñuka mama atarisha, kasna waysa upisha tiasha, kwintasha, wakak aka.$_{26}$

GE: Ah.$_{27}$

SG: Ari, kwintasha wakan.$_{28}$
{Paywa . . . $_{29}$

GE: {Ñawpa urasmanda.$_{30}$

SG: Ñawpa urasmanda shimira ñuka mamaga mas ali yachak aka.$_{31}$
Rukumanda pachakunami, paygunaga ña llakta illash-kamanda, llaktamanda tukushkamanda.$_{32}$

SG: I said, I forget what was from the time before, what my mother told, since I didn't sit conversing like that with others.$_{25}$
But those before, my mother got up, sitting and drinking waysa, and telling stories, she would cry/lament.$_{26}$

GE: Oh.$_{27}$

SG: Yes, telling stories she laments.$_{28}$ {Her . . . $_{29}$

GE: {About the time before?$_{30}$

SG: My mother knew the speech from the time before better.$_{31}$
Those from the old world, now they [told] about the absence of towns, about how it became a town.$_{32}$

In line 25 Serafina indicates I had misunderstood her, quoting herself, "I said, 'I forget what was from the time before, what my mother told, not sitting conversing like this with others.'" Rather than an issue of preference, her answer highlights the role of intergenerational transmission through conversation. As she explained she did not "sit conversing like this with others," she paused her ongoing weaving, raised her hand, and turned her open palm back and forth, using the gesture that indicates absence or lack. As the youngest child in her family, Serafina became a *wakcha*, a child who has lost one or both parents, relatively early in her life, leading to a loss of the familial relationships where this knowledge would be transmitted. The history Serafina references is also from the "time before" Napo "became a town," or was settled.

Serafina and members of AMUPAKIN highlighted the importance of repeatedly telling and refining one's stories in dialogic settings. Their attitudes regarding the intergenerational and interactional transmission of knowledge are akin to what Gershon (2010) has called media ideologies. Extending language ideology to media, Gershon defines media ideologies as "the metalanguage that emphasizes the technology or bodies through which we communicate," which highlight "how people understand both the communicative possibilities and the material limitations of a specific channel, and how they conceive of channels in general" (2010, 283). Face-to-face communication is itself a form of mediation. These anxieties over the mediation and remediation of narrative address local media ideologies. Narratives are preferably told among attentive audiences, and well-known traditional narratives will receive both phatic encouragement when told fluently as well as spontaneous corrections in the event of memory failure (see also Mannheim and Van Vleet 1998). Serafina did not remember the stories we heard on the radio from her own childhood. Instead, she described the stories of the old days she remembered hearing during her childhood. These were stories of the time before towns and about her known, named relatives who carried cargo by foot to Quito.

Knowledge is accumulated and inherited within families. As one woman explained, "We each tell what our particular grandparents told," which is connected to their individual *iyay*, intelligence or knowledge. Radio host Rita Tunay raised a related issue when she reported that many community members demanded payment to record their stories. When they began recording with communities, many people told her they did not want to share their knowledge. Rita convinced many to share their stories with the radio archive, because "we must teach our knowledge, we must transmit it to the children." The introduction of new technologies has shifted ideologies surrounding the public and private nature of such knowledge. By expanding the public of inherited narrative knowledge from the private sphere of the family, radio media may reconfigure how such stories are received. Media hold considerable promise to transmit the poetic structures, stylistic practices, and musicality of Upper Napo Kichwa verbal artistry. They may also remediate external ideologies of the openness of media and language.

Conclusion

There are many ideas circulating in Napo about how Kichwa people speak or should speak. These include beliefs about what it means to speak using "our own language" versus standardized forms. These also include ideas about how men and women speak. Such ideologies serve to differentiate between groups, while they erase cases that do not quite fit (Irvine and Gal 2000; Gal and Irvine 2019)—men who might sing while they cry or women who enjoy a spicy joke. Media are a site where Upper Napo Kichwa people debate and define culturally significant forms of talk and behavior. They are contentious. They can be emotionally devastating or humorous. What matters is that an Upper Napo Kichwa public is created through interactions with media in ways that extend, amplify, and transform their shared practices. Not just the production but also the reception of radio media in Napo is suffused with affect. Such media give rise to interpersonal interactions and help maintain a community of shared practices, simultaneously extended and intimate.

Like Fabian's suggestion that young people should "record" and "grasp" their elders' words, activists young and old increasingly utilize audio and visual media to inscribe a collective memory of the past in the present to shape the future. Despite some contradictions—like the transformation of knowledge through mediation—many members of a densely interacting, ideologically plural Upper Napo Kichwa community of practice are turning to radio media to create new vitalities for the words of their elders, alongside other significant forms of verbal artistry and practice. It is not just speech that is involved. On programs like *A New Path*, performance media are used to reconstitute contexts of use and interactional practices within new regimes of value, so that the voices of contemporary elders are not forgotten but amplified, as interlinked linguistic and embodied knowledge is brought to life on the air.

CHAPTER 6

Media and Collective Memory

Mayor Shiguango adjusted his thin-rimmed, rectangular glasses as he explained, "To revalorize (*revalorizar*) means that the culture already existed. We already have it. We already know it." An energetic man in his early fifties, Shiguango had worked as an agronomist before entering politics in Archidona. While working with *A New Path*, I noted that Mayor Shiguango and others in the municipal offices spoke frequently about the need to revalorize Kichwa, described in Spanish as *revalorización* and in Kichwa as *balichina*.[1] Many activists recognized that the linguistic and cultural practices they hoped to maintain still existed in households in Napo. What remained was to make them public and valuable, both economically and socially. They did this on the radio, in parades, at public performances, in Facebook posts and in YouTube music vid-

---

This is a modified and expanded version of an article to appear as "Reweaving Language and Lifeways in the Western Amazon" in *American Indian Culture and Research Journal* (2025). The present chapter expands on the arguments suggested there. This chapter also grows from several workshops and conference sessions I organized. I especially thank Tony Webster for his comments on previous versions of this essay, which have inspired some of the analyses here.

1. The Kichwa term *balichina* is itself a loanword based upon the Spanish verb *valer* (to cost), which was Kichwanized to *balina*, "to have value; to be precious." Combined with the causative suffix *-chi*, the resulting verb *balichina* literally means to give something value.

eos, through community cinema, and on morning TV programs. Unlike their written counterparts, which suggested one way of writing—and therein speaking—Kichwa, community media and performance contexts allowed for a diversity of voices to emerge through grassroots pedagogies grounded in intergenerational transmission.

Mayor Shiguango contrasted this sense of "revalorizar" with another term I had asked him about, *rescate* (Sp. "salvage, rescue") commonly used to describe language revitalization projects in Latin America. Shiguango explained that to him, "rescate would be when everything was already lost, I'm going to say, 'I'll salvage this piece,' right?" For Shiguango, this idea of salvage implied that culture and language was already gone, but, as he continued to explain, Kichwa people still maintained a great deal of knowledge, "My parents know how to make [fermented manioc] chicha, how to survive in the rainforest, how to weave a shigra [net bag]." He continued, "Am I going to say to myself, 'I'll salvage a shigra bag or a basket?' No. It's already there." For many people, the shigra is one of the most recognizable signs of Upper Napo Kichwa cultural practice. Men and women wear these bags in the forest to carry game meat or foraged plants. Elder and adult women frequently use shigra as their purse in town. This style is less popular among young women for daily wear. Shigra are commonly worn as part of traditional dress in formal, public, and performance contexts (see figures 2 and 10). For Shiguango, the goal of the radio program was "to value what we have and show it to the public so that they know it."

Although Shiguango avoided the term *rescate*, it still circulated in municipal offices and elsewhere in Napo. A sign in the window of *A New Path*'s studio, written in Spanish, described the program's mission using the word:

Nos preocupamos del desarrollo integral de nuestro Cantón
*Nuestra programación pretende **rescatar** la identidad, lengua, gastronomía*
*   y costumbres de todo un pueblo*

We are concerned with the holistic development of our canton
Our programing intends to **salvage** the identity, language, cuisine, and
    customs of an entire people

The conversations that I had in Napo, public discourse, and the programs *A New Path* produced opened central questions for my research: Why would programming most people experienced by listening focus so much on otherwise embodied and material practices—like cuisine and handicrafts—alongside language? And what was the relationship between economic value, development, and language maintenance and shift? Among Sarah Shulist's (2018) interlocutors in the Brazilian Amazon, access to housing and employment was often more pressing than language revitalization. In Archidona, planners and activists sought to address these issues together. Topics like subsistence and cooperative agriculture, hunting, food preparation, environmental conservation, historical narrative, and music, among others were the subjects of *A New Path's* daily broadcasts from the municipal offices. These programs were brought to life once a month on live performances of ruku kawsay, "traditional lifeways," produced with communities around Archidona. There, radio hosts and community participants remediated and reanimated the living memory of the speech and activities of the early morning wayusa hours (Ennis 2019b). These programs intended to reclaim social and cultural practices understood as integral to Kichwa identity and as productive forms of labor in a burgeoning community tourism and performance industry.

Napo Runa activities have turned to what some might still see as an "unexpected" (Deloria 2004; Webster and Peterson 2011) method to confront ongoing shift toward Spanish language and settler lifeways—live performances and the production of various forms of media, including community cinema, radio, television, and music. Philip Deloria's (2004) work on Native engagements with technology—from early automobiles to film—highlights how expectations of indigeneity reveal more about the underlying assumptions of the dominant society than they do about the actual lives and practices of Indigenous peoples. Such expectations shape still prevalent imaginaries of the supposed technological incompetence of Amazonian peoples, living in uncontacted, remote conditions. These expectations may be embedded in disciplinary approaches to revitalization understanding language in terms of distinction between *langue* and *parole*, or between actual speech and the conceptual system (Saussure 1966). As Bernard Perley has described, such approaches "dismember" Indigenous languages both into their constituent linguistic parts and from the communities who speak them (Perley 2013, 244). In Ecuador, the academic dismemberment of Kichwa in language planning and revitalization has primarily occurred through language standardization transforming the variations of regional dialects into a pan-Kichwa standard.

In Napo, the ways Kichwa activists and producers use media for language reclamation is unexpected because their work expands the focus of revitalization from language as a grammatical code to reclaiming language to communicate further social, ecological, and economic knowledge. To focus on Kichwa media work as solely a form of language revitalization would ignore that participants sought to reclaim and strengthen multiple forms of cultural knowledge. Napo Kichwa activists engage with broadcast and performance media as a community-oriented and community-directed approach to linguistic *and* cultural reclamation. Production, reception, and circulation of multimodal media events are ways of reanimating and therein "remembering" (Perley 2013) language in communities, reweaving indexical connections between linguistic and cultural practice. They are sites of memory and reconnection. Wesley Leonard has described language reclamation as "a larger effort by a community to speak a language and to set associated goals in response to community needs and perspectives" (Leonard 2012, 359). This "larger effort" to set goals for and beyond language in response to their own needs and perspectives of language was at stake in the Upper Napo ecology of media.

I first came to Napo in 2014 to study Kichwa language. As a graduate student, I carried several ways of knowing the world with me, particularly those of the academic fields of anthropology and linguistics growing out of a specific empiricist mindset (Smith 2012; Bauman and Briggs 2003). In 2015, I returned to study the use of media for language revitalization, with an emphasis on debates over linguistic code choices. Public messages like the sign on *A New Path*'s door, as well as conversations with the producers and hosts of local radio programs, and observations of their different media events quickly made it clear to me that much more than what I thought of as language was at stake in the media produced in Napo.

In Napo, I saw that language was inseparable from the environments in which people were socialized to use it. Telling a good joke, responding appropriately to the emotional overture of a lament, or learning how to appropriately ask questions of my interlocutors (Briggs 1986) were forms of communication that only became available to me as a language learner through repeated observations and embodied interactions, first at an immersive field school and later as a participant-observer in Kichwa households. This is one reason that interaction through and around radio programming was important for community-directed reclamation projects. The remediation of the wayusa upina on the airwaves revalued intimate spaces of intergenerational linguistic and cultural socialization. I also saw that Kichwa residents of Napo continued to confront settler colonial disruption to their local environments and social practices, which shape patterns of language use and vitality in the Amazon. Finding ways to strengthen practices—linguistic and otherwise—that had been disrupted in Napo was a primary goal of radio programs like *A New Path*, and the broader ecology of Kichwa media to which they contributed.

In Napo, reclaiming language was also about reclaiming those indexical connections to other forms of experience ruptured by historical and contemporary colonialism. As scholars have shown in other contexts, settler colonialism and social oppression matter a great deal for creating the conditions in which languages shift, while language revitalization often involves other forms of cultural revitalization (Davis 2017; Taff et al. 2018; Jacob 2013; Perley 2013; Simpson 2017). Napo Kichwa media producers and community members increasingly reclaim and reweave indexical connections between linguistic, cultural, and ecological knowledge through performance and broadcast media.

This final chapter explores how Napo Kichwa media and performance became multimodal sites of "living"—animating and reanimating—by "remembering" the words of the elders under dramatically different social and environmental conditions. One of the principal roles of Napo's media ecology is as a site of collective memory for language and otherwise embodied and material forms of knowledge. Napo performance media invite scholars and activists to reconsider conceptual approaches to language shift and reclamation, and to link language reclamation more explicitly to place-based forms of knowledge.

Mayor Shiguango suggested that publicizing the woven net bags known as shigra was one way to revalorize these practices. As a case study, I consider the reclamation of the fiber called pita to produce shigra and the ways it connects linguistic, historical, and environmental knowledge through embodied performances.[2] Tracking Upper Napo Kichwa women's production of pita across multiple performances and rehearsal spaces reveals how performers and media activists reclaim and revalorize language through other cultural practices and create emergent vitalities (Perley 2011, 2013) for both. The growth of pita in a local ecology of media allowed participants to reanimate and extend their lifeways, despite disruptions. Broadcast and performance media become a place-based, multimodal method for the reclamation of Upper Napo Kichwa language and lifeways grounded in their own socialization practices.

Reanimating Memory in Napo

"I wish you all good day," Serafina Grefa begins in a recording produced for *A New Path*'s radio archive sometime in 2014.[3] We sometimes heard the recording on the radio in her household in Chaupishungo, causing a commotion among listeners. Serafina continued, "So, they say that I am sixty-eight years old, . . . because of that, I'm going to tell you how our mothers, before, in the old days would make us get up. We got up at three on the dot, two on the dot." Serafina continued, describing how she and her family drank wayusa, then fermented aswa for breakfast, before heading to work in the forest or their fields. But, she said, "now in this time, the newly raised children, the newly raised daughters and sons, no matter what, they don't respect getting up at night, or making aswa at night and serving it, or preparing wayusa to serve." Serafina, however, claimed that she had "not forgotten" these practices.

In our conversation, Mayor Shiguango suggested that his parents still knew "how to weave a shigra." Serafina similarly emphasized her knowledge of material culture like woven bags. Through her narrative, Serafina recalled several gendered socialization practices. One of the most significant for women was the production of a fiber called pita and var-

---

2. This plant has been variously identified as *Aechmea* sp., Bromeliaceae (Kohn 2002, 415; Perreault 2000, 162) and *Furcraea andina* (Penuela et al. 2016, 87), as well as *Agave americana* (Oberem 1980, 94).

3. A full transcript of this recording is available in Ennis (2019b).

ious related products. She continued her recollections of her childhood socialization and described, "After [eating], we worked, to weave shigra bags, to weave *ishinga* [small nets], and like that, to [make] all of the shigra, to twist the pita fiber, to spin pita into thread, doing all of it, twisting, spinning, sitting there, I'm a weaver of shigra, of ishinga." Memory was central to Serafina's understanding of herself and her cultural practices. As she explained, "To this day I don't forget a single thing. I live doing that work."

Serafina's emphasis on living "the words of the elders" encapsulates the process I describe as reanimation in chapter 4. Reanimation describes how spatiotemporally distant events and perspectives are brought to life in the pragmatic present through discourse and other semiotic activity. Put most simply, reanimation answers the question: How does the past come to life in the present? One way is through the animation, in Goffman's (1981a) sense, of the words of one's elders. Reanimation does not imply that the past is only or exclusively in need of salvage or that it is dead and gone, brought back to life as a "zombie" (Perley 2012) in a documentarian archive. Rather, reanimation speaks to the ways that memories of the past are maintained, brought forward, nurtured, and kept alive through their reembodiment across generations. For speakers of Quechuan languages, including Upper Napo Kichwa, the past is "in front of one's eyes" (Huayhua 2020; cf. Canessa 2012). Bringing this past into the present can be accomplished discursively through narrative. Knowledge is also inscribed somatically (Uzendoski and Calapucha-Tapuy 2012). The embodiment of memory and repeated instantiations of material practices relink linguistic and cultural socialization from their academic dismemberment into separate spheres of knowledge. For people like Serafina, remembering and living memories of the elders included speaking "our own" language.

Serafina tells listeners in conclusion, "So, now I'll make you listen to just a little of the words of counsel [kamachishka shimi] of our elders that came before." As she speaks, her voice develops a rhythmic tone characterizing the speech genre of kamachina or counseling. As she reanimates her memories of this past counsel, she interweaves the voices of her elders with her own speech, slipping between first-person declaratives and citations of the speech of elders, a linguistic practice that characterizes kamachina speech and Amazonian narrative more generally (Nuckolls

2008). In some accounts of speech events and narrated events, the action of the narrated event is kept at arm's length from the speech event (Benveniste 1971; Jakobson 1971). However, in Kichwa narratives and performance, the action of the narrated event seems to break through to meet participants in the overarching speech event. These temporal laminations occur in underlined sections of lines 67 and 69, as Serafina moves between the space of the present and the past to the bring the counsel of her elders to life.

Excerpt of Serafina Grefa's kamachina recorded for *A New Path* (date unknown)

SG: Tukuy churiguna, tukuy wawaguna uyashkai rimauni.[65]
'Nakpi shinallara ima tunu ama chi llaki, ama chi turmindura tupanuchun nishami kayta rimani.[66]
Shinallara <u>kanguna uyak ringri asha uyak umayuk asha, uyasha kawsanunga.</u>[67]
Ñuka mamagunas shina nishami kamachikuna aka.[68]
Payguna ima tunumandas kanguna itiashka tupura may wawagunara kamachikpi <u>uyak wawa ashaga, uyasha kawsanunga nisha</u> rimashkarami, ñuka ansa ansa uyashkara kuna kangunara kanguna tukuy uyaushkai ansawara rimani.[69]
Chilla mashka ñukawak.[70]

SG: I am speaking when all the sons, all the children are listening.[65]
I say this because I don't want them to encounter hardship or sadness of any kind.[66]
Like this, <u>all of you as ones with ears that listen, as ones that pay heed, they will live listening.</u>[67]
My female relatives also would give advice speaking like this.[68]
For what you all consider whatever reason, wherever they counseled their children, <u>they said, "being a child that listens and pays heed, listening they will live"</u> and this speech, just a little of what I heard, with all of you listening, I now speak a little.[69]
Just that is what I have had to say.[70]

In line 69, the voices of Serafina's female relatives are directly embedded into her counsel, interweaving her memories with the present event.

Her citation of their voices in line 69 reinforces her own voice in line 67, which tells her interlocutors to "listen," as she reminds her audience that she too speaks with the words elders left behind. Although brief, this recording illustrates how speakers voice inherited knowledge in daily linguistic practice. It also points to the importance of such knowledge for contemporary reclamation projects in Napo, including *A New Path*'s efforts to "revalorize" and reconstitute the indexical linkages between elders' lifeways (ruku kawsay) and contemporary Kichwa lifeways (runa kawsay) through radio-mediated remembering. These are sites where Napo Runa transmit lessons about who they were and who they might be, grounded in intergenerational memories and lived experiences.

The transmission of narratives and embodied practices among Upper Napo Kichwa speakers contributes to the formation of a collective memory of their social world. In everyday moments of interaction, speakers reanimate the voices of people—often elders—who taught them something significant, including stories of the origins of animals and plants in the forest, prohibitions surrounding hunting and alimentation, the preparation of medicinal plants, material techniques for planting or weaving, among many other strands of familial, inherited knowledge that combine to make ñukanchi rukuguna sakishka shimi, "the words our elders left behind." When Kichwa adults and elders teach (yachachina) they both demonstrate (*rikuchina*) and converse (kwintana), bringing past practices and voices into the present. These forms of embodied and linguistic knowledge are sites of collective memory, what anthropologist Brigittine French describes as "a social construction constituted through a multiplicity of circulating sign forms, with interpretations shared by some social actors and institutions and contested by others in response to heterogeneous positions in a hierarchical social field in which representations of the past are mediated through concerns of the present" (2012, 340). They are collective in the dialogic sense advocated by Halbwachs, as it is in "society that [people] recall, recognize, and localize their memories" (1992 [1925], 38).[4] One form of dialogic contestation is over

---

4. Theorizations of collective memory (e.g., Connerton 1989; Climo and Cattell 2002; French 2012) generally trace their intellectual history to the French sociologist Maurice Halbwachs, who outlined a fundamentally dialogic theory of memory. According to Halbwachs, "It is to the degree that our individual thought places itself

the voices that will be animated in these collective memories. Standard-ized or regional? Purified through inclusion of neologisms or sometimes mixed with Spanish? These programs and performances are sites where concerns of the present—including social change and environmental disruption—speak to memories of the past.

A New Path remediated and reanimated elders' knowledge through radio, contributing to the creation of collective memories. The hosts of *A New Path*, alongside other cultural activists and media producers brought the interactional space-time of the wayusa upina to life each month as a site of cultural and linguistic socialization. In other daily me-dia practices, from the naming of radio shows to on-air exhortations to drink guayusa, the wayusa upina was a central point of reference for Up-per Napo Kichwa radio and other forms of media production. This mul-timodal, intertextual chronotope of the familial home—like that of the Bakhtinian (1981b) literary chronotope—entails and presupposes certain understandings of personhood and relationality, creating a tacit social ontology (Mannheim 2015; Agha 2007). These on-air reanimations, then, can reveal a great deal about how social personhood is constituted and understood among speakers of Upper Napo Kichwa.

During her narrative, Serafina slips into the speech genre called ka-machina, "counseling, ordering, disciplining," which is central to the practice of the wayusa upina, both on and off air. In face-to-face en-counters, kamachina is used to socialize children, novices, and oth-erwise errant social actors (such as killa, "lazy," wives and husbands) into the appropriate knowledge, behavior, habits, and interactional relationships that give shape to past and present social practices. This counsel is a means of knowing the past, because kamachina speech is based in the animation and reanimation of an elder's knowledge, including that of their own elders, in an interdiscursive chain. Linking

---

in these frameworks and participates in this memory that it is capable of the act of recollection" (1992 [1925], 38). From this perspective, Halbwachs argued that "in reality, the past does not recur as such, . . . everything seems to indicate that the past is not preserved but reconstructed on the basis of the present. . . . Collective frame-works . . . are precisely the instruments used by the collective memory to reconstruct an image of the past that is in accord, in each epoch, with the predominant thoughts of the society" (1992 [1925], 39–40).

MEDIA AND COLLECTIVE MEMORY

the wayusa hours with counseling is central to discourse about linguistic and cultural shift and efforts to reclaim and revalorize Napo Runa lifeways. This is evident in how many speakers frame recorded stories. This occurred in Serafina's recorded narrative of elders' practices, as the coda of her speech frames it explicitly as kamachina, rooted in the authority of her elders. As the knowledge called "the words left by our elders" has often been transmitted during the wayusa upina, it is seen as increasingly threatened in the context of shifting social relationships and daily habits.

Myth, History, and Collective Memory in Upper Napo Kichwa

The narratives animated in face-to-face interactions and on air partly reveal how my interlocutors grappled with cultural and linguistic shift through Upper Napo Kichwa social ontologies, remediated across narrative genres. Amazonian narratives have fascinated academics. The interrelationship of the seemingly stable genres of "myth" and "history" remains a topic of considerable discussion (Cadena 2015; Gow 2001; Fausto and Heckenberger 2007; Hill 1988; Lévi-Strauss 1966; Taylor 2008; Whitten 2008). In Napo, familial and personal narratives remediate underlying theorizations of how people become recognizable members of different social formations found in "mythic" narratives more commonly circulated among outsiders and academics (e.g., Viveiros de Castro 1998).

Speakers of Upper Napo Kichwa have found the stories left behind by their elders under increasing attack in the context of settler colonial expansion. This point was driven home to me during my interview with Roberto Cerda on the history of the bilingual education movement. During the interview, I mentioned my interest in the "stories" (Sp. cuentos) bilingual educators had collected as part of their language activism. He remarked in reply, "The stories, which according to the external understanding is myth, for us are a reality. They are true. So, for people with [this] awareness, we couldn't be quiet, or say that it is myth. It is not myth for us."

Stories belonging to the category of "what the elders told" describe that language, substance, material practice, and interpersonal interaction are ways that different categories of social beings are produced and transformed. In the stories told by elders, people of the distant past (*ñawpa timpu*) became beings who are today animals or plants because they failed to engage in proper social relationships or took up new habits, changes evidenced by a transformation in their external coverings (clothes, fur, feathers) or consumption. Similarly, contemporary elders reflect on how the things they ate and drank as children and the interactional relationships they maintained with their own elders, gave shape to the lives they live as the contemporary elders of Upper Napo Kichwa society. However, many children today, they say, are "forgetting" the words left behind by the elders and their ability to "live" (or animate) them in the present.

Not just complaints about intergenerational change or "kids these days," the discursive structures and narrative patterning of many stories reflect a concern that the relational field of Upper Napo Kichwa personhood is transforming due to linguistic, social, and environmental change. Stories of personal experience and recent history shape much Upper Napo Kichwa storytelling, as stories of the ways the world and its inhabitants took shape in the past, handed down by distant elders, are recounted infrequently, if at all, in some households. These historical stories are privileged forms of knowledge and are not shared as openly by some who know them. Stories from conversations among elders in the past, brought to life in various modalities in the present, are ways that Napo Runa storytellers mobilize a collective memory for future-oriented action through the socialization of novices into appropriate norms of interaction.

These narratives theorize Napo Runa personhood and social interaction. Michi Saagiig Nishnaabeg scholar Leanne Betasamosake Simpson has described that stories are theories. "A 'theory' in its simplest form is an explanation of a phenomenon," she writes, "and Nishnaabeg stories in this way form part of the theoretical basis of our intelligence" (2017, 151). Simpson emphasizes that theory is not just an analytic category but something "generated and regenerated continually through embodied practice and within each family, community, and generation of people" (2017, 151). As she explains, stories as theory are a form of knowledge that people grow into throughout their lives. First, someone may only understand the literal meaning; with time, they may come to understand the conceptual underpinning, and finally, the metaphorical meanings of the stories they encounter (2017, 151–52). It is with such understanding, Simpson suggests, that "they start to apply the processes and practices of the story in their own lives." Stories of cultural change like Serafina's are not just about the literal content chiding "lazy" children these days, but also about the conceptual and metaphorical meanings accessible through lived experience and teaching. They are theories of personhood and interaction, which encourage listeners to "live" their elders' remembered ways of being in the world.

Many participants in the Upper Napo Kichwa media industry sought to reclaim regional linguistic forms and the social environments where language is meaningfully used disrupted by settler colonialism. Theirs was a grassroots pedagogy, which highlighted significant practices within intergenerational spaces where linguistic, cultural, and ecological knowledge meet. The production of a natural fiber called pita is one site linking language to social relationships and material practices to contribute to remembering Upper Napo Kichwa language and lifeways.[5]

Woven Lifeways

"My mother would tell how her female relatives used to sell [pita] in Quito," Serafina reflected as she pounded and scraped the long leaves of a pita plant at home in Chaupishungo. The leaves can be pounded, scraped, and twisted to produce a durable natural fiber used to weave shigra bags, as well as nets (cf. Lincoln and Orr 2011). Serafina tended an

---

5. I have chosen to write this word as *pita*, which is the pronunciation I am most familiar with in Napo, and which coincides with the way the term is written in Spanish. As discussed in chapter 4 (see note 5), other forms may represent hypercorrection relative to Unified Kichwa. The word likely arrived in Kichwa through Spanish by way of an Arawakan term (Colmenero-Robles, Bazarte Martínez, and Rosas Medina 2020; Tremblay 2007). Arawakan languages were also spoken in the Northern Andes prior to European contact (Urban 2021; Renard-Casevitz, Saignes, and Taylor 1988), it may be possible that the term represents substrate influence or processes of inter-Indigenous language contact that pre-date the arrival of Europeans.

abundant pita plant close to her home. She would carefully harvest spiky leaves often more than five or even six feet in length. The plant towered over her frame when she harvested them.

The production of pita is not easy. Serafina and other members of AMUPAKIN demonstrated different stages of this process to tourists at their midwifery and educational center on the outskirts of Archidona. They harvested pita near their homes and prepared different stages of the multistep process for demonstrations and teaching. They also processed pita for their own use and sale. At home, the stages of pita production took Serafina several days to complete. After harvesting leaves, Serafina would trim and de-thorn them using her machete. After the leaves were de-thorned, she pulled the stalk across an upright pole, slapping its ends against the wood, softening its epidermis. Serafina then peeled the stalk apart, splitting its skin from a thick strip of fibers. She then bundled these strips together and tied them off with a discarded piece of the plant, before soaking them in a bucket of water. After soaking, she tied individual strips of fiber to a long wooden pole and scraped the fibers using a piece of wood, separating the plant's green flesh from the fibrous white core. She then washed the fibers again. After washing and drying, the pita was finally ready to be processed into thread. This process was again labor intensive. Serafina carefully separated thin strands of the plant fiber, which she then twisted into compact strands and then into multi-ply yarn. The final stages of this process involved tightening and rolling the threads of yarn against her leg (figure 12). As she explained the steps while working pita, Serafina said, "It is a lot of work, that's why we value our shigra," the bags woven from pita and carried by men and women in the Upper Amazon.

Indigenous peoples of the Upper Amazon have spun plant fiber into a valuable resource for hundreds of years, if not longer. Elders' recollections parallel reports from the early 1600s that Indigenous residents around the town of Archidona were famously producers of pita (Oberem 1980, 181). Colonial records suggest regional groups already used pita at the time of the Spanish invasion (Oberem 1980, 184). Beginning in the early 1600s through the early 1800s, Archidona residents were forced to pay "tributes" of pita or its equivalent in gold to priests and colonial landowners (Oberem 1980, 85, 105). In the 1800s, these tributes became in-

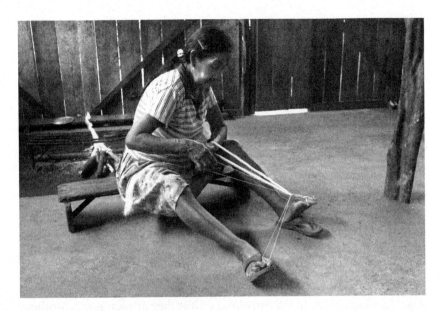

FIGURE 12 Serafina Grefa processing pita fiber by her fire in 2017. Photo by the author.

flated payments for trade goods Amazonian Kichwa people were forced to buy from missionaries and landowners (Oberem 1980, 112). Elders in Napo born in the 1940s and 1950s recount that their parents and grandparents were among the generations subjected to the practice of using Indigenous porters to carry goods—and people—on their backs across the Andean Highlands at the turn of the century (Muratorio 1991, 28). Like Serafina's relatives who sold pita in the Highlands, many Kichwa people traveled by foot over the peaks to sell Amazonian goods in Quito, the capital.

Pita is also a significant cultural item, despite its history as one of many products forcibly extracted through Amazonian labor. Serafina explained that during her childhood pita was commonly used as thread for clothing. During my time in Napo, pita was mostly used to weave the conical shigra bags and to produce necklaces and other forms of ornamentation.

In Serafina's household, like those of her colleagues and friends in AMUPAKIN, pita production is a gendered task. While she scraped the pita, Serafina continued:

Serafina Grefa comments on gender roles and pita, March 15, 2017

Shina katushkaramari ñuka mamaga	My mother used to tell of what they
kwintak aka.[1] Imarashami pitas	sold.[1] My mother used tell us, saying
aspisha, warmi tunu rashaga ganana	"You have to earn by scraping the pita
anmi nisha rimak aka ñuka mama.[2]	and doing a woman's kind of work."[2]

As in other narratives, Serafina embeds her mother's voice in line 2, reanimating her counsel on gendered labor. Pita was historically grown in distant secondary residences where families maintained their hunting and gardening grounds in the forest (Kohn 2002, 253–54). During my fieldwork in Archidona, women like Serafina tended pita near their homes. Land reform has reduced the territories people can access. Many people no longer had the option of maintaining a secondary home deeper in the forest. Others were unable to visit regularly. Women are also responsible for processing the fibers and hand-twisting them into cords, and for weaving shigra bags, often in the early hours while they drink wayusa. Mothers teach daughters to weave shigra bags by adding "daughter" knots onto "mother" threads, producing flexible and durable net bags.

Despite the importance of shigra and pita for Kichwa cultural history and practice, younger women's production of pita seems to be diminishing. Serafina was the only woman in her household who prepared pita during the year that I lived with her family. She and her daughters sometimes purchased pita, particularly colorfully dyed pita, from others. Serafina affirmed that she had demonstrated the steps to her daughters and that they knew how to complete the process. Some young women in her household transferred these skills to recycling soft plastics, hand-twisted into thin cords with similar techniques as those used to create pita thread. They wove these plastic cords into waterproof shigra, popular for use during fishing. Since Serafina's death, pita production has been too painful for her daughters. The burnished wood pole she used to weave was carefully set aside in a corner near the fire, waiting for the day a daughter's hand might take it up again.

Pita was a focus of cultural activism in Napo, woven through the regional ecology of media in beauty pageants, music, radio programs, and among the members of cultural organizations who often participated in local media. Cultural activists have turned to media as a vehicle to reclaim the production of pita and the use of shigra, utilizing a multimodal form of remembering that links together women's knowledge of their ecology and their economy.

Growing Pita in Napo's Media Ecology

The offices of the radio program *A New Path* were just one node within the broader ecology of Kichwa media in the Ecuadorian Amazon, which also included community films, a variety of radio programs, a morning TV news program, music and music videos, live performances, books, websites, and social media content. Since concluding my primary research in 2017, I have also witnessed a fluorescence of social and digital media production from Napo, particularly as young community activists use platforms like Instagram, TikTok, and YouTube to spread awareness about illegal mining and other serious environmental issues affecting Napo. Representations of weaving with pita and other materials could also be found across a variety of these settings. In 2023, for instance, the singer Sisa Kuty released the song "Awak Huarmi" (Weaver Woman), celebrating women's knowledge of traditional handicrafts, in this case, basketry. Kuty studied traditional Amazonian women's song and music with the founder of AMUPAKIN (Ennis 2021). This is one example of how the broader ecology of media in Napo interwove interactions and relationships outside of individual media technologies, platforms, or events, which had identifiable effects on participants' practices.[6]

While individual events featuring pita may seem somewhat ephemeral, the presence of this fiber throughout Upper Napo Kichwa community media served as an important way of remembering pita—either explicitly or implicitly—through interaction. Pita and shigra have become iconic elements of Upper Napo Kichwa performance media, worn by women young and old in cultural pageants, at political events, during dance performances, in community cinema, and during radio broadcasts produced for live audiences.

---

6. The song mixes two styles of writing Kichwa; the term *awak* (weaver) conforms to the standards of Unified Kichwa, while *huarmi* (woman) utilizes the prior Spanish-influenced script preferred by many people in Napo. Residents of Napo continue to negotiate the linguistic resources of standardization and regionally aligned forms.

Performing Pita

Pita gives its name to one of the local ñusta cultural pageants—discussed in chapter 4—indicative of its local importance. Members of the Unión de Comunidades Kichwas de Amarun Rumi elect the Pitak Waska Ñusta, or the Princess of Pita. Kichwa ñusta competitions combine charismatic spectacle with demonstrations of culturally significant practices and public oratory. These pageants often accompany yearly communal festivals. Celebrations of pita are woven into this ecology of media in ways that encourage the embodied remembering of the practice among participants, viewers, and listeners. Perhaps unsurprisingly, UCKAR's 2016 Pitak Waska pageant featured several instantiations of its namesake product.

During the 2016 festival season, the band Los Ángeles released the song "Pitaj Warmi" (Pita Woman). Los Ángeles is a popular Kichwa band from the community of San Rafael, one of the members of UCKAR. The song boldly proclaims, "The Princess of Pita has arrived" and describes a young woman presenting pita at a pageant to audience acclaim. It was a popular choice among pageant participants after release. Like other local music and media forms, the song mixes discussions of significant Kichwa cultural practices—in this case both pita production and cultural pageantry—with political discourse. After several verses, the singer calls out to "Ñukanchi alcalde Mashi Jaime Shiguango" (our mayor Comrade Jaime Shiguango), asking him to "dance hard." The singer similarly calls to "our organization UCKAR," showing the deep relationship between media and politics in Napo, which often leads pageant participants and media personalities toward political roles. The excerpt that follows presents lyrics from the song transcribed from a YouTube music video (James Yumbo [Jm Produce Full HD4K] 2019).[7] Comparison of this music video with recordings of live performances suggests the lyrics are somewhat flexible, emphasizing production and demonstration of pita.[8]

---

7. Notably, the video (2019) was produced by James Yumbo, cohost of *A New Path* and regular MC of pageants during my time in Napo. Indeed, James cohosted the 2016 Pitak Waska Ñusta pageant, again showing the deep interrelationship of participants and media forms within Napo's ecology of community media.

8. The title of this song can be found both as "Pitaj Warmi" and "Pitak Warmi." The lyrics to this song incorporate some features of Unified Kichwa, particularly the *-ta*

Excerpt of "Pitaj Warmi" by Los Ángeles

Pita warmika puruntupangui$_1$	Please get ready pita woman$_1$
Pita warmika puruntupangui$_2$	Please get ready pita woman$_2$
Pita karata apipangui$_3$	Please bring the pita plant$_3$
Pita waskata kawchungawa$_4$	To twist the pita vine$_4$
Kamba shutita kaparinukpi$_5$	When they call your name$_5$
Asi asilla llukshipangui$_6$	Please come out just laughing$_6$
Kamba shutita kaparinukpi$_7$	When they call your name$_7$
Kushi kushilla llukshipangui$_8$	Please come out just happy$_8$
Pita karata apasha risha$_9$	You go carrying the pita plant$_9$
Apukunata riksichingui$_{10}$	And show it to the leaders$_{10}$
Pita shigrata apasha risha$_{11}$	You go carrying the shigra$_{11}$
Apukunata gustachingui$_{12}$	And entertain the leaders$_{12}$

The music video features the lead singer alongside a young man and woman, dressed in traditional clothes of blue pacha and kushma. Likely filmed in a local community, various scenes show the lead singer and the young woman dancing near a large pita plant. The young woman also prepares pita as she dances, scraping the flesh from the fibers and twisting the cords, before donning a fully woven shigra. She and the other young participant dance at various points holding pita plants and leaves. Interspersed are clips from the 2017 Ñusta Chunta Warmi pageant, in which Los Ángeles performed live to accompany the representative from UCKAR.

The song was a popular choice among contestants at regional pageants, who demonstrated the various stages of pita production while dancing to it, eventually holding up a completed shigra. The song was also heard at community celebrations and on local radio programs. The ideological connection between shigra and pita, traditional Kichwa cultural and ecological practice, and performance media are enregistered through repeated performances. Such signs are multivalent—their meanings shift depending on contexts and audiences—existing within what Anna Babel (2018) calls a semiotic field. In Napo, pita and shigra have become signs

---

object marker. In live versions of this song, the singer can also be heard pronouncing the object marker as -*ra* when expected based on phonetic environment in Upper Napo Kichwa.

of identifiable personae, pointing variably to traditional ecological practices, rural lifeways, as well as glamorous performance media.

During the election of the Pitak Waska Ñusta in 2016, the contestant from Chaka Rumi was the first to demonstrate the production of pita as part of her performance with the traje de muyu (beaded-seed suit). The scene was part of a larger representation of the wayusa upina, featuring the young woman and several assistants preparing guayusa tea harvested from small trees that had been placed around the field where the pageant was held. The young woman repeated compressed versions of the stages of pita production while also dancing: collecting the leaves, striking and pulling them against a wooden pole, scraping the flesh, arranging and twisting the cords, and finally, weaving a shigra.

Likely owing to the pageant's name—the Princess of Pita—the next contestant also demonstrated pita production. Hailing from the community of San Rafael—also home to Los Ángeles—Karen Pizango danced with a male partner dressed in blue *kuru balon* (short pants; from Spanish, *pantalón corto*), slowly spinning across the field to the sound of flutes and bird calls. The gentle music suddenly transformed into the thumping rhythm of "Pitaj Warmi." Over the next four minutes, Karen danced and demonstrated the steps of scraping the pita, spinning the thread, and donning a shigra, as well as a skirt woven from pita threads. She then turned to a preteen girl who had been dancing in the background holding a large crown, and wrapped her in the woven skirt, suggesting an intergenerational transmission of practice in the performative space of the pageant. The young girl handed the crown off to the male participant, who crowned Karen as the dance concluded.

Karen won Princess of Pita in 2016. She ultimately won the crown in the township-wide pageant of Miss Peach Palm Princess (Ñusta Chunta Warmi). During the April 2017 Miss Peach Palm pageant, twenty-three-year-old Karen presented an amplified version of her prior performance, accompanied by two young men and two young women, and the singer and keyboardist of Los Ángeles. Her performance lives on in a video uploaded to YouTube (Omar Pizango 2017), further weaving together the various strands of Napo's ecology of media and its repertoire of memory (Taylor 2003). These performances incorporate forms of presentation that Perley has described as "charismatic Indigeneity" (2014). They are also sites of what he has referred to as "remembering" (Perley

2013), which can reconnect community members to social relationships, knowledge, and language.

While dancing with a shigra or miming the production of pita may seem like it could have limited effect on a young woman's knowledge, participation in pageants can shape women's lives. Some women in Napo have gone on to careers in media and politics through their work in cultural pageantry (see also Erazo and Benitez 2022). Others have become involved in cultural reclamation organizations. Still others—including a daughter-in-law in Serafina's household—have settled into the lives they performed on stage—tending manioc and weaving shigra by the morning fire. It is impossible to know how every young woman prepares, but at least some preparations involve interactions with family members and other knowledgeable elders to develop scenes and props. Many teenage performers, however, prepare with their families, consulting grandmothers, mothers, sisters, and cousins. Their families may even participate in pageantry, further drawing intergenerational communities together around a focal activity. There are of course also significant costs associated with these pageants—including significant financial expenditures required of participants. However, a key benefit of these performances is that they can foster spaces of intergenerational interaction, alongside more personal and public forms of remembrance.

Reweaving Pita on Air

In pageantry, participants present mimetic versions of cultural practices like weaving. Other forms of Kichwa media allow for a fuller expression of the interactional routines through which such knowledge is transmitted. These programs are sites of collective remembering, especially for women. Chapters 3 and 4 explored a September 2016 production of *A New Path* broadcast live from the community of Santa Rita to first consider the importance of listening in Kichwa language socialization, as well as how regional voices are animated and reanimated in Napo's media ecology. We return to this scene now to consider the forms of knowledge that participants chose to transmit in this production. These interactions partly occurred around the weaving of shigra, which emerged as an important part of gendered cultural knowledge, embedded in intergenerational interaction. In this way, we have also moved through my own lived theorization (Simpson 2017) of this material—from its literal meaning (the discourse of listening) to its conceptual meaning (the inclusion of regional voices) to its metaphorical meaning (the creation of collective memories).

This conversation is a segment of gendered counseling and disciplining of young people. Other portions of the program featured an elder man teaching adolescent boys similarly gendered practices. Meanwhile, the elder woman named Mama Olga led two preteen girls, their live audience, and at-home listeners in discussing and demonstrating the production of shigra, guided by producer and host Rita Tunay. Mama Olga explained the importance of the shigra and how her elders taught her the skill as an economic practice. Her description echoes scenes from beauty pageants and stories from *A New Path*'s narrative archive, showing how these performances remediate and reanimate collective memories.

"Santa Rita Wayusa Upina," kamachina excerpt 1.1–2, September 13, 2016

Rita: Imara kamachinuk akai ruku yayakuna ruku mamakuna kay punzhayanakunai, Mama Olga yallichipay ña?$_1$

Olga: Kay ñawpa punda, ña waysara upikanchi.$_2$ Ña chiwasha, kay ñukanchi ruku mamauna <u>ñawpa kasna rasha, shigrara awasha, mashti, katusha ganana anmi</u> nisha kamachikuna anmi.$_3$

Rita: What did [your] grandfathers and grandmothers counsel [you] when the dawn was breaking, Mama Olga please demonstrate, ok?$_1$

Olga: First, we drank guayusa.$_2$ Then after that, our female elders counsel us, saying "<u>first doing it like this, weaving shigra, um, selling [them], [you] have to earn [money]</u>."$_3$

Like Olga's underlined citation of her elder's advice in line 3, Serafina also reported her mother had counselled her that women must earn money by spinning pita, using very similar discursive structures. This suggests a broader gendered discourse of subsistence and labor, which has circulated in Napo and which Kichwa women seek to transmit on and off the air. This speech was also significant because Olga's voice follows the phonological and morphological contours of Upper Napo Kichwa dialect, less frequently heard in public performances. Live radio broadcasts provided a multimodal channel for language. They included embodied, oral, and aural dimensions, and revalued the voices of elder and rural speakers by bringing them into the public sphere.

Later in the show, Mama Olga implored the girls to observe the stages of pita production and to listen to her. Prompted by Rita, the exchange took place using enregistered routines for teaching and counseling. When Mama Olga checked the channel with the young girls (payaguna) in line 32 by asking, "Are you listening?" she had just explained the production of pita fiber.

"Santa Rita Wayusa Upina," shigra excerpt, September 13, 2016

Rita: Ña kuna kayma yallichishunchi imasnara tukun.[14]	**Rita**: So now over here let's demonstrate how it turns out.[14]
Olga: **Kasnami** tukun, shigrara awakpi.[15] Riki payauna rikupaychi.[16] **Kasna** rasha awashami, kangunawa apay risha rina anguichi, aychawara **kasna** rasha panga wambullandi apasha risha kaywai.[17] Apasha risha, wasii, maytusha kusasha mikuna anmi, kay shigrai apisha.[18] Riki, **kasna**.[19] Uyapanguichi payauna.[20]	**Olga**: **This is how** it turns out when the shigra is woven.[15] Look, please look girls.[16] Doing **like this**, weaving, you must go around carrying [it] with you, **like this** placing a leaf with the meat, you'll carry with this.[17] Carrying it, [once] in the home, wrapping in leaves and roasting, you must eat, receiving in this shigra.[18] Look, **like this**.[19] Please listen girls.[20]
Rita: Ña kuna kay rakulla payama kuyashun.[21] Chita apariy, apariy, chita apay risha.[22]	**Rita**: Ok now let's give it to this big girl.[21] Carry that, put it on, take it and carry it.[22]
Olga: Ña apariy apariy kayta.[23]	**Olga**: Ok, carry this, carry [it].[23]
Rita: Ña kuna ima waskara rurangui mama?[24]	**Rita**: So now, what vine do you make, ma'am?[24]
Olga: Payga pitami, pita waska.[25] **Kasna** ñawpa pundaga virdi karara pitisha, aspisha, chi taksashka washami kasna tukun.[26] Paya rikuy, rikuychi.[27] **Kasnmi**, **kasna** rashami kangunaga shigrara awashaga kan-	**Olga**: It's pita, pita vine.[25] **Like this**, first, the green flesh is cut, it's scraped, then after it's been washed, it turns out like this.[26] Girl look, look [plural].[27] **Like this**, doing it **like this**, now you all weaving the shigra

gunawak valirina.$_{28}$ Imas	[must] value what is yours.$_{28}$
maykan, maykanbas katusha	What we sell, we end up
ganana tukunchi kaywa.$_{29}$	earning with this.$_{29}$
. . .	. . .
Uyanguichichu payauna?$_{32}$	Are you listening girls?$_{32}$

As we have already seen, without Rita's prompting the exchange might have met the infelicitous fate of many conversations between grandparents and grandchildren, who often do not respond to queries of "are you listening?" from elders. But in this site of remembering, children were encouraged to listen and interact with their elders and their material practices. In line 23, Olga placed a shigra around the elder girl. The stages of pita were displayed for participants and live audiences, while those at home relied on their knowledge to imagine the scene on the air. In my own attempts at learning to spin pita and weave shigra, I became accustomed to Serafina's prompting "kasna" or "like this" as she demonstrated the steps, like Mama Olga does with the bolded items throughout lines 16, 17, 19, and 28. For audiences who were not present at the live broadcast, such deictic expressions pointing to specific interactions and participants could evoke memories of their own households, prior interactions with performative reanimations of these events, or perhaps even confusion. From technologically mediated events to daily interactions, pita and shigra emerged as linguistic and material sites for the multimodal production of women's collective memory in Napo. These uses of pita and shigra might seem fleeting in isolation, but they are connected to wider sites for the reclamation of women's knowledge.

Off-Stage Reclamation

Behind the scenes, organizations like AMUPAKIN train apprentices in practices like producing pita and weaving shigra in preparation for cultural presentations and community tourism, as well as for their own knowledge. AMUPAKIN participated in several of *A New Path*'s live radio performances and other public events around Napo, frequently creating sites of intergenerational interaction and training during preparations. Tourist visits provided income to participants in the organization, but community media events like radio programs were often unpaid.

MEDIA AND COLLECTIVE MEMORY

One morning, during my last month in Napo, I asked the midwives of AMUPAKIN to drink wayusa together to reflect on how their mothers had counselled them in the early morning hours.[9] What emerged was a fully embodied reanimation of the morning hours, which extended the interactional frames available to performers during live radio broadcasts. As we saw in chapter 3, the founder of the organization, María Antonia Shiguango, counseled one young woman for more than fifteen minutes, partly reminding her that pita should never be in short supply and that it should be planted near the house. In one segment of her counseling, she emphasized the importance of pita for a woman's development, linking it to the fulfillment of a woman's gender role:

María Antonia Shiguango, kamachina to Kelly Huatatoca, June 10, 2017

MS: May pita kawchuna, may ashanga awana, shushuna awana, shigra awana, tukuyra yachana anmi.[77] Shinakpi chigunara kasna tuta atarisha tiashami chigunara yachana an.[78] 'Na rakpi chigunara yachasha, chiga ali paktakta warmi tukun.[79]

MS: [The girl] must learn all of it, how to twist the pita, how to weave *ashanga* baskets, how to weave *shushuna* sieves, how to weave shigra bags.[77] So, all of those [things], getting up before dawn like this and being [by the fire], all of those must be learned.[78] When she does that, when she knows those things, then she will fully become a woman.[79]

---

9. Members of AMUPAKIN and I have written (Ennis et al. 2024) about the need to provide economic compensation to research colleagues and teachers in language and cultural revitalization research. Economic concerns are pressing for many people living in Napo, and participation in revitalization projects assumes time and economic stability. Utilizing research funds to pay participants and transcriptionists is one way to redistribute resources as scholars who make careers from the data of others' lives. Despite the cautions of methods manuals to avoid paying "informants," I contributed general payments to AMUPAKIN as an organization during my time there, paid participants in the wayusa upina for their time, and have continued to pursue grant funding for community-oriented media projects at AMUPAKIN's request.

Much like Olga, María Antonia checked the channel early in the exchange by asking Kelly, "Girl, are you listening?" María Antonia similarly spoke a distinctly Upper Napo variety of Kichwa to the young woman before her, who responded that she understood. While María Antonia spoke, Serafina and her colleagues were gathered around the fire, twisting pita and weaving shigra while women in their late teens and early twenties observed and assisted.

Organizations like AMUPAKIN, and the wide range of media events in which they participate in Napo, often bring elders together with young people for events focused on learning language through culture, based in routines of listening and watching. Listening and watching are two of the most significant ways young people are expected to learn. At AMUPAKIN, I observed young women assisting their elders—and speaking with them—in tasks like producing pita, weaving shigra, as well as other gendered cultural jobs such as chewing pulp for fermented manioc aswa or tending the organization's small medicinal and food gardens. AMUPAKIN also incorporated several younger volunteers and apprentices, many of whom were reclaiming regional linguistic practices through their daily interactions at the center with elder midwives and the preparations they undertook for various performance and tourist events.

Although individual media production and performance events appear transitory, the broader ecology of media in Napo has several important effects. Since my time in Napo, once cohost of *A New Path* and former ñusta contestant Rita Tunay became prefect of the province, partly aided by her recognizability and public-speaking skills. Women's political participation is one seemingly "unexpected" outcome of Indigenous media production. Likewise, the facilitation of new economic opportunities through media work, tourism, and the production of handicrafts might be "unexpected" ways that Amazonian Kichwa people are engaging media, one that more directly speak to the goal of "holistic development" in the region. Perhaps most importantly, this ecology of regional media opened new spaces for multimodal and intergenerational interaction beyond texts and classrooms. Such spaces were sites to reweave indexical connections between communities, language, and lifeways in the service of reclaiming an identity many people worried was being forgotten.

Conclusion: Reweaving and Remembering More Than Language

The ecology of community media has become a significant place of remembrance in Napo. The words of the elders are sometimes ephemeral, prone to being forgotten when the person who holds them dies, unless carefully remembered as the words "left behind." These are forms of knowledge that have adhered in living bodies and have been transmitted through narrative and embodied interactions. During one live-broadcast radio kamachina an elder speaker counseled a younger supplicant to honor and love his parents while they lived, as she told him, "You will not hear your father's speech after he dies." This lesson was reinforced for everyone—me included—who learned from and loved Serafina Grefa when she died in November of 2020, partly severing one of the strands of memory woven through Napo's ecology of media. Serafina's memory lives on in photos, videos, writings, and other forms of mediation that shape a large and shifting community archive of Napo Kichwa media, an archive of which I also hold a piece. However, as María Antonia cautioned Kelly in chapter 3, the words of the elders should be "planted in the heart," not just in entextualized media. This thread of memory has been picked up in various ways by her children and other loved ones, who now live the memory of Serafina and her elders' counsel. Serafina's advice is a thread that I hold onto and remember to guide my life, as well as my understanding of the time I spent studying community media in Napo.

Pita and shigra production provide a powerful organizing frame for reanimating women's environmental knowledge through the voices of elder and younger women. Multimodal media and performance create opportunities to recirculate language and otherwise embodied practices. For some young women, their participation can plant the seeds for future action as politicians, or as mothers and homemakers. Such events have emerged as their own cultural practice, connected to wider moments of media production and reception. In pageants and radio programs alike, participants reframe products like pita and shigra as the valuable items they once were, when they are seen by many as outdated. Such practices also seek to interrupt oppressive economic systems that devalue handicrafts and handspun materials, as well as the people who make them. They are grassroots ways of promoting the "integral development" of the region through women's political and economic empowerment.

In isolation, the individual events of beauty pageants, radio shows, performances, or daily interactions at cultural centers might not be enough to return regional Upper Napo Kichwa to active use among younger speakers or to improve intergenerational interaction and transmission. This, however, assumes that daily use or the creation of newly fluent speakers are the ultimate goals of all revitalization projects (Nettle and Romaine 2000; Grenoble and Whaley 2006; cf. Meek 2019), as I once thought. Creating new speakers is a long-term goal many people desire, but the idea of language reclamation also involves recognizing the existence of the multiple, even conflicting goals, that can be present in such projects, goals that may exceed or challenge the expectations of external advocates.

On the radio show *A New Path* the hosts frequently claimed that the programs existed so that audience members would not "forget" their elders' knowledge. Their programs, and the interconnected mediascape of which they are part, were grassroots sites of "remembering" in the face of dismemberment of language. For Perley, remembering is more than just recall, it is also about "*remembering* the social relations that linguistic science has dismembered from indigenous languages" (2013, 258, original emphasis). Programs like *A New Path* and organizations like AMUPAKIN brought together speakers, their linguistic varieties, and their embodied practices to reweave connections between them. This, too, was a form of reclamation of oppressed languages and lifeways, directed by community members in response to their own history, knowledge, and goals. They did this through existing preferences for living—animating—how they understood the past in the present through the embodied transmission of language and knowledge, often discussed as "the words left by the elders." The reclamation of pita and shigra as significant cultural practices in the face of recent settler colonial disruptions to local languages, ecologies, economies, and interaction points to how speakers of doubly oppressed languages like Upper Napo Kichwa engage in a reclamation of language that is also about more than language.

Like other methods, there are limits to such projects. Much of the media work in Napo—like the municipal program I have explored here—were supported through funding from the Ecuadorian government under the auspices of former president Rafael Correa's Citizens' Revolution, using resources from oil extraction that has helped to drive environmental degradation, urbanization, and cultural change in the Amazon (Riofrancos 2020). Cultural organizations like AMUPAKIN and others in Archidona often support themselves through community tourism, welcoming visitors from the United States or Europe, who are likely among those who consume fossil fuels and other minerals extracted from the Amazon (Zuckerman and Koenig 2016). But decolonization is perhaps best understood as a process of reclamation—of land and of sovereignty (Tuck and Yang 2012; Smith 2012), certainly, but also of language and culture—not an overnight solution. In the context of ongoing settler and extractive colonialism in the Amazon, the production and reception of community media are daily realizations of embodied forms of reclamation. They are hopeful and defiant acts against ongoing linguistic and social oppression. They are sites of memory against many pressures to "forget" and ways of living the words of the elders in the present.

Epilogue

Were you listening?
Did you understand?

Sitting by the fire, Mama Serafina attempted to teach me how to listen and to speak like an *achimama*, a wise woman, and how to live a good life, an ali kawsay, grounded in hard work, community, and conviviality. These were lessons reiterated through my time spent observing radio programs and other media events in Napo. I have told you just a little of what Serafina and others told me about the ways that Napo Runa communities live among shifting ecologies, so that you might better understand how interwoven "their" ecologies are with "ours," and the consequences this can have for language and other forms of social practice.

The people I have told you about in this book do not live in some distant place, "deep in the heart of the Amazon," isolated from global relationships or forces. The ongoing interaction of people through and across media technologies and platforms are one way our ecologies are interwoven. They are also interwoven through the circulation of different linguistic codes in Napo, and the internal and external ideologies and ontologies of language that shape their use. They are further woven together in the global market for resources that are rapidly being extracted from the region. Some parents hoped their children would interact within a multilingual ecology, one in which they speak a local variety of runa shimi, as well as Spanish and English. Napo's ecology of language also includes languages like Chinese, as Chinese-backed gold mining has further transformed the ecologies of the province.

After completing the fieldwork upon which this book is based in 2017, I returned to Napo once in 2019 and again in 2023. It is media, particularly community and social media, which have connected me to Napo in my absences. I have followed my friends and colleagues in Napo on air—or at least the digital airwaves over which Napo radio is often transmitted. Gloria Grefa continues to host broadcasts on La Voz de Napo. James Yumbo became the host of wayusa upina broadcasts sponsored by the administration of his former cohost, Rita Tunay, who was prefect of Napo between 2019 and 2023. James further shapes the local ecology of media in Napo as a video producer for groups such as Los Playeros Kichwas (The Kichwa Beachboys), directed by Fernandisco, another local radio host. A new generation of activists has also emerged to draw attention to the effects of extractive industries on local communities and environments in Napo through social media.

It is also social media platforms that have kept me connected to my friends and colleagues in Napo, as we communicate over Facebook Messenger and WhatsApp. It was through these channels that I learned of Serafina's death in November of 2020, after several weeks of illness and messages back and forth. The next day, AMUPAKIN posted an announcement to Facebook, describing Serafina as "an influential Kichwa woman, who always defended her cultural roots," who left an "irreplaceable legacy to those who knew her." Part of this "irreplaceable legacy" is what has been described in this text as "the words our elders left," passed across generations. One of Serafina's eldest daughters, who took up her place beside the fire during the wayusa upina, described this with the Spanish word as her "inheritance" or "legacy" (*herencia*). These are, ultimately, the words left by the elders, which many in Napo sought new ways to reanimate in face-to-face and otherwise mediated interactions.

Only future work can address how the young people and adults of today might apprehend their own practices as reanimations of the memories of their elders, through the words they left for them. It seems very likely, though, that their involvement in these didactic spaces and emergent forms of linguistic and cultural vitality will bolster their authority as those who have seen and know the past, which allows them to mean-

EPILOGUE

ingfully "live" (kawsana) the lifeways (*kawsay*) of their elders, even in a changing social, linguistic, and material world.

■ ■ ■

The production and reception of community media in Napo provides a complicated means of extending and amplifying language and memory in the region. Although community-produced media are said to strengthen Indigenous linguistic and cultural practices and articulate sovereignty (Wilson and Stewart 2008; Camp and Portalewska 2013), many of the on-the-ground effects of these media remain unclear. Attending to both the production and reception of Upper Napo Kichwa radio media demonstrates that community media have emerged as a powerful method for cultural activists and other community members to reclaim language as a living code. Where linguistic unification and formal education have provided dominant models for institutional language revitalization in Ecuador—and elsewhere (Lane et al. 2018)—many of these methods are removed from how many speakers conceptualize language in use and their relationships to different varieties. It is important to consider the methods and media of language reclamation within the complex ecologies of language and assemblages of linguistic ideologies where language use takes place.

By looking closely at the semiotic processes and modalities—discursive, embodied, and otherwise material—of different forms of Napo Kichwa verbal artistry and their remediation on the radio, I have provided a linguistically and ethnographically grounded confirmation of what Indigenous activists and allies across different corners of the globe have already proposed. Community media are an important method in what must be a multifaceted approach to addressing contemporary processes of language oppression and change. No one I interacted with became a more fluent speaker of Upper Napo Kichwa exclusively by listening to the radio, but community radio stations were significant sites of further interaction, transmission, and reclamation in several ways. Perhaps one of the most important was that producers and participants experienced these programs as sites where they were encouraged to speak Kichwa, especially regional varieties, in public settings. The case in Napo also reveals some more specific effects of community media production,

which may be helpful for participants involved in other language reclamation projects.

Media and Method in Language Reclamation

The processes and practices of language revitalization and reclamation
in Ecuador speak to larger issues in language planning in Indigenous and
other languages undergoing shift. Linguistic unification has been unde-
niably important for establishing the symbolic legitimacy of Ecuadorian
Kichwa in comparison to Spanish, a legitimacy underscored by its inclusion in the Ecuadorian constitution as an official language of intercultural communication (*Constitución de la República del Ecuador* 2008).
A major ideological shift is underway in Ecuador, in which speakers see
a language that they were recently discouraged from speaking elevated
to the symbolic level of Spanish. However, the elevation of one regional
code—or at least what is seen as the elevation of the Highland's code—
has raised debates over just what is being revitalized in these projects.

Despite the diverse, well-established efforts to address linguistic shift
through formal education—often seen as the site where Spanish has
been inculcated—ongoing processes of shift toward Spanish raise difficult questions about the effects of these projects. In the 2022 national
census, 659,361 people in all of Ecuador reported that they speak an
Indigenous language, a decline of more than 30,000 people from the
691,108 who self-reported speaking an Indigenous language in the 2010
census (INEC 2010, 2023). An unacknowledged irony of the use of standard language and formal education for language revitalization is that
these methods continue to separate novice speakers from the contexts
of use and relationships of close intergenerational transmission through
which linguistic and cultural knowledge were once more robustly transmitted.[1] Unified Kichwa is also often regimented toward the norms of

---

1. The right to access formal education is a significant political achievement and
ongoing site of activism in Napo, as well as Ecuador more broadly. I do not mean to
discount the importance of formal education, nor bilingual programs, for Kichwa
speakers, but rather to point out ways in which formal education can be supple-
mented by other forms of linguistic and cultural socialization, facilitated by com-

Spanish-language interactional spaces, layering an explicitly Kichwa code onto Spanish-language lexical and grammatical loans. Widely held literacy ideologies that emphasize the transparent relationship between written and oral codes—expressed in statements among my interlocutors such as "Kichwa is pronounced just as it is written"—have produced a situation in which written standardization is often extended to oral standardization. In this view, Unified Kichwa becomes the de facto standard for written and oral communication, though the ways this standard code is deployed by speakers may be quite heterogeneous. Such forms may sometimes be quite foreign to regional speakers in Napo, lines of differentiation undergirded by the ways they already ideologize dialectal variation and belonging. The complex ways that people relate to and evaluate different varieties can also provoke considerable anxiety in speakers, frequently hindering language use.

Language planners in Ecuador are aware of these debates. Luis Montaluisa—one of the main academic and political proponents of linguistic unification—identifies radio media as a method through which speakers could be socialized into dialectal differences. In his view, the diffusion of systematic training regarding regional differences could be aided by radios, allowing for the development of "polydialectal" speakers (2018, 209). However, Montaluisa also regularly references the development of "formal" and "informal" varieties of Kichwa (2018, 306), suggesting that the standard may continue to be treated as the "formal" prestige form in a case of emergent triglossia among Spanish, standard, and regional varieties. Language standardization is also emerging as a form of linguistic shift in Napo, where some young people are predominantly learning the standardized code. While also a form of linguistic vitality, such revitalization practices often fit uneasily alongside the ways that many regional speakers conceive of language as the oral speech left to them by their elders.

The complex assemblages of external and internal linguistic ideologies surrounding Unified and regional varieties are thus one answer to a question that began this book—*Why do speakers of minoritized languages,*

---

munity media. This suggestion is also tied to the practices of my interlocutors in AMUPAKIN, who dream of someday establishing an immersive educational center for young people, which focuses on the practices of ruku kawsay within the rainforest.

despite many well-established programs aimed at reinvigorating or re-awakening heritage languages, continue to shift to dominant, colonial languages, such as Spanish, and English? Text-based approaches to language revitalization focusing on standardization, literacy, and formal education have been some of the predominant methods for language revitalization in Ecuador, as they have been in many other contexts (K. A. King 2001; McCarty 2008; Grenoble and Whaley 2006). Many language activists described their efforts as circumscribed by an unsupportive state apparatus with limited funding and time for immersive education. Yet, the uneven acceptance of these methodologies also points to their awkward fit among many of the communities they are meant to serve. There is room for text-based methods in language reclamation. However, other forms of mediation have the potential to amplify linguistic and cultural practices and respond more effectively to speakers' diverse needs.

Ideological complexity, however, is not the only answer. Many of the parents and adults I spoke with placed a high value on bilingualism, but the language they explicitly taught to young children was Spanish. Despite ongoing efforts at multiple scales to change the economic and ideological regimes of value in which Kichwa is located, Spanish remains a politically, economically, and socially dominant code in many spaces. Addressing linguistic shift toward Spanish is not just about the reconstitution of a linguistic code, but also reconstituting and revaluing the contexts of use where that code had meaning (Meek 2010), as well as creating new contexts and forms of use for it (Perley 2011). In Napo, radio media production emerges as an important way to support the ongoing transmission of linguistic and cultural forms, in part because the broader Napo mediascape placed Kichwa in new regimes of economic and linguistic value. Both top-down and bottom-up efforts seek to make Kichwa a language of economic opportunity for elders and young people alike, in which they can speak both to an Upper Napo Kichwa public and to interested outsiders. Projects that make knowledge and use of Kichwa—and other Indigenous languages—an economically viable pathway for people in Napo would be one way to more robustly support language reclamation. Programs that provide stipends for language learners and knowledge keepers, for example, or grant funding that supports the participants involved in community-media production (Ennis et al. 2024) are possibilities for support that could be more robustly developed—

particularly in recognition of the harm done by colonial linguistic and environmental policies.

Media production is an important method to extend and amplify the abilities of existing speakers, as well as to draw participants together into situations where Kichwa is the dominant and expected code of interaction. Community media production has become a focal site for a broader community of practice to reclaim practices and generate linguistic vitalities. Local and community radio programs and broadcasts integrate speakers of various abilities, establishing mediated communities of practice, and contributing to the formation of various publics, as different listeners are hailed in distinct ways. Some people participate more actively, while others interact on a more limited or passive basis. Radio programs, particularly those like *A New Path*, which focused on the inclusion of local cultural organizations and community members, created significant opportunities for the transmission of knowledge among participants both onstage and behind the scenes, as well as to their various audience members.

These programs amplify the voices and knowledge of speakers of languages that are undergoing shift. Particularly in contexts like Napo where a relatively large number of fluent speakers are still present, community-produced media also provide various dialogic points of departure for listeners who commented upon and recirculated them. Language revitalization, then, can be as much about amplifying the abilities and reinvigorating the practices of the elderly members of a discursive community (Rouvier 2017; Meek 2010) as it is about producing young and otherwise novice speakers.

In Napo, I met several people who I originally thought of as "native" speakers of Kichwa, but who I learned had reclaimed speaking as adolescents and adults. This includes some of the hosts, producers, and performers whom I have introduced in this book. The literature on language revitalization is often concerned with the production of new speakers, emphasizing the need to ensure intergenerational transmission to children (Grenoble and Whaley 2006; Meek 2019). However, ongoing grassroots processes of language reclamation in Napo show that adults are important actors in reclamation projects, not just as fluent knowledge keepers but as more passive listeners who may be transformed into active speakers, sometimes through their engagement with media.

Even fluent elders may "remember" more within a community of shared practices like AMUPAKIN, which encouraged members to recall and reanimate their elders' knowledge. By extending the opportunity to listen to wider audiences, while uplifting the interactional spaces in which children are socialized as listeners, many participants in Napo's ecology of media sought to strengthen listening in Kichwa, as much as speaking. Such practices may also help to "plant" Kichwa in the hearts of a broader public, while working against the linguistic discrimination that Kichwa speakers continue to face in Napo.

The introduction of new forms of mediation entails a shift in associated ideologies of language and media. Much like the ways that Unified Kichwa has remediated hegemonic standard language ideologies at odds with ideologies of regional belonging, media production sometimes conflicts with ideologies of secrecy, value, and authority. The remediation of oral narratives and other modalities of cultural practice on air has entailed a reorganization of ideologies of secrecy around familial knowledge. Where value once hinged upon control of the circulation of knowledge, the valorization of Napo Runa knowledge and cultural practice involves its public circulation. While bringing these stories onto the airwaves places them into new regimes of public value, it can also separate them from the authoritative relationships of familial transmission, leading listeners like Serafina to question their truth.

The situation in Napo raises larger questions of Indigenous data sovereignty and protocols surrounding the circulation of Indigenous media, which are related to the increasing use of digital technologies to mediate Indigenous languages (Carroll, Duarte, and Max Liboiron 2024; Miller 2022; Duarte 2017; Wemigwans 2018; Christen 2012). Machine-assisted translation of Indigenous languages, for instance, could represent new possibilities to expand the use of these languages. It also potentially creates ideological and ontological disjunctures that must be clarified (Dauenhauer and Dauenhauer 1998; Kroskrity 2009; Ennis 2020) on a case-by-case basis. The ways contemporary media will shape social imaginaries and collective memories among speakers of Upper Napo Kichwa in the future remain to be explored. The introduction of new digital technologies involving such media suggest a more hopeful future, in which language and culture are remembered, rather than forgotten, albeit in new modalities and regimes of value.

Community media have a complicated but important role to play in the mediation of linguistic ecologies. Broadcast media are sometimes credited with transmitting a standard register of speech—think of the register of the nightly news in the United States. While I did find codes that mixed regional and standardized forms on Napo radio programs, I also found that participatory and community-based media afforded the transmission of regional speech. The use of the standardized register did not always index a simple acquiescence to the ideologies and goals of standardization but did index a complex negotiation of the expectations of different audience members. Even as these programs allow for the emergence of regional forms of speech and the knowledge of community members, they also help to consolidate and regiment a collective memory of the past, though one that is still polyvocal and plural. As such knowledge becomes increasingly mediated in the public sphere, it also shapes the ways that various publics apprehend and imagine the past, present, and future of the Upper Napo Kichwa social world. Ultimately, the production and reception of community media in Napo emerges as an active, affective, and interpersonal process, into and through which learners—of many ages, abilities, and ideological orientations—can be socialized, providing hopeful avenues for future reclamation in Kichwa communities and beyond.

APPENDIX
Guide to Orthographic Conventions and Morpheme Glosses

I have completed transcriptions for this text in consultation with Napo Runa colleagues. Several also benefited from the input of Adela Carlos-Rios, instructor of Southern Peruvian Quechua during my time at the University of Michigan. All errors, however, are my own.

Orthographic practices for Kichwa (Quichua) are complex. In this text, I have adopted some of the norms of Unified Kichwa (including many uses of *k* instead of Spanish-derived orthographic *qu* and *c*, but not for *g* when used by speakers), while also attempting to represent significant regional variations in phonological processes. I have adopted a convention from Michael Wroblewski (2014) to capitalize and bold forms that tend to be phonologically marked for my interlocutors. This approach, at times, produces a somewhat heterogeneous text, which attempts to capture language in use. Some of the significant differences between Unified Kichwa conventions and the orthography utilized in transcriptions are the shown in table A1.

Morpheme glosses shown in table A2 are based on the Leipzig Glossing Rules, and further adapted from Adelaar and Muysken (2004) as needed.

TABLE A1 Unified Kichwa Conventions and Orthography

Form	Unified Kichwa	UNK practical orthography
Locative	-pi	-i / -bi / -ibi / -pi
Plural	-kuna	-una / -guna / -kuna
Same subject	-shpa	-sha[a]
Near future ('going to')	-kri-	-nga(k) rau-
Second person singular	-nki	-ngui[b]
Agentive	-k	-k [-x]
Durative	-ku-	-u-[c]
Accusative	-ta	- ra / -da / -ta
Purposive	-nkapak	-ngak / -ngawa
Copula	kana	ana[d]

[a] Unified Kichwa uses *-sha* for the first-person singular future; this is one of the two future tenses in use in Napo.

[b] I have maintained the common Spanish-derived spelling "-ngui" for a form pronounced [-ŋgi] as it is one of the more common spellings in Napo and avoids confusion about the pronunciation of *g* for Spanish speakers.

[c] Durative -u- is commonly realized as a diphthong, as in [rawni] "I am doing" or as vowel lengthening [miku:ni] "I am eating."

[d] When *-mi* or *-chu* precede the copula, they are often reduced and appended to the beginning of the word; for example, 'mani' "I am" and 'chani' "I am not."

APPENDIX

TABLE A2 Morpheme Glosses

Morpheme code	Gloss	Form
1.S	1st person singular subject	-ni
2.S	2nd person singular subject	-ngui [-ŋgi]
3.S	3rd person singular subject	-n
1.PL	1st person plural subject	-nchi
2.PL	2nd person plural subject	-nguichi
3.PL	3rd person plural subject	-nun
ABL	ablative case	-manda
ADV	adverb	-ra / -da / -ta
AC	accusative case	-ra / -da / -ta
AG	agentive nominalizer	-k [-x]
CIS	cislocative (toward subject)	-mu-
COP	copula	a-
CAUS	causative	-chi
CONJ	conjunction	shinakpi / shinallara
DAT	dative	-ma
D.DOM	distal demonstrative	chi
P.DEM	proximate demonstrative	kay
DL	delimitative case ('just, only')	-lla
DS	different subject (switch reference)	-kpi
DUR	durative	-u- / -hu- / -ku-
EPST	epistemic marker	-mi / -dá
IMP	imperative	-ychi (plural) / -y (singular)
LOC	locative	-i / -ibi / -bi / -pi
NOM	nominalizer	-na / -shka
PA	past	-ka- / -ra- / -rka-
PL	plural	-guna / -una / -kuna
PRF	perfect	-shka
PURP	purposive	-ngak / -ngawa
Q	question marker	-chu
SS	same subject	-sha
TOP	topicalizer	-ga / -ka

REFERENCES

Abu-Lughod, Lila. 2004. *Dramas of Nationhood*. Chicago: University of Chicago Press.

Adelaar, Willem F. H., and Pieter Muysken. 2004. *The Languages of the Andes*. Cambridge: Cambridge University Press.

Agha, Asif. 2005. "Voice, Footing, Enregisterment." *Journal of Linguistic Anthropology* 15 (1): 38–59.

Agha, Asif. 2007. "Recombinant Selves in Mass Mediated Spacetime." *Language & Communication*, Temporalities in Text, 27 (3): 320–35.

Agha, Asif. 2011. "Commodity Registers." *Journal of Linguistic Anthropology* 21 (1): 22–53.

Aguirre, Windsor E., Gabriela Alvarez-Mieles, Fernando Anaguano-Yancha, Ricardo Burgos Morán, Roberto V. Cucalón, Daniel Escobar-Camacho, Iván Jácome-Negrete, et al. 2021. "Conservation Threats and Future Prospects for the Freshwater Fishes of Ecuador: A Hotspot of Neotropical Fish Diversity." *Journal of Fish Biology* 99 (4): 1158–89. https://doi.org/10.1111/jfb.14844.

Ahearn, Laura M. 2001. *Invitations to Love*. Ann Arbor: University of Michigan Press.

Albó, Javier. 1979. "The Future of the Oppressed Languages in the Andes." In *Language and Society Anthropological Issues*, edited by William Charles McCormack and S. A. Wurm, 309–30. The Hague, Netherlands: Mouton.

Alfred, Taiaiake, and Jeff Corntassel. 2005. "Being Indigenous: Resurgences Against Contemporary Colonialism." *Government and Opposition* 40 (4): 597–614.

Alvarado, Carlos. 1994. *Historia de Una Cultura a La Que Quiere Matar*. Quito, Ecuador: Editorial Quipus.

Anderson, Benedict R. O'G. 1983. *Imagined Communities: Reflections on the Origin and Spread of Nationalism*. London: Verso.

Andronis, Mary Antonia. 2004. "Iconization, Fractal Recursivity, and Erasure: Linguistic Ideologies and Standardization in Quichua-Speaking Ecuador." *Texas Linguistic Forum* 47:263–69.

Appadurai, Arjun. 1996. "Disjuncture and Difference in the Global Cultural Economy and Global Ethnoscapes." In *Modernity at Large: Cultural Dimensions of Globalization*, 27–65. Minneapolis: University of Minnesota Press.

Aschmann, Richard. 2020. "Ecuadorpi Rimaj Quichua Shimicunami/Idiomas Quichuas Hablados En Ecuador." Quichua. https://quichua.net/Q/Ec/.

Asociación de Mujeres Parteras Kichwas del Alto Napo (AMUPAKIN). 2017. *Ñukanchi Sacha Kawsaywa Aylluchishkamanda/Relaciones Con Nuestra Selva/Relating to Our Forest*, Edited by Georgia Ennis. Quito, Ecuador: Ministerio de Cultura y Patrimonio.

Austin, J. L. 1962. *How to Do Things with Words*. Oxford: Clarendon Press.

Babel, Anna. 2018. *Between the Andes and the Amazon: Language and Social Meaning in Bolivia*. Tucson: University of Arizona Press.

Bakhtin, Mikhail. 1981a. "Discourse in the Novel." In *The Dialogic Imagination: Four Essays*, edited by Michael Holquist, translated by Caryl Emerson and Michael Holquist, 259–75. Austin: University of Texas Press.

Bakhtin, Mikhail. 1981b. "Forms of Time and of the Chronotope in the Novel." In *The Dialogic Imagination: Four Essays*, edited by Michael Holquist, translated by Caryl Emerson and Michael Holquist, 84–279. Austin: University of Texas Press.

Ball, Christopher. 2014. "On Dicentization." *Journal of Linguistic Anthropology* 24 (2): 151–73.

Balogun, Oluwakemi M. 2012. "Cultural and Cosmopolitan: Idealized Femininity and Embodied Nationalism in Nigerian Beauty Pageants." *Gender & Society* 26 (3): 357–81. https://doi.org/10.1177/0891243212438958.

Balogun, Oluwakemi M. 2020. *Beauty Diplomacy: Embodying an Emerging Nation*. Globalization in Everyday Life. Stanford, Calif.: Stanford University Press.

Barker, Meghanne. 2019a. "Dancing Dolls: Animating Childhood in a Contemporary Kazakhstani Institution." *Anthropological Quarterly* 92 (2): 311–43.

Barker, Meghanne. 2019b. "Intersubjective Traps over Tricks on the Kazakhstani Puppet Stage: Animation as Dicentization." *Journal of Linguistic Anthropology* 29 (3): 375–96. https://doi.org/10.1111/jola.12227.

Basso, Keith H. 1979. *Portraits of "The Whiteman": Linguistic Play and Cultural Symbols Among the Western Apache*. Cambridge: Cambridge University Press.

Basso, Keith H. 1996. *Wisdom Sits in Places: Landscape and Language among the Western Apache*. Albuquerque: University of New Mexico Press.

Bateson, Gregory. 1972. "A Theory of Play and Fantasy." In *Steps to an Ecology of Mind*, 177–93. New York: Ballantine Books.

Bauman, R., and Charles L. Briggs. 1990. "Poetics And Performance As Critical Perspectives On Language And Social Life." *Annual Review of Anthropology* 19 (1): 59–88.

REFERENCES

Bauman, Richard, and Charles L. Briggs. 2003. *Voices of Modernity: Language Ideologies and the Politics of Inequality*. Cambridge: Cambridge University Press.

Becker, Marc. 2008. *Indians and Leftists in the Making of Ecuador's Modern Indigenous Movements*. Durham, N.C.: Duke University Press Books.

Becker, Marc. 2010. *Pachakutik Indigenous Movements and Electoral Politics in Ecuador*. Critical Currents in Latin American Perspectives. Lanham, Md.: Rowman & Littlefield.

Becker, Marc, and Silvia Tutillo. 2009. *Historia Agraria y Social de Cayambe*. Quito, Ecuador: FLASCO Ecuador.

Benveniste, Émile. 1971. "Relationships of Person in the Verb." In *Problems in General Linguistics*, translated by Mary Meek, 223–30. Problèmes de Linguistique Générale. English. Coral Gables, Fla.: University of Miami Press.

Bermúdez, Natalia. 2020. "Ideophone Humor: The Enregisterment of a Stereotype and Its Inversion." *Journal of Linguistic Anthropology* 30 (2): 258–72. https://doi.org/10.1111/jola.12275.

Bermúdez, Patricia, and Michael Uzendoski. 2018. "Kukama Runa: Polyphonic Aesthetics in Cine Comunitario Among the Napo Runa of Amazonian Ecuador." *Anthropology and Humanism* 43 (1): 74–89.

Besnier, Niko. 1995. *Literacy, Emotion and Authority: Reading and Writing on a Polynesian Atoll*. Cambridge: Cambridge University Press.

Biddle, Jennifer L., and Tess Lea. 2018. "Hyperrealism and Other Indigenous Forms of 'Faking It with the Truth.'" *Visual Anthropology Review* 34 (1): 5–14.

Biersack, Aletta. 1999. "Introduction: From the 'New Ecology' to the New Ecologies." *American Anthropologist* 101 (1): 5–18. https://doi.org/10.1525/aa.1999.101.1.5.

Boas, Franz. 1911. *Introduction to Handbook of American Indian Languages*. Edited by John Wesley Powell and Preston Holder. Handbook of American Indian Languages. Lincoln: University of Nebraska Press.

Bolter, J. David. 2001. *Writing Space: Computers, Hypertext, and the Remediation of Print*. Mahwah, N.J.: Lawrence Erlbaum Associates.

Bolter, J. David, and Richard. Grusin. 1999. *Remediation: Understanding New Media*. Cambridge, Mass.: MIT Press.

Bourdieu, Pierre. 1991. *Language and Symbolic Power*. Edited by John B. Thompson. Translated by Gino Raymond and Matthew Adamson. Cambridge, Mass.: Harvard University Press.

Boym, Svetlana. 2007. "Nostalgia and Its Discontents." *The Hedgehog Review* 9 (2): 7–18.

Briggs, Charles L. 1986. *Learning How to Ask: A Sociolinguistic Appraisal of the Role of the Interview in Social Science Research*. Studies in the Social and Cultural Foundations of Language, No. 1. Cambridge: Cambridge University Press.

Briggs, Charles L. 1988. *Competence in Performance: The Creativity of Tradition in Mexicano Verbal Art*. Philadelphia: University of Pennsylvania Press.

Briggs, Charles L., and Richard Bauman. 1992. "Genre, Intertextuality, and Social Power." *Journal of Linguistic Anthropology* 2 (2): 131–72.

Brown, Joshua R. 2022. *The Verticalization Model of Language Shift: The Great Change in American Communities*. Oxford: Oxford University Press.

Brown, Michael F. 2007. *Tsewa's Gift Magic and Meaning in an Amazonian Society*. Tuscaloosa: University of Alabama Press.

Bucholtz, Mary. 2000. "The Politics of Transcription." *Journal of Pragmatics* 32 (10): 1439–65. https://doi.org/10.1016/S0378-2166(99)00094-6.

Bucholtz, Mary, and Kira Hall. 2005. "Identity and Interaction: A Sociocultural Linguistic Approach." *Discourse Studies* 7 (4–5): 585–614.

Butler, Judith. 1993. "Gender Is Burning: Questions of Appropriation and Subversion." In *Bodies That Matter: On the Discursive Limits of "Sex"*, 121–42. New York: Routledge.

Cadena, Marisol de la. 2015. *Earth Beings: Ecologies of Practice across Andean Worlds*. Durham, N.C.: Duke University Press.

Calhoun, Kendra. 2019. "Vine Racial Comedy as Anti-Hegemonic Humor: Linguistic Performance and Generic Innovation." *Journal of Linguistic Anthropology* 29 (1): 27–49. https://doi.org/10.1111/jola.12206.

Camp, Mark, and Agnes Portalewska. 2013. "The Electronic Drum: Community Radio's Role in Reversing Indigenous Language Decline." *Cultural Survival Quarterly* 37 (1).

Canessa, Andrew. 2012. *Intimate Indigeneities: Race, Sex, and History in the Small Spaces of Andean Life*. Durham, N.C.: Duke University Press Books.

Carpenter, Lawrence K. 1982. "Ecuadorian Quichua: Descriptive Sketch and Variation." Master's thesis, University of Florida.

Carroll, Stephanie Russo, Marisa Elena Duarte, and Max Liboiron. 2024. "Indigenous Data Sovereignty." In *Keywords of the Datafied State*, edited by Jenna Burrell, Ranjit Singh, and Patrick Davison, 207–23. Data & Society Research Institute. http://dx.doi.org/10.2139/ssrn.4734250.

Chao, Sophie. 2022. *In the Shadow of the Palms: More-Than-Human Becomings in West Papua*. Durham, N.C.: Duke University Press.

Chernela, Janet. 2018. "Language in an Ontological Register: Embodied Speech in the Northwest Amazon of Colombia and Brazil." *Language & Communication*, Language in the Amerindian Imagination, 63 (November): 23–32.

Choksi, Nishaant. 2018. "Script as Constellation Among Munda Speakers: The Case of Santali." *South Asian History and Culture* 9 (1): 92–115.

Chomsky, Noam. 1965. *Aspects of the Theory of Syntax*. Cambridge, Mass.: MIT Press.

Christen, Kimberly. 2012. "Does Information Really Want to Be Free? Indigenous Knowledge Systems and the Question of Openness." *International Journal of Communication (19328036)* 6 (January): 2870–93.

Climo, Jacob, and Maria Cattell. 2002. *Social Memory and History: Anthropological Perspectives*. Walnut Creek, Calif.: Rowman Altamira.

Cognet, Arthur. 2021. "Jumandy, Le Héros National Des Napo Runa: Généalogie de La Création d'un Héros Amazonien Jumandy, El Héroe Nacional de Los Napo Runa: Genealogía de La Creación de Un Héroe Amazónico Jumandy, National

Hero of the Napo Runa: Genealogy of the Creation of an Amazonian Hero." *Bulletin de l'Institut Français d'études Andines* 50 (August): 25–45. https://doi.org/10.4000/bifea.13265.

Cohen, Colleen Ballerino, Richard Wilk, and Beverly Stoeltje, eds. 1995. *Beauty Queens on the Global Stage: Gender, Contests, and Power*. 1st ed. New York: Routledge.

Colmenero-Robles, Aurelio, Alicia Bazarte Martínez, and Imelda Rosas Medina. 2020. "La Asombrosa Fibra de Pita o Seda Mexicana." *Desarrollo Local Sostenible* 12 (35). https://www.eumed.net/rev/delos/35/fibra-pita-mexicana.html.

Conklin, Beth A. 1997. "Body Paint, Feathers, and VCRs: Aesthetics and Authenticity in Amazonian Activism." *American Ethnologist* 24 (4): 711–37. https://doi.org/10.1525/ae.1997.24.4.711.

Conklin, Beth A., and Laura Graham. 1995. "The Shifting Middle Ground: Amazonian Indians and Eco-Politics." *American Anthropologist* 97 (4): 695–710.

Connerton, Paul. 1989. *How Societies Remember*. Cambridge: Cambridge University Press.

Constitución de la República del Ecuador. 2008. Archivo Biblioteca. http://archivo biblioteca.asambleanacional.gob.ec/constituciones-del-ecuador.

Corr, Rachel. 2010. *Ritual and Remembrance in the Ecuadorian Andes*. First Peoples. Tucson: University of Arizona Press.

Coulthard, Glen Sean. 2014. *Indigenous Americas: Red Skin, White Masks: Rejecting the Colonial Politics of Recognition*. Minneapolis: University of Minnesota Press.

Dąbkowski, Maksymilian. 2021. "A'ingae (Ecuador and Colombia)—Language Snapshot." *Language Documentation and Description* 20:1–12.

Dalmases, Francesc Badia i. 2021. "How the Wind Power Boom Is Driving Deforestation in the Amazon." *EL PAÍS English Edition*, November 26, 2021. https://english.elpais.com/usa/2021-11-26/how-the-wind-power-boom-is-driving-deforestation-in-the-amazon.html.

Dauenhauer, Nora Marks, and Richard Dauenhauer. 1998. "Technical, Emotional, and Ideological Issues in Reversing Language Shift: Examples from Southeast Alaska." In *Endangered Languages: Current Issues and Future Prospects*, edited by Lenore A. Grenoble and Lindsay J Whaley, 57–98. Cambridge: Cambridge University Press.

Davis, Jenny L. 2017. "Resisting Rhetorics of Language Endangerment: Reclamation Through Indigenous Language Survivance." Edited by Wesley Leonard and Haley De Korne. *Language Documentation and Description* 14:37–58.

Davis, Jenny L. 2018. *Talking Indian: Identity and Language Revitalization in the Chickasaw Renaissance*. Tucson: University of Arizona Press.

De Korne, Haley, and Wesley Leonard. 2017. "Reclaiming Languages: Contesting and Decolonising 'Language Endangerment' from the Ground Up." Edited by Wesley Leonard and Haley De Korne. *Language Documentation and Description* 14:5–14.

De la Cadena, Marisol. 2000. *Indigenous Mestizos: The Politics of Race and Culture in Cuzco, Peru, 1919–1991*. Durham, N.C.: Duke University Press.

Debenport, Erin. 2015. *Fixing the Books: Secrecy, Literacy, and Perfectibility in Indigenous New Mexico.* Santa Fe, N.Mex.: SAR Press.

Debenport, Erin. 2017. "Perfecting Publics: Future Audiences and the Aesthetics of Refinement." In *Engaging Native American Publics: Linguistic Anthropology in a Collaborative Key,* edited by Paul V. Kroskrity and Barbra A. Meek, 130–45. London: Routledge.

Deloria, Philip Joseph. 2004. *Indians in Unexpected Places.* Lawrence: University Press of Kansas.

Deloria, Vine Jr. 2001. "American Indian Metaphysics." In *Power and Place: Indian Education in America,* edited by Daniel R. Wildcat and Vine Deloria Jr., 1–6. Golden, Colo.: Fulcrum Publishing.

Descola, Philippe. 1994. *In the Society of Nature: A Native Ecology in Amazonia.* Cambridge: Cambridge University Press.

Dorian, Nancy. 1977. "The Problem of the Semi-Speaker in Language Death." *International Journal of the Sociology of Language* 1977 (12).

Dorian, Nancy C., ed. 1989. *Investigating Obsolescence: Studies in Language Contraction and Death.* Studies in the Social and Cultural Foundations of Language 7. Cambridge: Cambridge University Press.

Duarte, Marisa Elena. 2017. *Network Sovereignty: Building the Internet Across Indian Country.* Seattle: University of Washington Press. http://ebookcentral.proquest .com/lib/pensu/detail.action?docID=4987329.

Duchene, Alexandre, and Monica Heller. 2008. "Discourses of Endangerment: Ideology and Interest in the Defence of Languages." In *Discourses of Endangerment: Ideology and Interest in the Defence of Languages,* edited by Alexandre Duchene and Monica Heller. London: Bloomsbury.

Eckert, Penelope, and Sally McConnell-Ginet. 1992. "Think Practically and Look Locally: Language and Gender as Community-Based Practice." *Annual Review of Anthropology* 21:461–90.

Eisenlohr, Patrick. 2004. "Language Revitalization and New Technologies: Cultures of Electronic Mediation and the Refiguring of Communities." *Annual Review of Anthropology* 33 (1): 21–45.

Eisenlohr, Patrick. 2015. "Mediating Disjunctures of Time: Ancestral Chronotopes in Ritual and Media Practices." *Anthropological Quarterly; Washington* 88 (2): 281–304.

Emlen, Nicholas Q. 2020. *Language, Coffee, and Migration on an Andean-Amazonian Frontier.* Tucson: University of Arizona Press.

Emlen, Nicholas Q., and Willem F. H. Adelaar. 2017. "Proto-Quechua and Proto-Aymara Agropastoral Terms." In *Language Dispersal Beyond Farming,* edited by Martine Robbeets and Alexander Savelyev, 25–45. Amsterdam: John Benjamins.

Ennis, Georgia. 2019a. "Multimodal Chronotopes: Embodying Ancestral Time on Quichua Morning Radio." *Signs and Society* 7 (1): 6–36.

Ennis, Georgia. 2019b. "Remediating Endangerment: Radio and the Animation of Memory in the Western Amazon." PhD dissertation, University of Michigan.

REFERENCES

Ennis, Georgia. 2020. "Linguistic Natures: Method, Media, and Language Reclamation in the Ecuadorian Amazon." *Journal of Linguistic Anthropology* 30 (3): 304–25. https://doi.org/10.1111/jola.12281.

Ennis, Georgia. 2021. "Affective Technologies: Kichwa Women's Media Activism in the Ecuadorian Amazon." *Resonance* 1 (4): 376–93. https://doi.org/10.1525/res .2020.1.4.376.

Ennis, Georgia. 2023. "Caring for Indigenous Languages in Settler Times by Georgia Ennis—American Ethnological Society." Edited by Magdalena Zegarra Chiaporri and Salwa Tareen. American Ethnologist, August 2023. https://american ethnologist.org/online-content/collections/uncaring-world/caring-for-indigenous -languages-in-settler-times-by-georgia-ennis/.

Ennis, Georgia, Gissela Yumbo, María Antonia Shiguango, Ofelia Salazar, and Olga Chongo. 2024. "Relating to the Forest: Possibilities and Limitations of Collaborative Community Media." In *Countering Modernity*, edited by Carolyn Smith-Morris and César Abadía, 59–84. New York: Routledge.

Ennis, Georgia C. 2025. "Reweaving Language and Lifeways in the Western Amazon." *American Indian Culture and Research Journal* 48 (1).

Erazo, Juliet. 2013. *Governing Indigenous Territories: Enacting Sovereignty in the Ecuadorian Amazon*. Durham, N.C.: Duke University Press.

Erazo, Juliet, and Ernesto Benitez. 2022. "Becoming Politicians: Indigenous Pageants as Training Sites for Public Life." *American Anthropologist* 124 (1): 154–64. https://doi.org/10.1111/aman.13676.

Fanon, Frantz. 1968. *The Wretched of the Earth*. Evergreen Black Cat Edition, B-342-K. New York: Grove Press.

Faudree, Paja. 2013. *Singing for the Dead: The Politics of Indigenous Revival in Mexico*. Durham, N.C.: Duke University Press.

Fausto, Carlos, and Michael Heckenberger. 2007. *Time and Memory in Indigenous Amazonia: Anthropological Perspectives*. Gainesville: University Press of Florida.

Ferguson, Jenanne. 2019. *Words Like Birds : Sakha Language Discourses and Practices in the City*. Lincoln: University of Nebraska Press.

Fill, Alwin, and Peter Mühlhäusler. 2006. *The Ecolinguistics Reader: Language, Ecology, and Environment*. London: Bloomsbury.

Fill, Alwin, and Hermine Penz. 2017. *The Routledge Handbook of Ecolinguistics*. Routledge. https://doi.org/10.4324/9781315687391.

Fisher, Daniel. 2016. *The Voice and Its Doubles Media and Music in Northern Australia*. Durham, N.C.: Duke University Press.

Fisher, Daniel. 2019. "To Sing with Another's Voice." *American Ethnologist* 46 (1): 34–46.

Fishman, Joshua A. 1991. *Reversing Language Shift: Theoretical and Empirical Foundations of Assistance to Threatened Languages*. Clevedon: Multilingual Matters.

Fitzgerald, Colleen M. 2017. "Understanding Language Vitality and Reclamation as Resilience: A Framework for Language Endangerment and 'Loss' (Commentary on Mufwene)." *Language* 93 (4): e280–97.

Flores, Nelson. 2013. "Silencing the Subaltern: Nation-State/Colonial Governmentality and Bilingual Education in the United States." *Critical Inquiry in Language Studies* 10 (4): 263–87.

Floyd, Simeon. 2008. "The Pirate Media Economy and the Emergence of Quichua Language Media Spaces in Ecuador." *Anthropology of Work Review* 29 (2): 34–41.

French, Brigittine M. 2003. "The Politics of Mayan Linguistics in Guatemala: Native Speakers, Expert Analysts, and the Nation." *Pragmatics* 13 (4): 483–98.

French, Brigittine M. 2010. *Maya Ethnolinguistic Identity Violence, Cultural Rights, and Modernity in Highland Guatemala.* Tucson: University of Arizona Press.

French, Brigittine M. 2012. "The Semiotics of Collective Memories." *Annual Review of Anthropology* 41:337–53.

Frey, Benjamin E. 2013. "Toward a General Theory of Language Shift: A Case Study in Wisconsin German and North Carolina Cherokee." PhD dissertation, University of Wisconsin–Madison.

Frey, Benjamin E. 2022. "Internal Verticalization and Community Maintenance: The Story of North Carolina Cherokee." In *The Verticalization Model of Language Shift: The Great Change in American Communities,* edited by Joshua R. Brown, 139–65. Oxford: Oxford University Press.

Fuller, Matthew. 2005. *Media Ecologies: Materialist Energies in Art and Technoculture.* Cambridge, Mass.: MIT Press.

Gal, Susan. 1979. *Language Shift: Social Determinants of Linguistic Change in Bilingual Austria.* Language, Thought, and Culture. New York: Academic Press.

Gal, Susan. 2006. "Contradictions of Standard Language in Europe: Implications for the Study of Practices and Publics." *Social Anthropology* 14 (2): 163–81.

Gal, Susan, and Judith T. Irvine. 2019. *Signs of Difference: Language and Ideology in Social Life.* Cambridge: Cambridge University Press. https://doi.org/10.1017/9781108649209.

Gal, Susan, and Kathryn A. Woolard. 2001. *Languages and Publics: The Making of Authority.* London: Routledge. https://doi.org/10.4324/9781315759647.

Galarza, Emily, Marcela Cabrera, Rodrigo Espinosa, Edgar Espitia, Gabriel M. Moulatlet, and Mariana V. Capparelli. 2021. "Assessing the Quality of Amazon Aquatic Ecosystems with Multiple Lines of Evidence: The Case of the Northeast Andean Foothills of Ecuador." *Bulletin of Environmental Contamination and Toxicology* 107 (1): 52–61. https://doi.org/10.1007/s00128-020-03089-0.

Galla, Candace Kaleimamoowahinekapu. 2019. "Materials Development for Indigenous Language Learning and Teaching: Pedagogy, Praxis, and Possibilities." In *Handbook of Indigenous Education,* edited by Elizabeth Ann McKinley and Linda Tuhiwai Smith, 357–75. Singapore: Springer. https://doi.org/10.1007/978-981-10-3899-0_12.

Galli, Elisa. 2012. *Migrar Transformándose: Género y Experiencas Oníricas Entre Los Runas de La Amazonía Ecuatoriana.* Quito, Ecuador: Abya-Yala.

Garrett, Paul B. 2005. "What a Language Is Good for: Language Socialization, Language Shift, and the Persistence of Code-Specific Genres in St. Lucia." *Language in Society* 34 (3): 327–61.

REFERENCES

Garrett, Paul B. 2007. "'Say It like You See It': Radio Broadcasting and the Mass Mediation of Creole Nationhood in St. Lucia." *Identities* 14 (1–2): 135–60.

Gatti, Luciana V., Luana S. Basso, John B. Miller, Manuel Gloor, Lucas Gatti Domingues, Henrique L. G. Cassol, Graciela Tejada, et al. 2021. "Amazonia as a Carbon Source Linked to Deforestation and Climate Change." *Nature* 595 (7867): 388–93. https://doi.org/10.1038/s41586-021-03629-6.

Gershon, Ilana. 2010. "Media Ideologies: An Introduction: Media Ideologies: An Introduction." *Journal of Linguistic Anthropology* 20 (2): 283–93.

Gershon, Ilana. 2015. "What Do We Talk About When We Talk About Animation." *Social Media + Society* 1 (1).

Ginsburg, Faye. 1997. "From Little Things, Big Things Grow: Indigenous Media and Cultural Activism." In *Between Resistance and Revolution: Cultural Politics and Social Protest*, edited by Richard Fox and Orin Start, 118–44. New Brunswick, N.J.: Rutgers University Press.

Ginsburg, Faye, Lila Abu-Lughod, and Brian Larkin. 2002. *Media Worlds: Anthropology on New Terrain*. Berkeley: University of California Press.

Goffman, Erving. 1959. *The Presentation of Self in Everyday Life*. New York: Doubleday.

Goffman, Erving. 1974. *Frame Analysis: An Essay on the Organization of Experience*. New York: Harper & Row.

Goffman, Erving. 1981a. "Footing." In *Forms of Talk*, 124–59. Philadelphia: University of Pennsylvania Press.

Goffman, Erving. 1981b. "Radio Talk." In *Forms of Talk*, 197–327. Philadelphia: University of Pennsylvania Press.

Goody, Jack, and Ian Watt. 1963. "The Consequences of Literacy." *Comparative Studies in Society and History* 5 (3): 304–45.

Gow, Peter. 2001. *An Amazonian Myth and Its History*. Oxford: Oxford University Press.

Graham, Laura R. 2002. "How Should an Indian Speak? Amazonian Indians and the Symbolic Politics of Language in the Global Public Sphere." In *Indigenous Movements, Self-Representation, and the State in Latin America*, edited by Kay B. Warren and Jean Jackson, 181–228. Austin: University of Texas Press.

Graham, Laura R., and H. Glenn Penny. 2014. *Performing Indigeneity: Global Histories and Contemporary Experiences*. Lincoln: University of Nebraska Press.

Grenoble, Lenore A., and Lindsay J. Whaley. 2006. *Saving Languages: An Introduction to Language Revitalization*. Cambridge: Cambridge University Press.

Grzech, Karolina. 2016. "The Non-Evidential Meaning of the Tena Kichwa 'Direct Evidential.'" *York Papers in Linguistics* 3 (June), 73–94.

Grzech, Karolina. 2017. "¿Es Necesario Elegir Entre La Estandarización de Las Lenguas Minoritarias y La Vitalidad de Sus Variedades? Estudio de Caso Del Kichwa de Alto Napo." *Onomázein Revista de Lingüística Filología y Traducción* 37 (amerindias), 16–34.

Grzech, Karolina, Anne Schwarz, and Georgia Ennis. 2019. "Divided We Stand, Unified We Fall? The Impact of Standardisation on Oral Language Varieties: A Case Study of Amazonian Kichwa." *Revista de Llengua i Dret, Journal of Language and Law* 7:123–45.

Gumperz, John J. 1989. "Conversational Code-Switching." In *Discourse Strategies*, 59–99. Cambridge: Cambridge University Press.

Guzmán Gallegos, María Antonieta. 1997. *Para Que La Yuca Beba Nuestra Sangre: Trabajo, Género y Parentesco En Una Comunidad Quichua de La Amazonía Ecuatoriana / María Antonieta Guzmán Gallegos*. Quito, Ecuador: Ediciones Abya-Yala.

Habermas, Jürgen. 1989. *The Structural Transformation of the Public Sphere: An Inquiry into a Category of Bourgeois Society*. Translated by Thomas Burger. Cambridge, Mass.: MIT Press.

Haboud, Marleen, and Nicholas Limerick. 2017. "Language Policy and Education in the Andes." In *Language Policy and Political Issues in Education*, 435–47. Encyclopedia of Language and Education. Cham, Switzerland: Springer.

Halbwachs, Maurice. 1992. *On Collective Memory*. Chicago: University of Chicago Press.

Hale, Ken, Michael Krauss, Lucille J. Watahomigie, Akira Y. Yamamoto, Colette Craig, LaVerne Masayesva Jeanne, and Nora C. England. 1992. "Endangered Languages." *Language; Washington* 68 (1): 1–42.

Hall, Edward Twitchell. 1990. *The Silent Language*. New York: Anchor Books.

Harris, Olivia. 1980. "The Power of Signs: Gender, Culture and the Wild in the Bolivian Andes." In *Nature, Culture, and Gender*, edited by Carol P. MacCormack and Marilyn Strathern, 70–94. Cambridge: Cambridge University Press.

Harrison, Regina. 1989. *Signs, Songs, and Memory in the Andes: Translating Quechua Language and Culture*. Austin: University of Texas Press.

Hartikainen, Elina I. 2017. "Chronotopic Realignments and the Shifting Semiotics and Politics of Visibility in Brazilian Candomblé Activism." *Signs and Society* 5 (2): 356–89.

Harvey, Penelope. 1994. "The Presence and Absence of Speech in the Communication of Gender." In *Bilingual Women*, edited by Pauline Burton, Ketaki Kushari Dyson, and Shirley Ardener, 44–64. London: Routledge.

Hauck, Jan David, and Guilherme Orlandini Heurich. 2018. "Language in the Amerindian Imagination: An Inquiry into Linguistic Natures." *Language & Communication*, Language in the Amerindian Imagination, 63 (November):1–8.

Haugen, Einar. 1966. "Dialect, Language, Nation." *American Anthropologist*, New Series, 68 (4): 922–35.

Haugen, Einar. 1972. *The Ecology of Language*. Redwood City, Calif.: Stanford University Press.

Heath, Shirley Brice. 1982. "What No Bedtime Story Means: Narrative Skills at Home and School." *Language in Society* 11 (1): 49–76.

Heggarty, Paul, and David Beresford-Jones. 2010. "Agriculture and Language Dispersals: Limitations, Refinements, and an Andean Exception?" *Current Anthropology* 51 (2): 163–91.

Herzfeld, Michael. 2016. *Cultural Intimacy: Social Poetics and the Real Life of States, Societies, and Institutions*. 3rd ed. London: Routledge. https://doi.org/10.4324/9781315647289.

High, Casey. 2018. "Bodies That Speak: Languages of Differentiation and Becoming in Amazonia." *Language & Communication* 63 (March).

Hill, Jane H. 2002. "'Expert Rhetorics' in Advocacy for Endangered Languages: Who Is Listening, and What Do They Hear?" *Journal of Linguistic Anthropology* 12 (2): 119–33.

Hill, Jane H. 2005. "Intertextuality as Source and Evidence for Indirect Indexical Meanings." *Journal of Linguistic Anthropology* 15 (1): 113–24. https://doi.org/10.1525/jlin.2005.15.1.113.

Hill, Jane H., and Kenneth C. Hill. 1986. *Speaking Mexicano: Dynamics of a Syncretic Language in Central Mexico*. Tucson: University of Arizona Press.

Hill, Jonathan D. 1988. *Rethinking History and Myth: Indigenous South American Perspectives on the Past*. Urbana: University of Illinois Press.

Hinton, Leanne. 2013. *Bringing Our Languages Home: Language Revitalization for Families*. Berkeley, Calif.: Heyday.

Hirschkind, Charles. 2006. *The Ethical Soundscape: (Cassette Sermons and Islamic Counterpublics)*. Cultures of History. New York: Columbia University Press.

Hornberger, Nancy, and Serafín M. Coronel-Molina. 2004. "Quechua Language Shift, Maintenance, and Revitalization in the Andes: The Case for Language Planning." *Journal of the Sociology of Language* 167:9–67.

Hornberger, Nancy, and Kendall A. King. 1996. "Language Revitilisation in the Andes: Can Schools Reverse Language Shift?" *Journal of Multilingual and Multicultural Development* 17 (6): 427–41.

Hornberger, Nancy, and Kendall A. King. 1998. "Authenticity and Unification in Quechua Language Planning." *Language, Culture and Curriculum* 11 (3): 390–410.

Hornborg, Alf. 2005. "Ethnogenesis, Regional Integration, and Ecology in Prehistoric Amazonia: Toward a System Perspective." *Current Anthropology* 46 (4): 589–620.

Howard, Rosaleen. 2007. *Por Los Linderos de La Lengua*. Lima, Peru: Institut Français D'études Andines.

Huarcaya, Sergio Miguel. 2018. "Land Reform, Historical Consciousness and Indigenous Activism in Late Twentieth-Century Ecuador." *Journal of Latin American Studies* 50 (2): 411–40.

Huayhua, Margarita. 2020. "Collaborating on Presenting Reanimated Native Andean History." Society for Cultural Anthropology. February 6, 2020. https://culanth.org/fieldsights/collaborating-on-presenting-reanimated-native-andean-history.

Hurston, Zora Neale. 2018. *Barracoon: The Story of the Last "Black Cargo."* Edited by Deborah G. Plant. 1st ed. New York: Amistad.

Inoue, Miyako. 2004. "What Does Language Remember?: Indexical Inversion and the Naturalized History of Japanese Women." *Journal of Linguistic Anthropology* 14 (1): 39–56.

Instituto Nacional de Estadistica y Censos (INEC). 2001. "Base de Datos de Resultados Del Censo de Población y Vivienda 2001 En El Software Redatam." Censo de Población y de Vivienda- cpv 2010-Aplicación de R+SP xPlan. Quito, Ecuador: Instituto Nacional de Estadísticas y Censos de Ecuador: Centro Latinoamericano de Desarrollo Empresarial-Comisión Económica para América Latina y el Caribe (CELADE-CEPAL). http://redatam.inec.gob.ec/.

Instituto Nacional de Estadistica y Censos (INEC). 2010. "Base de Datos de Resultados Del Censo de Población y Vivienda 2010 En El Software Redatam." Censo de Población y de Vivienda- cpv 2010-Aplicación de R+SP xPlan. Quito, Ecuador: Instituto Nacional de Estadísticas y Censos de Ecuador: Centro Latinoamericano de Desarrollo Empresarial-Comisión Económica para América Latina y el Caribe (CELADE-CEPAL). http://redatam.inec.gob.ec/.

Instituto Nacional de Estadistica y Censos (INEC). 2023. "Tabulados Nacionales—Autoidentificación Cultural." https://www.censoecuador.gob.ec/wp-content/uploads/2023/12/02_2022_CPV_Autoidentificacion_cultural.xlsx.

Instituto Nacional de Estadistica y Censos (INEC). n.d.-a. "Cantón Tena." Instituto Nacional de Estadística y Censos. Accessed December 8, 2017. https://www.ecuadorencifras.gob.ec/documentos/web-inec/Bibliotecas/Fasciculos_Censales/Fasc_Cantonales/Napo/Fasciculo_Tena.pdf.

Instituto Nacional de Estadistica y Censos (INEC). n.d.-b. "Resultados Del Censo 2010 de Población y Vivienda En El Ecuador: Fascículo Provincial Napo." Instituto Nacional de Estadística y Censos. Accessed December 8, 2017. https://www.ecuadorencifras.gob.ec/wp-content/descargas/Manu-lateral/Resultados-provinciales/napo.pdf.

Irvine, Judith. 1989. "When Talk Isn't Cheap: Language and Political Economy." *American Ethnologist* 16 (2): 248–67.

Irvine, Judith. 1993. "Insult and Responsibility: Verbal Abuse in a Wolof Village." In *Responsibility and Evidence in Oral Discourse*, edited by Jane H. Hill and Judith Irvine, 105–34. Cambridge: Cambridge University Press.

Irvine, Judith. 1996. "Shadow Conversations: The Indeterminacy of Participant Roles." In *Natural Histories of Discourse*, edited by Michael Silverstein and Greg Urban. Chicago: University of Chicago Press.

Irvine, Judith. 2006. "Speech and Language Community." In *Encyclopedia of Language and Linguistics*, edited by Keith Brown, 2nd ed., 689–98. Oxford: Elsevier.

Irvine, Judith, and Susan Gal. 2000. "Language Ideology and Linguistic Differentiation." In *Regimes of Language: Ideologies, Politics, and Identities*, edited by Paul V. Kroskrity, 35–83. Santa Fe, N.Mex.: School of American Research.

Jacob, Michelle M. 2013. *Yakama Rising: Indigenous Cultural Revitalization, Activism, and Healing*. Tucson: The University of Arizona Press.

Jaffe, Alexandra. 1999. *Ideologies in Action: Language Politics on Corsica*. Berlin: Mouton de Gruyter.

Jakobson, Roman. 1961. "Closing Statement: Linguistics and Poetics." In *Style in Language*, edited by Thomas Sebeok, 350–77. Cambridge, Mass.: MIT Press.

Jakobson, Roman. 1968. "Poetry of Grammar and Grammar of Poetry." *Poetics Today* 2 (1a): 83–85.

Jakobson, Roman. 1971. "Shifters, Verbal Categories, and the Russian Verb." In *Selected Writings II: Word and Language*, 130–47. v. The Hague, Netherlands: Mouton.

REFERENCES

Jarrett, Christopher. 2019. "The Social Life of Guayusa from Amazonian Ecuador: An Examination of Livelihoods, Landscapes, and Politics." San Antonio: University of Texas.

Jarrett, Christopher, Ian Cummins, and Eliot Logan-Hines. 2017. "Adapting Indigenous Agroforestry Systems for Integrative Landscape Management and Sustainable Supply Chain Development in Napo, Ecuador." In *Integrating Landscapes: Agroforestry for Biodiversity Conservation and Food Sovereignty*, edited by Florencia Montagnini, 283–309. Advances in Agroforestry. Cham, Switzerland: Springer International Publishing. https://doi.org/10.1007/978-3-319-69371-2_12.

Keane, Webb. 2005. "Signs Are Not the Garb of Meaning: On the Social Analysis of Material Things." In *Materiality*, edited by Daniel Miller. Durham, N.C.: Duke University Press.

Keane, Webb. 2013. "Ontologies, Anthropologists, and Ethical Life." *HAU: Journal of Ethnographic Theory* 3 (1): 186–91.

King, Jeanette. 2001. "Te Kohanga Reo: Maori Language Revitalization." *The Green Book of Language Revitalization in Practice*, 119–31.

King, Kendall A. 2001. *Language Revitalization Processes and Prospects: Quichua in the Ecuadorian Andes*. Clevedon, UK: Multilingual Matters.

Kirksey, Eben. 2015. *Emergent Ecologies*. Durham, N.C.: Duke University Press.

Kirsch, Stuart. 2006. *Reverse Anthropology: Indigenous Analysis of Social and Environmental Relations in New Guinea*. Stanford: Stanford University Press.

Kohlberger, Martin. 2016. "Prescriptivism as a Nation-Building Tool in the Upper Amazon: The Case of Shiwiar." *Journal of Multilingual and Multicultural Development* 37 (3): 263–73. https://doi.org/10.1080/01434632.2015.1068785.

Kohn, Eduardo. 2002. "Natural Engagements and Ecological Aesthetics Among the Ávila Runa of Amazonian Ecuador." PhD dissertation, University of Wisconsin–Madison.

Kohn, Eduardo. 2007. "Animal Masters and the Ecological Embedding of History Among the Ávila Runa of Ecuador." In *Time and Memory in Indigenous Amazonia: Anthropological Perspectives*, edited by Carlos Fausto and Michael Heckenberger. Gainesville: University Press of Florida.

Kohn, Eduardo. 2013. *How Forests Think: Toward an Anthropology Beyond the Human*. 1st ed. Berkeley: University of California Press.

Kohn, Eduardo, and Manuela Lavinas Picq. 2020. "An Oil Spill in the Time of Coronavirus." *Al Jazeera*, July 14, 2020. https://www.aljazeera.com/opinions/2020/7/14/an-oil-spill-in-the-time-of-coronavirus.

Konefal, Betsy. 2009. "Subverting Authenticity: Reinas Indigenas and the Guatemalan State, 1978." *Hispanic American Historical Review* 89 (1): 41–72. https://doi.org/10.1215/00182168-2008-044.

Kottak, Conrad P. 1999. "The New Ecological Anthropology." *American Anthropologist* 101 (1): 23–35. https://doi.org/10.1525/aa.1999.101.1.23.

Krauss, Michael. 1992. "The World's Languages in Crisis." *Language; Washington* 68 (1): 4–10.

Kroskrity, Paul V. 2000. *Regimes of Language: Ideologies, Polities, and Identities.* Santa Fe, N.Mex.: School of American Research Press.

Kroskrity, Paul V. 2007. "Language Ideologies." In *A Companion to Linguistic Anthropology*, 496–517. Malden, Mass.: Wiley-Blackwell.

Kroskrity, Paul V. 2009. "Language Renewal as Sites of Language Ideological Struggle: The Need for 'Ideological Clarification.'" In *Indigenous Language Revitalization: Encouragement, Guidance & Lessons Learned*, edited by Jon Reyhner and L. Locklard, 71–83. Flagstaff: Northern Arizona University.

Kroskrity, Paul V. 2011. "Facing the Rhetoric of Language Endangerment: Voicing the Consequences of Linguistic Racism." *Journal of Linguistic Anthropology* 21 (2): 179–92.

Kroskrity, Paul V. 2018. "On Recognizing Persistence in the Indigenous Language Ideologies of Multilingualism in Two Native American Communities," in "Indigenous Multilingualisms," edited by Ruth Singer and Jill Vaughan, special issue, *Language & Communication* 62 (September): 133–44.

Kroskrity, Paul V., and Margaret C. Field. 2009. *Native American Language Ideologies: Beliefs, Practices, and Struggles in Indian Country.* Tucson: University of Arizona Press.

Kulick, Don. 1992. *Language Shift and Cultural Reproduction: Socialization, Self, and Syncretism in a Papua New Guinean Village.* Cambridge: Cambridge University Press.

Lane, Pia, James Costa, Haley De Korne, and Taylor & Francis. 2018. *Standardizing Minority Languages Competing Ideologies of Authority and Authenticity in the Global Periphery.* 1st ed. New York: Routledge.

LaPoe, Victoria L., and Benjamin Rex LaPoe. 2017. *Indian Country.* East Lansing: Michigan State University Press.

Leonard, Wesley. 2012. "Framing Language Reclamation Programmes for Everybody's Empowerment." *Gender and Language* 6 (2): 339–67. https://doi.org/10.1558/genl.v6i2.339.

Leonard, Wesley. 2017. "Producing Language Reclamation by Decolonising 'Language.'" *Language Documentation and Description* 14 (September): 15–36.

Lévi-Strauss, Claude. 1966. *The Savage Mind.* Chicago: University of Chicago Press.

Ley Orgánica de Comunicación. 2013. https://www.telecomunicaciones.gob.ec/wp-content/uploads/2020/01/Ley-Organica-de-Comunicaci%C3%B3n.pdf

Liboiron, Max. 2021. *Pollution Is Colonialism.* Durham, N.C.: Duke University Press.

Limerick, Nicholas. 2017. "Kichwa or Quichua? Competing Alphabets, Political Histories, and Complicated Reading in Indigenous Languages." *Comparative Education Review* 62 (1): 103–24.

Limerick, Nicholas. 2020. "Speaking for a State: Standardized Kichwa Greetings and Conundrums of Commensuration in Intercultural Ecuador." *Signs and Society* 8 (2): 185–219. https://doi.org/10.1086/708164.

Lincoln, Kathryn, and Blair Orr. 2011. "The Use and Cultural Significance of the Pita Plant (Aechmea Magdalenae) Among Ngöbe Women of Chalite, Panama." *Economic Botany* 65 (1): 13–26. https://doi.org/10.1007/s12231-010-9144-x.

REFERENCES

Lippi-Green, Rosina. 2011. *English with an Accent: Language, Ideology and Discrimination in the United States.* 2nd ed. London: Routledge.

López, Víctor, Fernando Espíndola, Juan Calles, and Janette Ulloa. 2013. *Amazonía Ecuatoriana Bajo Presión.* Quito, Ecuador: EcoCiencia. https://biblio.flacsoandes.edu.ec/libros/digital/56384.pdf.

Lu, Flora. 2007. "Integration into the Market Among Indigenous Peoples: A Cross-Cultural Perspective from the Ecuadorian Amazon." *Current Anthropology* 48 (4): 593–602. https://doi.org/10.1086/519806.

Lum, Casey Man Kong. 2005a. "Notes Towards an Intellectual History of Media Ecology." In *Perspectives on Culture, Technology and Communication: The Media Ecology,* edited by Casey Man Kong Lum, 1–60. Cresskill, N.J.: Hampton.

Lum, Casey Man Kong. 2005b. *Perspectives on Culture, Technology and Communication: The Media Ecology.* Cresskill, N.J.: Hampton.

Macdonald, Theodore. 1979. "Processes of Change in Amazonian Ecuador: Quijos Quichua Indians Become Cattlemen." PhD dissertation, University of Illinois at Urbana-Champaign.

Macdonald, Theodore. 1999. *Ethnicity and Culture Amidst New "Neighbors": The Runa of Ecuador's Amazon Region.* Boston: Allyn and Bacon.

Mackey, William F. 2006. "The Ecology of Language Shift." In *The Ecolinguistics Reader: Language, Ecology, and Environment,* edited by Alwin Fill and Peter Mühlhäusler, 67–74. London: Bloomsbury.

Maffi, Luisa. 2002. "Endangered Languages, Endangered Knowledge." *International Social Science Journal* 54 (173): 385–93. https://doi.org/10.1111/1468-2451.00390.

Maffi, Luisa. 2005. "Linguistic, Cultural and Biological Diversity." *Annual Review of Anthropology* 29:599–617.

Manna Producciones. 2019. "Pitaj Warmi—Los Angeles Vol 1 New Music Jmproducciones 4KHD." YouTube. https://www.youtube.com/watch?v=0jXxlMGxJVE.

Mannheim, Bruce. 1998. "'Time, Not the Syllables, Must Be Counted': Quechua Parallelism, Word Meaning, and Cultural Analysis." *Michigan Discussions in Anthropology* 13 (1): 238–81.

Mannheim, Bruce. 2015. "The Social Imaginary, Unspoken in Verbal Art." In *The Routledge Handbook of Linguistic Anthropology,* edited by Nancy Bonvillain, 44–61. Routledge.

Mannheim, Bruce. 2017. "Three Axes of Variability in Quechua: Regional Diversification, Contact with Other Indigenous Languages, and Social Enregisterment." In *The Andean World,* edited by Linda J. Seligmann and Kathleen Fine-Dare. Milton Park, UK: Routledge.

Mannheim, Bruce. 2018a. "Ontological Foundations for Inka Archaeology." In *Andean Ontologies: New Perspectives from Archaeology, Ethnohistory and Bioarchaeology,* edited by María Cecilia Lozada and Tantaleán Henry, 240–70. Gainesville: University of Florida press.

Mannheim, Bruce. 2018b. "Preliminary Disciplines." *Signs and Society* 6 (1): 111–19.

Mannheim, Bruce, and Krista Van Vleet. 1998. "The Dialogics of Southern Quechua Narrative." *American Anthropologist* 100:326–46.

Manning, Paul, and Ilana Gershon. 2013. "Animating Interaction." *HAU: Journal of Ethnographic Theory* 3 (3): 107–37.

Marcus, George E. 1995. "Ethnography in/of the World System: The Emergence of Multi-Sited Ethnography." *Annual Review of Anthropology* 24 (January): 95–117.

Martinez, Raul. 2019. "The Verbal Art of Kichwa Reclamation." *Anthropology News,* September 19, 2019.

McCarty, Teresa. 2008. "Language Education Planning and Policies by and for Indigenous Peoples." *Encyclopedia of Language and Education* 1:150.

McCarty, Teresa. 2018. "Community-Based Language Planning: Perspectives from Indigenous Language Revitalization." In *The Routledge Handbook of Language Revitalization,* edited by Leanne Hinton, Leena Huss, and Gerald Roche, 23–35. New York: Routledge.

McLuhan, Marshall. 1964. *Understanding Media: The Extensions of Man.* New York: Signet.

Meek, Barbra. 2007. "Respecting the Language of Elders: Ideological Shift and Linguistic Discontinuity in a Northern Athapascan Community." *Journal of Linguistic Anthropology* 17 (1): 23–43.

Meek, Barbra. 2010. *We Are Our Language.* Tucson: University of Arizona Press.

Meek, Barbra. 2011. "Failing American Indian Languages." *American Indian Culture and Research Journal* 35 (2): 43–60. https://doi.org/10.17953/aicr.35.2.m27 2376nl73v332t.

Meek, Barbra. 2017. "Native American Languages and Linguistic Anthropology: From the Legacy of Salvage Anthropology to the Promise of Linguistic Self-Determination." In *Engaging Native American Publics: Linguistic Anthropology in a Collaborative Key,* edited by Paul Kroskrity and Barbra Meek, 3–24. London: Routledge, Taylor & Francis Group.

Meek, Barbra A. 2019. "Language Endangerment in Childhood." *Annual Review of Anthropology* 48 (1): 95–115. https://doi.org/10.1146/annurev-anthro-102317-050041.

Meek, Barbra. 2025. "On Re-Languaging: From Documentation to Decolonization." *American Indian Culture and Research Journal* 48 (1).

Mezzenzana, Francesca. 2017. "Difference Revised: Gender and Transformation Among the Amazonian Runa." *Ethnos* 83 (5): 1–20.

Mezzenzana, Francesca. 2020. "Between Will and Thought: Individualism and Social Responsiveness in Amazonian Child Rearing." *American Anthropologist* 122 (3): 540–53. https://doi.org/10.1111/aman.13345.

Miller, Tiffany D. Creegan. 2022. *The Maya Art of Speaking Writing: Remediating Indigenous Orality in the Digital Age.* Tucson: University of Arizona Press.

Milroy, James. 2001. "Language Ideologies and the Consequences of Standardization." *Journal of Sociolinguistics* 5 (4): 530–55.

Milroy, James, and Lesley Milroy. 1999. *Authority in Language: Investigating Standard English.* London: Routledge.

Milton, Kay. 1997. "Ecologies: Anthropology, Culture and the Environment." *International Social Science Journal* 49 (154): 477.

Ministerio de Educación del Ecuador. 2009. *RUNAKAY KAMUKUNA: Yachakuk-kunapa Shimiyuk Kamu.*

Ministerio de Educación del Ecuador. 2010a. *Kichwata Yachamanta Grámatica Pedagógica.* Quito.

Ministerio de Educación del Ecuador. 2010b. *Manual de Metodología de Enseñanza de Lenguas.* Quito.

Ministerio de Educación del Ecuador. 2013. *Modelo Del Sistema de Eduación Intercultural Bilingüe.*

Moll, Yasmin. 2018. "Television Is Not Radio: Theologies of Mediation in the Egyptian Islamic Revival." *Cultural Anthropology* 33 (2): 233–65.

Montaluisa, Luis. 2018. "La Estandarización Ortográfica Del Quichua Ecuatoriano: Consideraciones Históricas, Dialectológicas y Sociolingüísticas." San Miguel: Pontifica Universidad Católica del Perú.

Moore, Robert. 2016. "Rebranding Belfast: Chromatopes of (Post-)Conflict." *Signs and Society* 4 (S1): S138–62.

Muehlmann, Shaylih Ryan. 2016. "'Languages Die like Rivers: Entangled Endangerments in the Colorado Delta." In *Endangerment, Biodiversity and Culture*, edited by Fernando Vidal and Nélia Dias, 41–61. London: Routledge.

Mufwene, Salikoko S. 2001. *The Ecology of Language Evolution.* Cambridge: Cambridge University Press.

Mufwene, Salikoko S. 2017. "Language Vitality: The Weak Theoretical Underpinnings of What Can Be an Exciting Research Area." *Language* 93 (4): e202–23.

Mühlhäusler, Peter. 1995. *Linguistic Ecology: Language Change and Linguistic Imperialism in the Pacific Region.* Milton, UK: Taylor & Francis Group.

Muniz, Maria Luiza de Castro. 2022. "Jatari Kichwa: Flujos (y Contraflujos) Comunicativos Amazónicos, desde la Radio Comunitaria." In *Oralidades y Escrituras Kichwas*, edited by Fernando Garcés V. and Armando Muyolema C., 147–69. Quito, Ecuador: Abya-Yala.

Muratorio, Blanca. 1991. *The Life and Times of Grandfather Alonso, Culture and History in the Upper Amazon.* Rucuyaya Alonso y La Historia Social y Económica Del Alto Napo, 1850–1950. New Brunswick, N.J.: Rutgers University Press.

Muratorio, Blanca. 1995. "Amazonian Windows to the Past: Recovering Women's Histories of the Ecuadorean Amazon." In *Articulating Hidden Histories: Exploring the Influence of Eric R. Wolf*, edited by Rayna Rapp and Jane Schneider, 322–35. Berkeley: University of California Press.

Muratorio, Blanca. 1998. "Indigenous Women's Identities and the Politics of Cultural Reproduction in the Ecuadorian Amazon." *American Anthropologist*, New Series, 100 (2): 409–20.

Muysken, Pieter. 2000. "Semantic Transparency in Lowland Ecuadorian Quechua Morphosyntax." *Linguistics* 38 (5): 973.

Muysken, Pieter. 2011. "Change, Contact, and Ethnogenesis in Northern Quechua." In *Ethnicity in Ancient Amazonia*, edited by Alf Hornborg and Jonathan D. Hill, 237–56. Boulder: University Press of Colorado.

Nettle, Daniel, and Suzanne Romaine. 2000. *Vanishing Voices: The Extinction of the World's Languages*. Oxford: Oxford University Press.

Nevins, M. Eleanor. 2004. "Learning to Listen: Confronting Two Meanings of Language Loss in the Contemporary White Mountain Apache Speech Community." *Journal of Linguistic Anthropology* 14 (2): 269–88. https://doi.org/10.1525/jlin.2004.14.2.269.

Nozawa, Shunsuke. 2013. "Characterization." *Semiotic Review* 3 (November).

Nozawa, Shunsuke. 2016. "Ensoulment and Effacement in Japanese Voice Acting." In *Media Convergence in Japan*, edited by Patrick W. Galbraith, 169–99. Tokyo: Kinema Club.

Nuckolls, Janis. 1996. *Sounds Like Life: Sound-Symbolic Grammar, Performance, and Cognition in Pastaza Quechua*. New York: Oxford University Press.

Nuckolls, Janis. 2008. "Deictic Selves and Others in Pastaza Quichua Evidential Usage." *Anthropological Linguistics* 50 (1): 67–89.

Nuckolls, Janis, and Tod D. Swanson. 2020. *Amazonian Quichua Language and Life: Introduction to Grammar, Ecology, and Discourse from Pastaza and Upper Napo, Ecuador*. Lanham, Md.: Lexington Books.

Oberem, Udo. 1980. *Los Quijos: Historia de La Transculturación de Un Grupo Indígena En El Oriente Ecuatoriano*. Otavalo, Ecuador: Instituto Otavaleño de Antropología.

O'Brien, Jean M. 2010. *Firsting and Lasting: Writing Indians out of Existence in New England*. Minneapolis: University of Minnesota Press.

Ochs, Elinor. 1988. *Culture and Language Development: Language Acquisition and Language Socialization in a Samoan Village*. Cambridge: Cambridge University Press.

Ochs, Elinor. 1992. "Indexing Gender." In *Rethinking Context: Language as an Interactive Phenomenon*, edited by Alessandro Duranti and Charles Goodwin. Cambridge: Cambridge University Press.

Ochs, Elinor, and Lisa Capps. 2001. *Living Narrative: Creating Lives in Everyday Storytelling*. Cambridge, Mass.: Harvard University Press.

Ochs, Elinor, and Bambi Schieffelin. 1984. "Language Acquisition and Socialization: Three Developmental Stories and Their Implications." In *Culture Theory: Essays on Mind, Self, and Emotion*, edited by Richard A. Shweder and Robert Alan LeVine, 276–320. Cambridge: Cambridge University Press.

Omar Pizango, dir. 2017. "Ñusta Chonta Warmy 2017–2018 Karen Pisango Archidona La Bella." YouTube. https://www.youtube.com/watch?v=_rWu08s66Bc.

Ong, Walter J. 1982. *Orality and Literacy: The Technologizing of the Word*. London: Methuen.

Orlove, Benjamin S. 1980. "Ecological Anthropology." *Annual Review of Anthropology* 9:235–73.

Orr, Carolyn. 1978. *Dialectos Quichuas Del Ecuador: Con Respecto a Lectores Principiantes*. Quito, Ecuador: Instituto Lingüístico de Verano.

Orr, Carolyn, and Betsy Wrisley. 1981. *Vocabulario Quichua Del Oriente Del Ecuador*. 2nd ed. Quito, Ecuador: Instituto Lingüístico de Verano.

REFERENCES

Overing, Joanna. 2000. "The Efficacy of Laughter: The Ludic Side of Magic Within Amazonian Sociality." In *The Anthropology of Love and Anger: The Aesthetics of Conviviality in Native Amazonia*, edited by Joanna Overing and Alan Passes, 64–81. London: Routledge.

Overing, Joanna, and Alan Passes. 2000. *The Anthropology of Love and Anger: The Aesthetics of Conviviality in Native Amazonia*, xiv, 305. London: Routledge.

Oxford English Dictionary. n.d. "remediation (n.)." Accessed June 24, 2024. https://www.oed.com/dictionary/remediation_n?tab=meaning_and_use.

Palmer, Gus. 2017. "There's No Easy Way to Talk about Language Change or Language Loss: The Difficulties and Rewards of Linguistic Collaboration." In *Engaging Native American Publics: Linguistic Anthropology in a Collaborative Key*, edited by Paul V. Kroskrity and Barbra Meek, 27–40. London: Routledge.

Papacharissi, Zizi. 2015. *Affective Publics: Sentiment, Technology, and Politics*. New York: Oxford University Press.

Papacharissi, Zizi. 2016. "Affective Publics and Structures of Storytelling: Sentiment, Events and Mediality." *Information, Communication & Society* 19 (3): 307–24. https://doi.org/10.1080/1369118X.2015.1109697.

Patrick, Donna, Kumiko Murasugi, and Jeela Palluq-Cloutier. 2018. "Standardization of Inuit Languages in Canada." In *Standardizing Minority Languages: Competing Ideologies of Authority and Authenticity in the Global Periphery*, edited by Pia Lane, James Costa, and Haley De Korne, 135–53. New York: Routledge.

Peeke, M. Catherine. 1973. *Preliminary Grammar of Auca*. Publication number 39. Norman, Okla.: Summer Institute of Linguistics.

Peeke, M. Catherine, Stephen H. Levinsohn, and Carolyn Orr. 1991. *Estudios Gramaticales En Napo Quichua y Huaorani*. Quito, Ecuador: Instituto Lingüístico de Verano.

Peirce, Charles S. 1955. *Philosophical Writings of Peirce*. Edited by Justus Buchler. New York: Dover Publications.

Penuela, Maria, Anne Schwarz, María Benavides, Alvaro Monteros, Ruth Cayapa, and Nardelia Romero. 2016. *Guía de La Agrodiversidad. Tres Comunidades Kichwa: Alto Tena, Atacapi, Alto Tena y Pumayacu*. Tena, Ecuador: Universidad Regional Amazónica IKIAM.

Pequeño, Andrea. 2007. *Imágenes en Disputa. Representaciones de Mujeres Indígenas Ecuatorianas*. Quito, Ecuador: Abya-Yala.

Pequeño, Andrea. 2013. "Historias de Misses, Historia de Naciones." *Íconos—Revista de Ciencias Sociales* 20:114.

Perley, Bernard. 2011. *Defying Maliseet Language Death: Emergent Vitalities of Language, Culture, and Identity in Eastern Canada*. Lincoln: University of Nebraska Press.

Perley, Bernard. 2012. "Zombie Linguistics: Experts, Endangered Languages and the Curse of Undead Voices." *Anthropological Forum* 22:133–49.

Perley, Bernard. 2013. "Remembering Ancestral Voices: Emergent Vitalities and the Future of Indigenous Languages." In *Responses to Language Endangerment: In Honor of Mickey Noonan*. Studies in Language Companion Series no. 142, edited by Elena Mihas, Bernard Perley, Gabriel Rei-Doval, and Kathleen Wheatley, 243–70. Amsterdam: John Benjamins. https://doi.org/10.1075/slcs.142.13per.

Perley, Bernard. 2014. "Living Traditions A Manifesto for Critical Indigeneity." In *Performing Indigeneity: Global Histories and Contemporary Experiences*, edited by Laura R. Graham and H. Glenn Penny, 32–54. Lincoln: University of Nebraska Press.

Perreault, Thomas. 2000. "Shifting Ground: Agrarian Change, Political Mobilization, and Identity Construction Among Quichua of the Alto Napo, Ecuadorian Amazonia." PhD dissertation, University of Colorado at Boulder.

Perreault, Thomas. 2005. "Why Chacras (Swidden Gardens) Persist: Agrobiodiversity, Food Security, and Cultural Identity in the Ecuadorian Amazon." *Human Organization; Oklahoma City* 64 (4): 327–39.

Peterson, Leighton C. 1997. "Tuning In to Navajo: The Role of Radio in Native Language Maintenance." In *Teaching Indigenous Languages*, edited by Jon Reyhner, 214–21. Flagstaff: Northern Arizona University.

Peterson, Leighton C. 2017. "Reflections on Navajo Publics, 'New' Media, and Documentary Futures." In *Engaging Native American Publics: Linguistic Anthropology in a Collaborative Key*, edited by Paul V. Kroskrity and Barbra A. Meek, 169–83. London: Routledge.

Picq, Manuela Lavinas. 2018. *Vernacular Sovereignties: Indigenous Women Challenging World Politics.* Tucson: University of Arizona Press.

Postman, Neil. 2000. "The Humanism of Media Ecology." *Proceedings of the Media Ecology Association* 1:10–16.

Powdermaker, Hortense. 1962. *Copper Town: Changing Africa; the Human Situation on the Rhodesian Copperbelt.* New York: Harper & Row.

Quijano, Aníbal. 2000. "Coloniality of Power and Eurocentrism in Latin America." *International Sociology* 15 (2): 215–32. https://doi.org/10.1177/026858090001 5002005.

Rappaport, Roy A. 1967a. *Pigs for the Ancestors: Ritual in the Ecology of a New Guinea People.* New Haven, Conn.: Yale University Press.

Rappaport, Roy A. 1967b. "Ritual Regulation of Environmental Relations Among a New Guinea People." *Ethnology* 6 (1): 17–30.

Rasch, Elisabet Dueholm. 2020. "Becoming a Maya Woman: Beauty Pageants at the Intersection of Indigeneity, Gender and Class in Quetzaltenango, Guatemala." *Journal of Latin American Studies* 52 (1): 133–56. https://doi.org/10.1017/S00222 16X19000919.

Raygorodetsky, Gleb. 2018. "Indigenous Peoples Defend Earth's Biodiversity—but They're in Danger." *National Geographic*, November 16, 2018. https://www .nationalgeographic.com/environment/article/can-indigenous-land-stewardship -protect-biodiversity-.

Reeve, Mary-Elizabeth. 1988. "Caucha Uras: Lowland Quichua Histories of the Amazon Rubber Boom." In *Rethinking History and Myth: Indigenous South American Perspectives on the Past*, edited by Jonathan D. Hill, 19–34. Champaign: University of Illinois Press.

REFERENCES

Renard-Casevitz, France-Marie, Thierry Saignes, and Anne Christine Taylor. 1988. *Al Este de Los Andes: Relaciones Entre Las Sociedades Amazónicas y Andinas Entre Los Siglos XV y XVII.* Quito, Ecuador: Ediciones Abya-Yala; Instituto Francés de Estudios Andinos.

Rice, Keren. 2011. "Documentary Linguistics and Community Relations." *Language Documentation & Conservation* 5:187–207.

Riofrancos, Thea N. 2020. *Resource Radicals: From Petro-Nationalism to Post-Extractivism in Ecuador.* Radical Américas. Durham, N.C.: Duke University Press.

Roche, Gerald. 2019. "Articulating Language Oppression: Colonialism, Coloniality and the Erasure of Tibet's Minority Languages." *Patterns of Prejudice* 53 (5): 487–514. https://doi.org/10.1080/0031322X.2019.1662074.

Roche, Gerald. 2020. "Abandoning Endangered Languages: Ethical Loneliness, Language Oppression, and Social Justice." *American Anthropologist* 122 (1): 164–69. https://doi.org/10.1111/aman.13372.

Rogers, Mark. 1996. "Beyond Authenticity: Conservation, Tourism, and the Politics of Representation in the Ecuadorian Amazon." *Identities-Global Studies in Culture and Power* 3 (1–2): 73–125.

Rogers, Mark. 1998. "Spectacular Bodies: Folklorization and the Politics of Identity in Ecuadorian Beauty Pageants." *Journal of Latin American Anthropology* 3 (2): 54–85.

Roitman, Karem, and Alexis Oviedo. 2017. "Mestizo Racism in Ecuador." *Ethnic and Racial Studies* 40 (15): 2768–86. https://doi.org/10.1080/01419870.2016.1260749.

Rouvier, Ruth. 2017. "The Role of Elder Speakers in Language Revitalisation." *Language Documentation and Description* 14:88–110.

Rumsey, Alan. 2010. "Lingual and Cultural Wholes and Fields." In *Experiments in Holism*, edited by Ton Otto and Nils Burbandt, 145–71. Oxford: Blackwell.

Salomon, Frank. 1983. "El Quichua de Los Andes Ecuatoriales: Algunos Aportes Recientes." *Revista Andina* 2:393–405.

Sapir, Edward. 1912. "Language and Environment." *American Anthropologist* 14 (2): 226–42.

Saussure, Ferdinand de. 1966. *Course in General Linguistics.* Edited by Charles Bally, Albert Sechehaye, and Albert Riedlinger. Translated by Wade Baskin. Cours de Linguistique Générale. New York: McGraw-Hill.

Sawyer, Suzana. 2004. *Crude Chronicles: Indigenous Politics, Multinational Oil, and Neoliberalism in Ecuador.* Durham, N.C.: Duke University Press.

Schackt, Jon. 2005. "Mayahood Through Beauty: Indian Beauty Pageants in Guatemala." *Bulletin of Latin American Research* 24 (3): 269–87. https://doi.org/10.1111/j.0261-3050.2005.00135.x.

Seitz, Barbara. 1982. "Llaquichina Songs of the Sachua Huarmi (Jungle Woman) and Their Role in Transformational Communication Events in the Ecuadorian Oriente." PhD dissertation, Indiana University.

Shenton, Jamie E. 2019. "Strong Kichwa Women Are Made, Made Up, and Make Others: Feminist Theory Meets Amazonian Ethnography of Gender, Bodies, and

Social Change." *Anthropological Quarterly* 92 (1): 5–34. https://doi.org/10.1353/anq.2019.0000.

Shulist, Sarah. 2018. *Transforming Indigeneity: Urbanization and Language Revitalization in the Brazilian Amazon.* Toronto: University of Toronto Press.

Sierra, Rodrigo. 2000. "Dynamics and Patterns of Deforestation in the Western Amazon: The Napo Deforestation Front, 1986–1996." *Applied Geography* 20 (1): 1–16. https://doi.org/10.1016/S0143-6228(99)00014-4.

Silverstein, Michael. 1979. "Language Structure and Linguistic Ideology." In *The Elements: A Parasession on Linguistic Units and Levels,* edited by Paul R. Clyne, William F. Hanks, and Carol L. Hofbauer, 193–247. Chicago: Chicago Linguistic Society.

Silverstein, Michael. 1981. "The Limits of Awareness." In *Sociolinguistic Working Papers,* 84:1–30. Austin: Southwest Educational Development Laboratory.

Silverstein, Michael. 1996. "Monoglot 'Standard' in America: Standardization and Metaphors of Linguistic Hegemony." In *The Matrix of Language—Contemporary Linguistic Anthropology,* edited by Donald Brenneis and Ronald K. S. Macaulay, 284–306. Boulder, Colo.: Westview Press.

Silvio, Teri. 2007. "Remediation and Local Globalizations: How Taiwan's 'Digital Video Knights-Errant Puppetry' Writes the History of the New Media in Chinese." *Cultural Anthropology* 22 (2): 285–313.

Silvio, Teri. 2010. "Animation: The New Performance?" *Journal of Linguistic Anthropology* 20 (2): 422–38.

Simpson, Audra. 2007. "On Ethnographic Refusal: Indigeneity, 'Voice' and Colonial Citizenship." *Junctures: The Journal for Thematic Dialogue* 9 (January): 67.

Simpson, Audra. 2011. "Settlement's Secret." *Cultural Anthropology* 26 (2): 205–17.

Simpson, Leanne Betasamosake. 2017. *As We Have Always Done: Indigenous Freedom Through Radical Resistance.* Minneapolis: University of Minnesota Press.

Smith, Linda Tuhiwai. 2012. *Decolonizing Methodologies: Research and Indigenous Peoples.* London: Zed Books.

Spence, Justin. 2018. "Language Learning Through the Archives." In *The Routledge Handbook of Language Revitalization,* edited by Leanne Hinton, Leena Huss, and Gerald Roche, 178–87. New York: Routledge.

Spiller, Maximiliano. 1974. *Historia de La Misión Josefina Del Napo 1922–1974.* Vol. 1. Quito: Artes Graficas Equinoccio.

Spitulnik, Debra. 1997. "The Social Circulation of Media Discourse and the Mediation of Communities." *Journal of Linguistic Anthropology* 6 (2): 161–87.

Steward, Julian. 1955. "The Concept and Method of Cultural Ecology." In *The Environment in Anthropology,* 2nd ed., edited by Nora Haenn, Richard R. Wilk, and Allison Harnish, 12–17. A Reader in Ecology, Culture, and Sustainable Living. New York: New York University Press.

Steward, Julian, and Alfred Metraux. 1948. "Tribes of the Peruvian and Ecuadorian Montaña." In *Handbook of South American Indians,* 535–656. Washington, D.C.: Smithsonian Institution.

Swanson, Tod D. 2009. "Singing to Estranged Lovers: Runa Relations to Plants in the Ecuadorian Amazon." *Journal for the Study of Religion, Nature and Culture* 3 (1): 36–65.

Swanson, Tod D., and Jarrad Reddekop. 2023. "Feeling with the Land: Llakichina and the Emotional Life of Relatedness in Amazonian Kichwa Thinking." *Journal of the American Academy of Religion* 90 (4): 954–72. https://doi.org/10.1093/jaarel/lfad032.

Taff, Alice, Chee Melvatha, Jaeci Hall, Martin Kawenniyóhstha Nicole Hall, and Annie Johnston. 2018. "Indigenous Language Use Impacts Wellness." In *The Oxford Handbook of Endangered Languages*, edited by Kenneth Rehg and Lyle Campbell, 862–83. New York: Oxford University Press.

Taylor, Anne Christine. 1999. "The Western Margins of Amazonia from the Early Sixteenth to the Early Nineteenth Century." In *The Cambridge History of the Native Peoples of the Americas*, edited by Frank Salomon and Stuart B. Schwartz, 188–256. Cambridge: Cambridge University Press.

Taylor, Anne-Christine. 2008. "On Whitten's 'Interculturality and the Indigenization of Modernity.'" *Tipití: Journal of the Society for the Anthropology of Lowland South America* 6 (1).

Taylor, Diana. 2003. *The Archive and the Repertoire: Performing Cultural Memory in the Americas*. Illustrated edition. Durham, N.C.: Duke University Press.

Tedlock, Dennis. 1983. *The Spoken Word and the Work of Interpretation*, ix, 365. Philadelphia: University of Pennsylvania Press.

Tedlock, Dennis, and Bruce Mannheim. 1995. *The Dialogic Emergence of Culture*. Urbana: University of Illinois Press.

Thiong'o, Ngugi wa. 1998. "Decolonising the Mind." *Diogenes* 46 (184): 101. https://doi.org/10.1177/039219219804618409.

Todd, Zoe. 2016. "An Indigenous Feminist's Take on the Ontological Turn: 'Ontology' Is Just Another Word For Colonialism." *Journal of Historical Sociology* 29 (1): 4–22.

Tremblay, Marie Julie. 2007. "Contextualización de los Préstamos Léxicos de Origen Indígena." *Tinkuy: Boletín de Investigación y Debate* 4:77–96.

Tsing, Anna. 2012. "Unruly Edges: Mushrooms as Companion Species: For Donna Haraway." *Environmental Humanities* 1 (1): 141–54. https://doi.org/10.1215/22011919-3610012.

Tuck, Eve, and K. Wayne Yang. 2012. "Decolonization Is Not a Metaphor." *Decolonization: Indigeneity, Education & Society* 1 (1): 1–40.

Turner, Terence. 1991. "Representing, Resisting, Rethinking: Historical Transformations of Kayapó Culture and Anthropological Consciousness." In *Colonial Situations: Essays on the Contextualization of Ethnographic Knowledge*, edited by George W. Stocking, 285–313. Madison: University of Wisconsin.

United Nations Educational, Scientific and Cultural Organization (UNESCO). n.d. "Indigenous Languages Decade (2022–2032)." UNESCO. Accessed January 9, 2024. https://www.unesco.org/en/decades/indigenous-languages.

Urban, Matthias. 2021. "Language Classification, Language Contact and Andean Prehistory: The North." *Language and Linguistics Compass* 15 (5): e12414. https://doi.org/10.1111/lnc3.12414.

Urla, Jacqueline. 2012. *Reclaiming Basque Language, Nation, and Cultural Activism.* Reno: University of Nevada Press.

Uzendoski, Michael. 2004. "The Horizontal Archipelago: The Quijos/Upper Napo Regional System." *Ethnohistory* 51 (2): 317–57.

Uzendoski, Michael. 2005. *The Napo Runa of Amazonian Ecuador.* Interpretations of Culture in the New Millennium. Urbana: University of Illinois Press.

Uzendoski, Michael. 2009. "La Textualidad Oral Napo Kichwa y Las Paradojas de La Educación Bilingüe Intercultural En La Amazonia." In *Repensando Los Movimientos Indígenas,* edited by Carmen Martínez Novo, 147–71. Quito, Ecuador: FLACSO.

Uzendoski, Michael. 2018. "Amazonia and the Cultural Politics of Extractivism: Sumak Kawsay and Block 20 of Ecuador." *Cultural Studies* 32 (3): 364–88.

Uzendoski, Michael, and Edith Felicia Calapucha-Tapuy. 2012. *The Ecology of the Spoken Word: Amazonian Storytelling and Shamanism Among the Napo Runa.* Urbana: University of Illinois Press.

Uzendoski, Michael, and Norman E. Whitten. 2014. "From 'Acculturated Indians' to 'Dynamic Amazonian Quichua-Speaking Peoples.'" *Tipití: Journal of the Society for the Anthropology of Lowland South America* 12 (1): 1–13.

Vicariato Apostólico de Napo. 1995. *Devocionario Quichua.* Napo, Ecuador: Vicariato Apostólico de Napo.

Viveiros de Castro, Eduardo. 1998. "Cosmological Deixis and Amerindian Perspectivism." *Journal of the Royal Anthropological Institute* 4:469–88.

Vizenor, Gerald Robert. 1994. *Manifest Manners: Postindian Warriors of Survivance.* Hanover, N.H.: University Press of New England.

Vizenor, Gerald Robert. 2009. *Native Liberty: Natural Reason and Cultural Survivance.* Lincoln: University of Nebraska Press.

Voegelin, C. F., and Florence M. Voegelin. 1964. "Languages of the World—Native American Fascicle One." https://eric.ed.gov/?id=ED010352.

Warner, Michael. 2002. *Publics and Counterpublics.* New York: Zone Books.

Webster, Anthony. 2009. *Explorations in Navajo Poetry and Poetics.* Albuquerque: University of New Mexico Press.

Webster, Anthony. 2017. "'I Don't Write Navajo Poetry, I Just Speak the Poetry in Navajo' Ethical Listeners, Poetic Communion, and the Imagined Future Publics of Navajo Poetry." In *Engaging Native American Publics: Linguistic Anthropology in a Collaborative Key,* edited by Paul V. Kroskrity and Barbra A. Meek, 150–68. London: Routledge.

Webster, Anthony, and Leighton Peterson. 2011. "Introduction: American Indian Languages in Unexpected Places." *American Indian Culture and Research Journal* 35 (2): 1–18.

Weismantel, Mary. 2001. *Cholas and Pishtacos: Stories of Race and Sex in the Andes.* Chicago: University of Chicago Press.

REFERENCES

Wemigwans, Jennifer. 2018. *A Digital Bundle: Protecting and Promoting Indigenous Knowledge Online*. Regina, Saskatchewan: University of Regina Press.

Whitten, Norman E. 2008. "Interculturality and the Indigenization of Modernity: A View from Amazonian Ecuador." *Tipití: Journal of the Society for the Anthropology of Lowland South America* 6 (1).

Whitten, Norman E. 1976. *Sacha Runa: Ethnicity and Adaptation of Ecuadorian Jungle Quichua*. Urbana: University of Illinois Press.

Whyte, Kyle. 2018. "Settler Colonialism, Ecology, and Environmental Injustice." *Environment and Society* 9 (1): 125–44. https://doi.org/10.3167/ares.2018.090109.

Williams, Caroline. 2019. "'They Grow as Speakers, as Leaders': A Case Study of Experiential Leadership in the Miss World Eskimo–Indian Olympics Pageant." *The American Indian Quarterly* 43 (2): 204–35.

Wilson, Pamela, and Michelle Stewart. 2008. *Global Indigenous Media: Cultures, Poetics, and Politics*. Durham, N.C.: Duke University Press.

Wolf, Eric. 1972. "Ownership and Political Ecology." *Anthropological Quarterly* 45 (3): 201–5. https://doi.org/10.2307/3316532.

Wolfe, Patrick. 2006. "Settler Colonialism and the Elimination of the Native." *Journal of Genocide Research* 8 (4): 387–409. https://doi.org/10.1080/146235206010 56240.

Wolfram, Walt, and Natalie Schilling-Estes. 1995. "Moribund Dialects and the Endangerment Canon: The Case of the Ocracoke Brogue." *Language* 71 (4): 696–721. https://doi.org/10.2307/415741.

Woolard, Kathryn A. 1998a. "Introduction: Language Ideology as a Field of Inquiry." In *Language Ideologies: Practice and Theory*, edited by Bambi B. Schieffelin, Kathryn A. Woolard, and Paul V. Kroskrity, 3–47. New York: Oxford University Press.

Woolard, Kathryn A. 1998b. "Simultaneity and Bivalency as Strategies in Bilingualism." *Journal of Linguistic Anthropology* 8 (1): 3–29.

Wortham, Erica Cusi. 2013. *Indigenous Media in Mexico: Culture, Community, and the State*. Durham, N.C.: Duke University Press.

Wroblewski, Michael. 2012. "Amazonian Kichwa Proper: Ethnolinguistic Domain in Pan-Indian Ecuador." *Journal of Linguistic Anthropology* 22 (1): 64–86.

Wroblewski, Michael. 2014. "Public Indigeneity, Language Revitalization, and Intercultural Planning in a Native Amazonian Beauty Pageant." *American Anthropologist* 116 (1): 65–80.

Wroblewski, Michael. 2022. *Remaking Kichwa: Language and Indigenous Pluralism in Amazonian Ecuador*. London: Bloomsbury Academic.

Yánez, Consuelo. 1991. "The Implementation of Language Policy: The Case of Ecuador." *International Review of Education / Internationale Zeitschrift Für Erziehungswissenschaft / Revue Internationale de l'Education* 37 (1): 53–66.

Zuckerman, Adam, and Kevin Koenig. 2016. *From Well to Wheel: The Social, Environmental, and Climate Costs of Amazonian Crude*. Oakland, Calif.: Amazon Watch. https://amazonwatch.org/assets/files/2016-amazon-crude-report.pdf.

INDEX

Note: Page numbers in *italics* refer to illustrative matter.

Achuar language, 65. *See also* Chicham (Jivaroan) language family
affective publics, 176–77, 183, 186
affectivity, 5, 78, 175–77, 179, 180–86, 239
agglutinative, defined, 60
Agha, Asif, 15, 129
agricultural industries, 33, 55, 59
Aguinda, Catalina, 51–54
Aguinda, Mariano, *22, 99*; on linguistic variations, 61–63; as research interlocuters, 21, *22*–23
Ali Ñambi (radio program), 102. See also *A New Path* (radio program); radio programs
AllyTV, 101, 147
Alvarado, Carlos, 174
amarun, 194–95
Amazonian Kichwa language, 65–66
Amazonian Power (radio program), 84–87, 102. *See also* radio and language reclamation; radio programs
Amazon rainforest, 6, 33, 39
Andean Highlands, 6

Andoa language, 65. *See also* Zaparoan language family
Antisuyu Ushay/Poder Amazónico (Amazonian Power; radio program), 84–87, 102. *See also* radio and language reclamation; radio programs
Archidona shimi, 66
asichina, 89, 187. *See also* humor
assimilation, 12, 54, 57n5, 68n14. *See also* settler colonialism
Association of Kichwa Midwives of the Upper Napo (AMUPAKIN): cultural presentations by, 111, 155, 224–26; as ethnographic fieldsite, 19–20; humor and, 187–88; live wayusa upina performance at, 152–53, *154*, 157–58
aswa (chicha), 14, 22, 68, 107–8, 151, 206, 226
auka, 67, 67n11, 68
author's positionality, 21
"Awak Huarmi" (song), 217, 217n6
Aymara, 154
Ayuda en Acción (organization), 86, 87n2

Babel, Anna, 6, 219
balichina, 201, 201n1. *See also* revalorization
basketry, 134, 152, 202, 217
Basque, 127, 128
Basso, Keith, 52, 190
beauty pageants. *See* cultural pageantry
bilingualism and bilingual education: children's learning processes and, 123–24, 236; cultural pageantry and, 30, 71, 129, 142, 144, 161; cultural practices and, 30; prevalence of, 67, 67n12, 68; Unified Kichwa and education in, 9, 15, 36, 66, 69–71, 124–27. *See also* Kichwa language; Spanish language
biocultural diversity, 40
biodiversity, 40, 43
blast fishing, 38
boas (snake), 193–95
Boas, Franz, 11
Bobonaza Kichwa language, 66
Briggs, Charles, 173
burla shuti (nicknames), 89, 96, 187. *See also* nicknames

Calapucha-Tapuy, Edith Felicia, 79
Canelos Kichwa, 65n10, 66
Catholic missionaries, 49n4, 56–57. *See also* Josephine Order (Catholic) missionaries
cattle, 33, 55, 59
cell phones, 77, 96, 99–100, 101, 106
Cerda, Gabriela, 147
Cerda, Patricio, 36–39
Cerda, Roberto, 127, 128, 211
chagra, 35, 152. *See also* agricultural industries; environmental knowledge
charismatic Indigeneity, as term, 143, 220
Chavez, Edison, 89, 147
chiaw, 193–95. *See also* ideophones
Chicham (Jivaroan) language family, 7, 64, 65, 66, 69
Chickasaw, 116

Chinese language, 55, 232
Christianity. *See* missionization
chronotopes, 16–17, 25, 210
chunda (peach palm), 25, 35, 149
Citizens' Revolution (social policy), 51, 229
Claro, 100
clothing, 16, 25, 148–52, 155, 220
Coca Kichwa, 172
collective memory, 14–17, 201–13, 221–22, 227–29. *See also* intergenerational transmission; language; linguistic ecologies; media ecologies; print ecologies
colonialism. *See* settler colonialism
community media programs, 4–6, 18, 23–28, 31, 84–87, 227–29, 233, 237–39. *See also* collective memory; media ecologies; radio and language reclamation
CONAIE (Confederación de Nacionalidades Indígenas del Ecuador), 103–4, 124
CONFENIAE (Confederación de Nacionalidades Indígenas de la Amazonía Ecuatoriana), 103
Correa, Rafael, 51, 71, 229
counseling. *See* kamachina
crying, 100, 178, 180–86, 200. *See also* laments
cultural intimacy, 177, 190–91
cultural maintenance processes, 12–13, 12n3
cultural pageantry, 142–52; bilingualism and, 30, 71, 129, 142, 144, 161; clothing and dress in, 16, 25, 148–52, 220; description of, 15, 148–52; Festival Intercultural de la Chonta, 30, 142; history of, 145; Ñusta Chunta Warmi (Archidona), 142, 144–45, 148, 149, 162, 169, 219, 220; Ñusta Napu Marka, 142; Ñusta Pitak Warmi, 167; Ñusta Wayusa Warmi (Tena), 142, 148; participation in, 147; as part of media

ecology, 216, 222, 228; performance of, 29, 30, 71, 88, 142–43, 147, 148–49, 152–59, 173, 218–21; Pitak Waska Ñusta, 161, 162, 218, 220; regional events, 142; speeches and language in, 159–68; Sumak Ñusta Chunta Warmi, 141–42, 220; tourism and, 158–59; Unified Kichwa and, 129, 142; variations in, 147–48. *See also* cultural performance and representation; embodied performance
cultural performance and representation, 29, 30, 71, 88, 142–43, 147, 148–49, 152–59, 173, 218–21. *See also* cultural pageantry; embodied performance

dance performance, 150–51, 161
data sovereignty, 238
Davis, Jenny, 43, 45–46
decolonization, 11, 44, 229. *See also* settler colonialism
deforestation, 33, 39. *See also* Amazon rainforest
Deloria, Philip, 6, 203
Deloria, Vine, Jr., 127
demographics, 48n3. *See also* population statistics; racial categories
Devocionario Quichua, 82, 83, 102, 105, 106
Dorigatti, Humberto, 83, 83n1
dress, 16, 25, 148–52, 155, 220

earthquakes, 189
ecologies, as concept, 40–43. *See also* linguistic ecologies; media ecologies; print ecologies; settler colonialism
economic compensation for research participants, 225n9
economy. *See* wage economy
Ecuadorian Ministry of Culture and Patrimony, 20
elders' knowledge. *See* collective memory; intergenerational transmission

embodied performance, 30, 109, 142–43, 147, 173, 205–6, 222–23, 225. *See also* cultural pageantry; cultural performance and representation; pita; radio and language reclamation; wayusa upina
emergent vitalities, 9, 175–77, 182–83. *See also* language revitalization
Emlen, Nicholas, 6
employment opportunities, 54–55. *See also* wage economy
encomienda, 49
endangerment discourses, 11–12
English language, 55, 85, 236
environmental anthropology, 40–41
environmental knowledge: effects of colonialism on, 37, 39, 46; humor and, 187; media and reclamation of, 31, 75–76, 77, 216–17; pageants and, 149, 151; transmission of, 9, 20–21. *See also* chagra; intergenerational transmission; pita
extractive colonialism, 39, 50–55, 229. *See also* mineral extraction; settler colonialism

Facebook, 75–76, 81, 87, 100–101, 111, 185, 232. *See also* social media
femininity, 25, 149, 152, 179, 182, 185. *See also* women
Fernandisco, 84–87, 87n2, 232
Festival Intercultural de la Chonta, 30, 142. *See also* Intercultural Peach Palm Festival; Sumak Ñusta Chunta Warmi
fishing techniques, 38–39
Fishman, Joshua, 5, 176
FOIN (Federación de Organizaciones Indígenas del Napo), 103
food, 34, 68. *See also* aswa (chicha)
formal education, 27, 71, 103, 109, 137, 234–36, 234n1. *See also* bilingualism and bilingual education; literacy; standardized language; Unified Kichwa

francias, 68n15. *See also* rancia
French, Brigittine, 209
Frey, Benjamin, 44
future/past, 154, 156

gardening. *See* chagra
gender. *See* femininity; women
gold, 55. *See also* mineral extraction;
  settler colonialism
gowns, 150, 151. *See also* dress
Grefa, Augosto, 132
Grefa, César, 12–13, 90
Grefa, Gloria, 82–84, 102, 105, 232
Grefa, Serafina, *20, 22, 99, 215*; about, 33;
  death of, 31, 185, 227, 232; on humor,
  188–89, 192–93; on intergenerational
  narratives, 197–99; kamachina by,
  207–11; on Kichwa lifeways, 206–7;
  laments and, 181–84; on language,
  107–8, 116–19; legacy of, 232; pita
  production of, 213–16; as research
  interlocutor, 3–4, 21, 22–23, 30–31
grief. *See* crying; laments
Gringo Changa (mountain), 51
gringo, 52–54, 68, 190
guayusa drinking. *See* wayusa upina

hacienda system, 50, 58n6, 85
Halbwachs, Maurice, 209n4
Hall, Edward, 188
Haugen, Einar, 41
Herzfeld, Michael, 177, 191
Highland Kichwa language, 6–7, 9, 36,
  106, 124, 125, 128. *See also* Kichwa lan-
  guage; Unified Kichwa
*Historia de una Cultura a la que se Quiere
  Matar* (publication), 174
huasipungo system, 58n6
Huayhua, Margarita, 154
huiracocha, 67n13
humor, 187–93
hunting, 35
Hurston, Zora Neale, 38n2

ideophones, 192, 194–96
in betweenness, 6
Indigenous, as term, 5n2
Indigenous coalitions, 103–4
Indigenous erasure rhetoric, 40
Indigenous language statistics, 7–8,
  8, 234. See also *names of specific
  languages*
El Indio Amázonico (the Amazonian
  Indian), 12–13
intercultural code, 144, 159
Intercultural Peach Palm Festival, 30, 142,
  149. *See also* Festival Intercultural de la
  Chonta; Ñusta Chunta Warmi pageant
  (Archidona)
intergenerational transmission, 116–17,
  136, 196–200, 209–13, 221–24. *See
  also* collective memory; environmental
  knowledge; wayusa upina
intertextuality, 14, 15, 26, 51–52, 79, 96,
  111, 173, 187
Inuit, 127
invented tradition, 15–16, 16n5
ira akcha, 67, 67n13
iyarina, 12–13. *See also* collective memory; kungarina

Jesuit Mission of Maynas, 49. *See also*
  Catholic missionaries
Jesuits, 49n4. *See also* Catholic
  missionaries
Los Jilgueritos, 181–82, 184
joking, 187–93
Josephine Order (Catholic) missionaries,
  49n4, 50, 56–57, 81, 83
Jumandi (Jumandy; cultural hero), 13n4,
  48, 191

kachu (genre), 177, 189, 193
kamachina, 119–20, 155–57, 207–11, 225,
  227. *See also* wayusa upina
Kambak (musical group), 83
Kaska language, 122–23

INDEX

Kichwa, as term, 4n1

Kichwa language, 4–10; mixed orthography, 38n2; morphological and phonological variations in, 28, 60–61, 62, 124, 128, 129, 222; radio programs and, 80–97; regional variations of, 59–69, 172; statistics on speakers of, 7–8, 8, 66, 234. *See also* bilingualism and bilingual education; collective memory; language; linguistic ecologies; Unified Kichwa; Upper Napo Kichwa language

Kichwa lifeways: collective memory of, 14–17, 25–26, 201–13, 221–22, 227–29; cultural performance of, 152–54, 156–59; language embodiment as, 4; in Napo Runa communities, 12; pita and shigra production, 4, 23, 134–35, 155, 162, 171, 202, 205–7, 213–28; radio listening and, 97–103; settler colonial effects on, 34–36, 45–59. *See also* ruku kawsay; wayusa upina

Kichwa pageants. *See* cultural pageantry

kungarina, 12–13, 116–17, 156. *See also* collective memory; iyarina

Kuty, Sisa, 217

kwintu (genre), 193

laments, 100, 176, 177, 179–86

land reform and settlement, 50, 58–59. *See also* settler colonialism

language embodiment. *See* embodied performance

language ideologies, 17, 109, 114; assemblages of, 125–36; defined, 125; media ideologies and, 199

language oppression, 36, 44–45, 59

language reclamation, 11, 138, 204–5, 229, 233–39. *See also* collective memory; Kichwa language; radio and language reclamation

language revitalization, 11, 234; emergent vitalities, 175–77; Fishman on mass

media and, 176; goals of, 109–10, 127; Meek on, 17; pedagogical models of, 115–16; settler ecologies and debates on, 69–73. *See also* Kichwa language; language reclamation; language standardization

language socialization, 29–30, 119–23, 129–30, 138

language standardization, 9, 104–5, 113–16, 124–27, 137, 234–39. *See also* Kichwa language; Unified Kichwa

language statistics, 7, 8, 66, 234

Leonard, Wesley, 11, 204. *See also* language reclamation

Let's Return Home (radio program), 84. *See also* radio and language reclamation; radio programs

Ley de Tierras Baldías y Colonización (Law of Empty Lands and Colonization; 1936), 58n6

Liboiron, Max, 39

lifeways. *See* Kichwa lifeways

linguistic anthropology, 11, 18–19, 26–27, 38n2, 43, 51, 119

linguistic diversity, 38n2, 42, 70, 73, 128, 136–39, 168–73

linguistic ecologies, 36–45, 50, 63–71, 231–32. *See also* ecologies, as concept; Kichwa language; language; Unified Kichwa

listening, discourse of, 99, 116–23, 135–36, 221, 222–24, 226, 231

literacy, 79–80. *See also* formal education; language

llakichina, 180

Llaki Shungu (musical group), 83

Llaucana Cocha (The Saltlick Lake), 37–38

La Llave del Futuro (radio program), 86–87. *See also* radio and language reclamation; radio programs

Lopez, Dario, 88, 186

Los Ángeles (band), 218–19

Lower Napo Kichwa language, 60–61, 106. *See also* Kichwa language; Unified Kichwa

Lowland Ecuadorian Kichwa language, 66, 124

lumu, 35. *See also* aswa (chicha); manioc

Maffi, Luisa, 40

makikutuna (clothing), 150–51, 161

Maliseet language, 175–76

Mama Olga (performer), 134–35, 155–58, 169–71, 173, 222–24, 226

Mancino (radio host), 84, 85–86, 87n2

manioc, 14, 35, 68. *See also* aswa (chicha)

Mannheim, Bruce, 117, 173–74, 181

Maori, 116

"María Ñukapa Mama" (song), 83

material ecologies, 35, 36, 41, 42, 50, 59. *See also* ecologies, as concept

Maynas, 49

media ecologies, 77–80, 200; Amazonian Power radio program, 84–87; community media programs in, 4–6, 18, 23–28; growing pita and, 217–26; listening and participation in, 97–103; A New Path radio program, 19, 27, 32, 34, 75–77, 87–97; pita in, 217–26; radio stations in, 80–84. *See also* ecologies, as concept; *A New Path* (radio program); radio and language reclamation

mediascapes, 78

Meek, Barbra, 15, 17, 19, 44, 46

mestizaje, 67, 68n14. *See also* assimilation

metathesis, 124–25

Method for the Intercultural Bilingual Education System (publication), 104

mineral extraction, 50–55, 217, 229. *See also* extractive colonialism; settler colonialism

mishu (white-mestizo) knowledge systems, 12–13, 68, 127

missionization, 48–50, 49n4, 54, 56–58, 69. *See also* settler colonialism

Miss Peach Palm Princess pageant, 141–42, 220. *See also* cultural pageantry; Ñusta Chunta Warmi pageant (Archidona)

Moll, Yasmin, 15, 16n5

Montaluisa, Luis, 104, 128–29, 235

morphological variations, 28, 60–61, 62, 124, 128, 129, 222. *See also* Kichwa language

Movistar, 100

Muehlmann, Shaylih, 39

multimodal sites of living, 205–6. *See also* reanimation

Muratorio, Blanca, 146, 149, 185n3

Mushuk Ñampi. See *A New Path* (radio program)

music and musicality, 177–84

myth, 26, 187, 211

Nación Originaria Quijos (NAOQUI), 67

Napo, overview, 3–10, 46–49

Napo Runa, as term, 7

National Directorate of Bilingual and Intercultural Education, 124

ñawpa, 154. *See also* past/future

neologisms, 106, 124, 127, 141, 164, 167n7, 170, 210

net bags. *See* shigra

A New Path (radio program): about, 19, 75–77, 87–97; collective memories by, 210; creation of, 34; goals of, 27, 186–87, 202–3, 228; humor on, 186–87, 190, 191–92; songs and music on, 177–84; wayusa upina and, 32, 90–91, 97–98, 130–36, 152–53, 154, 173, 175. *See also* community media programs; media ecologies; radio and language reclamation; radio programs

nicknames: burla shuti, 89, 96, 187; francias, 68n15; gringu, 68; rancia, 68, 68n15, 115

Northern Athapascan language, 122–23

Nuckolls, Janis, 194–96

Ñusta Chunta Warmi pageant (Archidona), 141–42, 144–45, 148, 149, 162, 169, 219, 220. *See also* chunda; cultural pageantry

Ñusta Napu Marka provincial pageant, 142. *See also* cultural pageantry

Ñusta Pitak Warmi pageant (UCKAR), 167. *See also* cultural pageantry; Pitak Waska Ñusta

Ñusta Wayusa Warmi pageant (Tena), 142, 148. *See also* cultural pageantry

Oas (cultural group), 65

oil industry, 50–51, 229. *See also* mineral extraction

ontologies of language, 126–27

Orellana province, 64, 66, 81, 87

Orr, Carolyn, 60

pacha (clothing), 148–49

pagarachu, 108, 141n1, 167

paju, 178, 191

Papacharissi, Zizi, 176

Pastaza Kichwa, 60, 60n8, *61,* 67n12, *105,* 106, 124, 195

Pastaza province, 50, 65n10, 66, 81, 87, 178

past/future, 154, 156

patrilocality, 35

patrón, 49–50, 85

paya/payaguna, 157–58

peach palm, 25, 35, 149

Peircean realism, 14

performance. *See* cultural performance and representation; embodied performance

Perín, Mario, 81, 83

Perley, Bernard, 9, 43, 72, 143, 176, 192, 203–4, 220, 228

Peru, 117, 117n1, 154

phonological variations, 28, 60–61, 62, 124, 128, 129, 222. *See also* Kichwa language

Picq, Manuela, 146

pita, 31, 149, 162–64, 162n5, 205–7, 206n2, 213–28, 213n5

"Pitaj Warmi" (song), 218–19, 218nn7–8

Pitak Waska Ñusta, 161, 162, 218, 220. *See also* cultural pageantry

Pizango, Karen, 162–63, 167, 220

Los Playeros Kichwas (musical group), 83, 84, 232

population statistics, 7, *8,* 46–49, 66

print ecologies, 103–9. *See also* ecologies, as concept

privates, formation of, 24

Protestant missionaries, 56

Provincial Directorate of Bilingual and Intercultural Education in Napo (DIPEIB-N), 144

publics, 24–25

puppetry, 16, 154, 158

Quichua, as term, 4n1. *See also under* Kichwa

Quijos (cultural group), 64

Quijos (region), 48. *See also* Napo, overview

racial categories, 67–68, 148n3

radio and language reclamation, 4, 17–28; affectivity of, 175–77; broadcast programs, 84–87, 175; environmental knowledge and, 31, 75–76, 77, 216–17; regional differentiation of, 116–23; Shiguango on, 34; songs and music on, 177–84; La Voz de Napo, 81–84, 232. *See also* community media programs; embodied performance; media ecologies; *A New Path* (radio program)

radio programs: *Ali Ñambi* (radio program), 102; *Antisuyu Ushay* (Amazonian Power), 84–87, 102; *La Llave del Futuro,* 86–87; risachina, 102–3; *Wasima Tigrashun* (Let's Return Home), 84; *See also A New Path* (radio program) radio stations: La Voz de Napo (The Voice of Napo), 81–84, 232; Radio Arcoíris (Rainbow Radio), 81, 86; Radio Canela (Cinnamon Radio), 81; Radio Ideal (Ideal Radio), 81; Radio Jatari, 91n5, 102, 107; Radio Líder, 87n2; Radio Olímpica (Olympic Radio), 81, 84

rancia, 68, 68n15, 115

Rayu Shinalla (television program), 77, 101

reanimation, 14–17, 206–13, 221–24, 232–33

reducción (Indigenous reduction/reservation), 7, 49, 65

remediation, 10–14, 222

rescate, 202. *See also* salvage, as term

research methods, 19–21, 204, 225n9

revalorization, 110, 201–3

riksina, 147

road construction, 51–54

Roche, Gerald, 44

rubber industry, 49

rukuguna (elders), as term, 95

ruku kawsay, 12, 57, 149, 155, 203, 209, 235n1. *See also* Kichwa lifeways

"Ruku Kawsay" (song by Grefa), 12–13, 90. *See also* Grefa, César

ruku mama, 119

runa, 7, 66, 67, 67n11

runa kawsay, 12, 209. *See also* Kichwa lifeways

runa shimi, as term, 7, 66

Salazar, Ofelia, 54

saludo, 18

salvage, as term, 202.

salvage linguistics, 11. *See also* linguistic anthropology

San Pedro community, 37–39

Santa Rita community, 133–36, 169–70, 221

seed ensemble, 16, 150, *151*, 220. *See also* clothing; cultural performance and representation

settler colonialism: cultural practices and, 14, 155, 211; defined, 39; fiber production and, 214–15; history of, 46–48; land reform and settlement, 58–59; linguistic ecologies and, 14, 33–34, 35, 41–42, 211; mineral extraction, 50–55, 217, 229; missionization and, 48–50, 49n4, 54, 56–58, 69. *See also* assimilation; decolonization; Spanish language

shamanic knowledge, 95, 147. *See also* yachak

Shell Oil, 50

shigra, 4, 23, 134–35, 155, 162, 171, 202, 205–7, 213–28

Shiguango, Jaime, 34, 75, 87n3, 139, 160, 201–2

Shiguango, María Antonia, *20*, 21, 35, 119–22, 125, 155, 225–26

Shiwiar language, 65

shoes, 25, 157

Shuar-Candoan language, 64, 65

Shulist, Sarah, 203

shunguyuk wawa, 117–18. *See also* sunqu

Simpson, Leanne Betasamosake, 212–13

social ecologies, 27, 35, 36, 42, 44, 50, 59. *See also* ecologies, as concept

sociality and speech, 114–15, 136, 159–68

social media, 6, 18, 77–78, 217, 232. *See also* Facebook

somatic poetry, 79

songs and music, 177–84

Southern Athapaskan language, 123

Southern Peruvian Quechua, 117, 117n1

Spanish language: about shift toward use of, 7, 8, 33, 34, 235–36; missionization and, 57; racial binary and, 68; radio and, 75, 80, 83–84, 85–86; settler colonialism and wage economy in, 55, 72–73, 231; television programs in, 100–101. *See also* bilingualism and bilingual education; linguistic ecologies; settler colonialism

INDEX

spatial patterns, 154. *See also* future/past; ñawpa

speech and sociality, 114–15, 136, 159–68

spicy speech, 187–93

Spiller, Maximiliano, 56

standardized language, 9, 104–5, 113–16, 124–27, 234–39. *See also* Kichwa language; Unified Kichwa

statistics on language speakers, 7, *8*, 66, 234

stories. *See* collective memory; environmental knowledge; intergenerational transmission; language; myth

subsistence practices, 35, 144. *See also* chagra

Sumaco volcano, *52*

Sumak Ñusta Chunta Warmi. *See* Ñusta Chunta Warmi pageant (Archidona)

Summer Institute of Linguistics, 56, 60

sunqu, 117, 117n1

swidden agriculture, 35, 144. *See also* chagra

Taff, Alice, 44

technological engagements, 203–4. *See also* media ecologies

television programs, 77, 101

televisions, 100–101

temporal patterns, 154, 156. *See also* future/past; ñawpa

Tena shimi, 66. *See also* Amazonian Kichwa language

Terralingua, 40

Texaco-Gulf, 50

textuality, 25, 51, 79, 173

theory, defined, 212–13

to remember/forget, as process, 12–13, 12n3, 197–99. *See also* iyarina; kungarina

tourism, 158–59, 229

Tukanoan language, 64, 65, 114–15

Tunay, Rita, *91, 133*; as *A New Path* host, 19, 88, 94–96, 130–36; as pageantry

MC, 142; political career of, 147, 232; on process of recording knowledge, 199; on Unified Kichwa, 70, 113; on wayusa upina, 98, 130–31

Tupian language, 64

uchu churana, 149

uchu shimi, 187–93

UCKAR (Union of Kichwa Communities of Amarun Rumi), 162–64, 167, 218

ukuy, 75–76

UNESCO Indigenous Languages Decade, 40

Unified Kichwa: about standardization project of, 9–10, 33, 34, 104–5, 113–16, 124, 234–35; codification process of, 104, 137–38; cultural pageant speeches in, 159–68; goals of, 124, 125, 128; ideology and ontology in, 124–27; linguistic ecologies and, 59, 69–71; neologisms in, 106, 124, 127, 141, 164, 167n7, 170, 210; as term, 4n1. *See also* Kichwa language; linguistic ecologies; Upper Napo Kichwa language

Upper Napo Kichwa language, 4–5, 7, 60–61, 105–6, 113. *See also* Kichwa language; Unified Kichwa

uyana, 122. *See also* listening, discourse of

Uzendoski, Michael, 11, 79

vacant lands, 58

verbal art, 79

La Voz de Napo (radio station), 81–84, 232; risachina (prayer) programs of, 102–3. *See also* radio and language reclamation

wage economy, 28, 35–36, 44, 50, 54–55, 59, 71, 72, 117

wakana, 180, 181, 185–86, 185n3. *See also* laments

wakay siki, 184

wallka, 150. *See also* clothing

Wao Tededo (Huaorani/Waorani) language, 7, 66, 67n12, 69
Wasima Tigrashun (Let's Return Home; radio program), 84. *See also* radio and language reclamation; radio programs
Wayra Churis, 91
wayusa *(Ilex guayusa)*, 3, 158
wayusa upina: about, 4, 23; kamachina and, 119–21; *A New Path* radio program and, 90–91, 97–98, 130–36, 152–53, 154, 155, 171, 173, 210–11; performance at pageants of, 142, 149–50, 156–58; settler colonialism and, 35–36. *See also* embodied performance; kamachina
weaving, 4, 23, 134–35, 155, 162, 171, 202, 205–7, 213–28
Weismantel, Mary, 67–68
Western Apache, 190
White Mountain Apache, 123
Whyte, Kyle, 39, 55
Wolfe, Patrick, 39
women: author's positionality, 21; cultural dress of, 16, 25, 148–52, 220; gender roles and, 215–16, 225–26; as media personalities, 147; music and songs of, 179–84; in Napo Kichwa structure, 37n1; performances in cultural pageantry by, 149–50, 152, 159; pita production by, 215–16; political careers of, 147, 160; use of humor by, 187–93. *See also* collective memory; environmental knowledge; femininity; intergenerational transmission

yachachina, 18, 84, 90
yachak, 95
"Yapa Wakak Mama/Llanto y cariño de mama" (song), 181–82, 184. *See also* laments
Yumbo, James, 19, 88, 94–96, 142, 218, 218n7, 232
yupaychana, 108, 141, 165, 167, 172

Zaparoan language family, 64, 65, 66
zombie linguistics, 11, 43, 207

ABOUT THE AUTHOR

Georgia C. Ennis is an assistant professor of anthropology in the Department of Anthropology and Sociology at Western Carolina University, where she coordinates the Multimodal Ethnographic Learning and Design (MELD) Lab, an ethnographic media center focused on applied ethnographic media production. In 2017, she edited the collaborative trilingual community media project *Ñukanchi sacha kawsaywa aylluchishkamanda/Relaciones con nuestra selva/Relating to our forest* with the Association of Kichwa Midwives of the Upper Napo. *Rainforest Radio* is her first book.